# INTELLECTUAL PROPERTY

A Reference Handbook

Selected Titles in ABC-CLIO's
**CONTEMPORARY
WORLD ISSUES**
Series

*Adoption*, Barbara A. Moe
*Capital Punishment*, Michael Kronenwetter
*Chemical and Biological Warfare*, Al Mauroni
*Childhood Sexual Abuse*, Karen L. Kinnear
*Conflicts over Natural Resources*, Jacqueline Vaughn
*Domestic Violence*, Margi Laird McCue
*Energy Use Worldwide*, Jaina L. Moan and Zachary A. Smith
*Euthanasia*, Martha L. Gorman and Jennifer Fecio McDougall
*Food Safety*, Nina E. Redman
*Genetic Engineering*, Harry LeVine III
*Gun Control in the United States*, Gregg Lee Carter
*Human Rights Worldwide*, Zehra F. Kabasakal Arat
*Illegal Immigration*, Michael C. LeMay
*Internet and Society*, Bernadette H. Schell
*Mainline Christians and U.S. Public Policy*, Glenn H. Utter
*Mental Health in America*, Donna R. Kemp
*Nuclear Weapons and Nonproliferation*, Sarah J. Diehl and James
    Clay Moltz
*Policing in America*, Leonard A. Steverson
*Sentencing*, Dean John Champion
*U.S. Military Service*, Cynthia A. Watson
*World Population*, Geoffrey Gilbert

For a complete list of titles in this series, please visit
**www.abc-clio.com**.

Books in the Contemporary World Issues series address vital issues in today's society such as genetic engineering, pollution, and biodiversity. Written by professional writers, scholars, and nonacademic experts, these books are authoritative, clearly written, up-to-date, and objective. They provide a good starting point for research by high school and college students, scholars, and general readers as well as by legislators, businesspeople, activists, and others.

Each book, carefully organized and easy to use, contains an overview of the subject, a detailed chronology, biographical sketches, facts and data and/or documents and other primary-source material, a directory of organizations and agencies, annotated lists of print and nonprint resources, and an index.

Readers of books in the Contemporary World Issues series will find the information they need in order to have a better understanding of the social, political, environmental, and economic issues facing the world today.

# INTELLECTUAL PROPERTY

## A Reference Handbook

Aaron Schwabach

**CONTEMPORARY WORLD ISSUES**

A B C CLIO

Santa Barbara, California
Denver, Colorado
Oxford, England

Library of Congress Cataloging-in-Publication Data

Schwabach, Aaron.
  Intellectual property : a reference handbook / Aaron Schwabach.
    p. cm. — (Contemporary world issues)
  Includes bibliographical references and index.
  ISBN 978-1-59884-045-2 (hardcover : alk. paper) —
  ISBN 978-1-59884-046-9 (ebook : alk paper)  1. Intellectual property —
United States.  2.  Intellectual property (International law)  I. Title.
  KF2979.S39 2007
  346.7304—dc22
                                        2007001209

11  10  09  08  07   1  2  3  4  5  6  7  8  9  10

ABC-CLIO, Inc.
130 Cremona Drive, P.O. Box 1911
Santa Barbara, California 93116-1911

This book is also available on the World Wide Web as an ebook.
Visit www.abc-clio.com for details.

This book is printed on acid-free paper ∞

Manufactured in the United States of America

*This book is dedicated to*
*Qienyuan, Veronica, Jessica, and Daniel.*

# Contents

*Preface,* xiii

1 **Background and History, 1**
Development of Intellectual Property Rights and
    Concepts, 1
  Copyright: Invention of the Printing Press, 1
  Trademark: From Bakers' Marks to Metatags, 8
  Patent, 12
Intellectual Property Law in the United States Today, 14
  Copyright Overview, 14
  Trademark Overview, 26
  Patent Overview, 34
Summary, 41
Treaties, 42
Regulations, 43
Statutes and Legislative Materials, 43
Cases, 44
Sources and Further Reading, 46

2 **Problems, Controversies, and Solutions, 49**
Patent, Copyright, and Computer Programs, 50
  Is the Look and Feel of a Computer Program or a
    Website Copyrightable?, 53
  Is a Method of Doing Business Patentable?, 58
  Is an Electronic Database Copyrightable?, 62
Can Content Owners Restrict or Prohibit the Sale of
    Copying Devices?, 66
Copyright's Front Line: File Sharing, 69

Copy Protection and Copyright, 82
Trademarks and the Web: Infringement and Fair Use
    Online, 87
Trademarks and the Web: Cybersquatting, 90
Summary, 92
Treaties, 93
Statutes and Other Governmental Materials, 94
Cases, 94
Sources and Further Reading, 96

3   **Worldwide Perspective, 99**
Intellectual Property and International Law, 99
The World Wide Web, 104
The International Copyright Regime, 106
The International Trademark Regime, 114
The International Patent Regime, 116
Protection of Other Forms of Intellectual Property under
    U.S. and International Law, 119
Summary, 123
Treaties, 123
European Union, ICANN, WIPO, and WTO
    Documents, 126
Statutes and Legislative Materials, 127
Cases, 128
Sources and Further Reading, 128

4   **Chronology, 131**

5   **Biographies, 149**
Clara Barton, 149
Ernest Bourget, 151
Filippo Brunelleschi, 153
Laurens Coster, 155
Annie Ellsworth, 156
Johannes Gutenberg, 158
Victor Hugo, 159
Jon Lech Johansen, 160
Mary Kies, 162
Antonio Meucci, 163
Eadweard Muybridge, 164
Dmitri Sklyarov, 167
Jack Valenti, 169

Terri Welles, 171

Samuel Winslow and Joseph Jenks, 173

6   **Data and Documents, 175**

Copyright, 176

Copyright Act of 1976, 17 U.S.C. § 102. Subject matter
of copyright: In general, 176

Copyright Act of 1976, 17 U.S.C. § 106. Exclusive rights
in copyrighted works, 176

Copyright Act of 1976, 17 U.S.C. § 107. Limitations on
exclusive rights: Fair use, 177

Digital Millennium Copyright Act, 17 U.S.C. § 1201.
Circumvention of copyright protection systems, 178

TRIPs: Agreement on Trade-Related Aspects of
Intellectual Property Rights, 185

Part II: Standards Concerning the Availability, Scope
and Use of Intellectual Property Rights, 185

*Metro-Goldwyn-Mayer Studios, Inc. v. Grokster, Ltd.*, 125
S.Ct. 2764 (2005), 186

Trademark, 198

15 U.S.C. § 1125. False designations of origin, false
descriptions, and dilution forbidden, 198

Trademark Dilution Revision Act of 2006, 203

Trademark Dilution Revision Act of 2006, H.R.683, One
Hundred Ninth Congress of the United States of
America, 204

TRIPs: Agreement on Trade-Related Aspects of
Intellectual Property Rights, 208

Part II: Standards Concerning the Availability, Scope
and Use of Intellectual Property Rights, 208

*Abercrombie & Fitch Co. v. Hunting World, Inc.*, 537 F.2d
4, 210

Patent, 213

Patent Act, 35 U.S.C. § 101. Inventions patentable, 214

Patent Act, 35 U.S.C. § 102. Conditions for
patentability; novelty and loss of right to patent, 214

Patent Act, 35 U.S.C. § 103. Conditions for
patentability; non-obvious subject matter, 215

TRIPs: Agreement on Trade-Related Aspects of
Intellectual Property Rights, 216

Part II: Standards Concerning the Availability, Scope
and Use of Intellectual Property Rights, 216

*In re Alappat*, 33 F.3d 1526, 218
Endnotes, 222

7   **Directory of Organizations, 225**

8   **Resources, 255**
Books, 255
    Similar Works, 256
    Other Titles, 259
Journal, Magazine, and News Website Articles and
    Pamphlets, 260
Journals, 264
U.S. Materials, 275
    Federal Statutes, 276
    Federal Cases, 291
    State Case, 295
Treaties and Other International Agreements, 295
Other International and Foreign Materials, 298
Internet Corporation for Assigned Names and Numbers
    Materials, 299
Other Web Resources, 300

*Glossary*, 303
*Index*, 307
*About the Author*, 318

# Preface

The human desire to claim property rights in an idea is innate, as any child who has ever told another "Stop copying me!" knows. Legal recognition of property in ideas, however—intellectual property—is a comparatively recent phenomenon, appearing centuries of millennia after the recognition of property rights in objects and land.

Revolutions in technology bring about revolutions in law. The human race has experienced four great revolutions in information technology. The first, lost in prehistory and probably predating our emergence as a species, was language. The ability to attach specific sound-symbols to specific thoughts is what makes human civilization—including legal systems—possible. The second revolution, the invention of writing, made more complex legal systems possible. When written documents could only be copied by hand, however, the incentive for making unauthorized copies of entire works was limited—although disputes did arise, including the possibly mythical dispute between St. Columba and St. Finnian (discussed in Chapter 2) that may have led to three thousand deaths.

The third revolution in information technology was the invention of movable-type printing. The ability to reproduce printed works quickly and easily created an incentive for printers to copy the works of others, and a corresponding incentive for the authors of those works to prevent unauthorized copying. Some countries (Korea and England, for example) reacted by granting monopolies to approved printers and forbidding all others from operating printing presses. In addition to controlling unauthorized copying, this had the fringe benefit of preventing the printing of any material criticizing the government. In many countries several centuries passed before these monopolies were replaced by freedom of the press and modern copyright regimes.

The three best-known forms of intellectual property—copyright, patent, and trademark—appeared in Europe during the Renaissance. After the printing revolution had taken place in east Asia, but before it reached Europe, Europe's commercial revolution led to laws requiring the use of symbols and words to identify the products of particular bakeries, breweries, and eventually other businesses. And the increase in the rate of technological change in the fifteenth century (the century that saw, among other innovations, the arrival of the printing press in Europe) led the Italian city-states to issue patents to inventors, granting them exclusive rights to their inventions for limited periods of time.

The fourth revolution in information technology is happening right now. The advent of personal computing and the Internet has solved the problem expressed by Abbott Joseph Liebling, who in 1960 complained that "Freedom of the press is guaranteed only to those who own one." Today billions of people own "presses"; the barrier to universal distribution of any content they may choose to create is not expense, but the difficulty of getting people interested—a problem commercial presses have always faced. This revolution in information technology poses a dual problem for traditional media. First, much Web content borrows and incorporates existing material, and the extent to which such borrowing should be permitted has not yet been fully resolved. Second, many users create no content of their own, but merely make and pass along unauthorized copies of existing content. Existing law clearly frowns on this copying, but enforcement is difficult.

The fourth information technology revolution has also accelerated the internationalization of intellectual property law. The international nature of trade in intellectual property has been apparent since at least the mid-nineteenth century; in the digital age, however, barriers to international exchange of information have vanished entirely.

Intellectual property law has adapted more quickly to the fourth information revolution than to the first three. The response time to the first revolution might have been measured in tens or hundreds of thousands of years; the response to the second revolution, in millennia; and the response to the third, in centuries, or at least decades. The legal system responded to the appearance of the Internet, and especially the World Wide Web, much more quickly. Within five years of the appearance of the first easily usable Web browser, the United States had enacted the Digital Millennium Copyright Act and other statutes, which were designed to extend and strengthen copyright protection, and the Anticybersquatting Consumer Protection Act, which was designed to protect the interests of trademark holders in what was then called "cyberspace."

This book serves as a reference guide to humanity's attempts, up to and throughout the twentieth century and into the twenty-first, to balance the interests of consumers and producers and create a workable national and international intellectual property law system. Intellectual property law is currently in crisis; this book is designed to serve as a starting point for future research, and the resources provided here will make it possible to locate up-to-the-minute information in a wide variety of areas.

Chapter 1 begins with a historical overview of the development of intellectual property and the laws regulating it. It looks at the three traditional categories of intellectual property: copyright from the invention of the printing press in China more than 1,200 years ago to the Digital Millennium Copyright Act and the Sonny Bono Copyright Term Extension Act of 1998; trademark from the Bakers Marking Law of 1266 (requiring bakers in England to place identifying marks on their bread) to the Anticybersquatting Consumer Protection Act and search-engine spamming; and patent from the fifteenth-century Florence of Filippo Brunelleschi to business-method patents for one-click ordering. Chapter 1 also includes an overview of the law currently in force in the United States in each of these three areas of intellectual property law.

Chapter 2 looks at specific problems with intellectual property law and the success (or lack of success) of the current legal regime in addressing these problems. It looks first at a relative failure: the slow and awkward adaptation of the intellectual property regime, from the 1960s through the 1980s, to computer software. Software is functional; thus, it might seem to be a proper subject for patent. On the other hand it is composed of text and can be expressive; thus it might also seem to be a proper subject for copyright. The failure of the courts, lawmakers, and administrators of the United States and Europe to resolve—or even understand—this conflict when it first arose led to the disastrous Supreme Court decision in *Gottschalk v. Benson*, which apparently held (although much later the Court backtracked) that software could not be patented. This rule was then adopted in the

European Patent Convention. Rather than acknowledging the problem and perhaps creating a new form of intellectual property protection for software, the U.S. and European patent systems—and those of the rest of the world as well—allowed copyright to become the primary vehicle for protection of rights in computer programs, with results that have distorted the industry and arguably hindered progress.

Chapter 2 also covers "look and feel" copyright, database protection, business methods patents, and the conflict of interest between copyright owners and equipment manufacturers, before looking at perhaps the fiercest intellectual property battle of recent years: the battle over online file sharing. Chapter 2 also discusses online trademark issues (cybersquatting, metatags, and search-engine spamming).

Chapter 3 looks at international intellectual property law and the organizations that administer it. The three traditional forms of intellectual property are protected to varying degrees. The Berne Convention and other copyright treaties create nearly seamless and nearly universal copyright protection; almost all works are protected almost everywhere. Patent protection is less comprehensive, and the trademark regime still less so. The Patent Cooperation Treaty and other patent treaties have created a single patent-filing system, but obtaining global (or somewhat global) patent protection is still a dauntingly complex, difficult, and expensive task. The global trademark regime is the least comprehensive of all, with no single filing system covering a majority of the world's countries. Chapter 3 also looks at other forms of intellectual property outside the three traditional categories.

Chapter 4 provides a chronology of milestone events in the development of intellectual property law. Chapter 5 provides biographical sketches of inventors, activists, authors, and others who have played a role in the development of intellectual property law. Chapter 6 provides annotated excerpts from important documents in international intellectual property law, along with explanatory text. A full library of primary source materials in U.S. and international intellectual property law would not fit in this book, but all of these materials can be found on the Internet and in libraries. The resources listed in Chapters 7 and 8 will enable readers to find them. Chapter 7 describes and provides contact information for a variety of international and national government and nongovernment organizations. Chapter 8 provides a bibliography, with descriptions of suggested books for further reading; a list of articles, journals, and primary source materials; and a guide to the most comprehensive online resources.

I'd like to thank all of the people who helped make this book possible, including my research assistants, Candace Michaux and Kaiya Tollefson; my editors, Dayle Dermatis and Cami Cacciatore; Professors Julie Cromer, Deven Desai, K. J. Greene, and Sandra Rierson, my colleagues at Thomas Jefferson School of Law; and especially my family. I hope that you enjoy reading this book as much as I did writing it (or possibly more) and that it will serve as a starting point for further explorations in intellectual property law.

# 1

# Background and History

## Development of Intellectual Property Rights and Concepts

Intellectual property is the intangible but legally recognized right to property in the products of one's intellect. Intellectual property rights allow the originator of certain ideas, inventions, and expressions to exclude others from using those ideas, inventions, and expressions without permission. The three traditionally recognized forms of intellectual property are copyright, trademark, and patent. Copyright protects expressive works—movies, music, plays, books, and the like. Trademark protects marks that are placed on goods to distinguish them from other goods, generally by identifying the maker or distributor. Patent protects inventions. Both U.S. and international law also protect less well-known forms of intellectual property, such as trade secrets, know-how, and certain industrial designs.

### Copyright: Invention of the Printing Press

As a practical matter, an author's right to prohibit or profit from the copying of his or her work required little or no protection before the invention of mechanical means of copying. Manually copying books or paintings was too laborious for piracy to be profitable. The invention of copying technologies, however, has led to an ever-escalating legal regime of copyright protection as authors seek to protect their works.

The first of these technologies was the printing press. Early printing techniques, which were used in China and Japan as long as 1,400 years ago, used block printing: A single block was carved with all of the images and characters on a page. It could then be used to make multiple copies—prints—of that page. The perfection of the block-printing technique can be seen in the world's oldest surviving printed book, the *Diamond Sutra*, published by Wang Jie in AD 868 and bearing the words "reverently made for universal free distribution." (The *Diamond Sutra*, which is now in the collection of the British Library, can be viewed at http://www.bl.uk/onlinegallery/ttp/digitisation.html.) The text is astonishingly clear and can be easily read by any twenty-first century person who can read Chinese, although the use of the language is somewhat archaic and hard to follow.

Although block printing made reproduction of pictures and texts possible, it was the advent of movable type that brought about cheap, high-volume reproduction of printed text and ultimately gave rise to modern copyright laws. In AD 1041, a Chinese inventor named Bi Sheng built the world's first printing press using movable type; about two centuries later the world's oldest surviving book printed with movable text, *The New Code of Etiquette*, was published in Korea by Yi Gyu-bo. Because the Chinese (and, at the time, Korean) language uses thousands of characters, each representing a word, rather than a few dozen letters, setting up pages with movable type in Chinese is more time-consuming, and thus more expensive, than it is for languages that use an alphabet. Korea's adoption of a phonetic alphabet (now called *hangul* but at the time called *hunmin jeongeum*) in 1446 (two years after its invention) made printing with movable type much easier and cheaper. The Korean government responded to this information explosion, and the problem of unauthorized copying, in the same way that the British government would later respond to the same problem: Only government-authorized printers could print books (Choi 2003, 646). The concept of "copyright" in the modern sense seems to have first appeared in Korea in the 1880s, and the end of the government-granted monopoly or oligopoly on printing came with the Japanese annexation in the early twentieth century.

### The Origin of Anglo-American Copyright Law: The Stationer's Company and the Statute of Anne

The copyright law of the United States descends from the copyright law of Britain. Between 1430 and 1450, Europeans, including Johannes Gutenberg and Laurens Coster (see Chapter 5), built movable-type printing presses in Europe. Gutenberg published the first of his famous Bibles in 1455. (The British Library's two Gutenberg Bibles may be viewed at http://prodigi.bl.uk/treasures/gutenberg/search.asp.) In 1474 the British printer William Caxton published the first book printed in English using movable type—an English translation of Raoul Lefèvre's *The Recuyell of the Historyes of Troye*. (The British Library's copy is not yet available online, but a copy of Geoffrey Chaucer's *Canterbury Tales,* printed by Caxton in 1476, may be viewed at http://www.bl.uk/treasures/caxton/homepage.html.)

The introduction of movable type to Britain led to the problem of copying, and more than eight decades after Caxton's *Canterbury Tales* was printed the British government opted for the solution that the Korean government had chosen about two centuries earlier (Choi 2003, 646). In 1557 the British government granted the Stationer's Company a royal monopoly on book publishing. This monopoly lasted well over a century, until 1695. By the time the monopoly expired, printing had arrived in the British North American colonies, with the publication of the Eliot Indian Bible (a translation of the Bible into Algonquin) in Cambridge, Massachusetts, from 1661 to 1663.

From 1695, when the Stationer's Company's monopoly expired, until 1710, no copyright law existed in Britain and alternative publishers flourished. The Stationer's Company lobbied for further legal protection, with only partial success. In 1710 the British parliament passed its first copyright act, the Statute of Anne (Leaffer 1999, 4–5).

The Statute of Anne preserved the rights of the Stationer's Company in works already published until 1731 (an additional twenty-one years) but effectively undermined the position of the Stationer's Company by viewing copyright as originating with the writing rather than the publication of the work. The purpose of the statute was to encourage "learned men to compose and write useful work." For works created after the date of the statute, copyright was to endure for fourteen years and was renewable for a second fourteen-year term if the author was still alive at the end of the first. It was not until 1774, however, that the hold of the Stationer's Company over works it had previously published was finally broken by the holding in *Donaldson v. Beckett* that the term of copyright is invariably finite (Leaffer 1999, 4–5).

### The Beginning of U.S. Intellectual Property Law: The Patent and Copyright Clause of the U.S. Constitution

Shortly thereafter, the Constitution of the newly independent United States granted Congress the power "To promote the Progress of Science and useful Arts, by securing for limited Times to Authors and Inventors the exclusive Right to their respective Writings and Discoveries" (U.S. Const. art. I, § 8, cl. 8). This clause, known as the Patent and Copyright Clause, provided the basis for the 1790 Copyright Act, which provided authors and their assignees with copyright protection for books, charts, and maps for a term identical to that set out in the Statute of Anne: a fourteen-year copyright, renewable once for an additional fourteen years. As new technological developments enabled new forms of copying, additional forms of subject matter were added to the Copyright Act. In 1865, for example, photographs were added to the list of copyrightable subject matter.

As Anglo-American copyright law was developing along these lines, however, it was growing increasingly out of step with copyright law on the European continent. While Anglo-American law focused on the benefit of copyright (for a limited term) to society, French law focused on its benefit to the author. Concepts of copyright in France dated back at least to the reign of Francis I, who in 1537 instituted the concept of *dépôt légale*, requiring that all printers deposit a copy of each work they published and offered for sale in France with the Bibliothèque Nationale at the Château de Blois. This *dépôt légale* later served as a form of copyright registration. In the following centuries a state-regulated printing oligopoly developed along the lines of those in Britain, Korea, and elsewhere. By edict of 30 August 1777, the French crown extended printing-monopoly privileges on a quite different basis than that in the Statute of Anne. The right to publish a work was not defined by a set term of years, but if granted to or assigned to a publisher, it lasted for the lifetime of the author, and if granted to and held by the author, it was perpetual (Ginsburg 1990, 997). Decrees during the French Revolution limited the author's rights somewhat and recognized and expanded the public domain—the body of works not protected by copyright and available for copying (Ginsburg 1990, 1005–1009). Authors in France came to enjoy rights known as moral rights, including the right to be identified as the author of a work, the right to protect the work from changes, and the right to withdraw a work from distribution. In the United States, copyright continued to be viewed as an economic rather than a moral right. The U.S. legal system, while adopting copyright registration requirements derived from the *dépôt légale,* remained unreceptive to moral rights and to the idea of a lifetime (or longer) term of copyright protection.

Despite differences in national copyright laws, however, the ease with which copyrights could be violated outside the country in which they were granted made it increasingly apparent that some sort of international copyright law was needed. In 1886 a group of European countries adopted the Berne Convention, the foundation of the regime that still governs international copyright today—but because U.S. copyright law differed so greatly from that in other countries, the United States was not to join the Convention until another century had passed.

### The Copyright Act of 1909

The Copyright Act of 1909 doubled the term of U.S. copyright, from the fourteen-year, once-renewable term originally set by the Statute of Anne to a twenty-eight-year term, also renewable once. It did not, however, adopt the Berne Convention's minimum term (for individually authored works) of the life of the author plus fifty years (Leaffer 1999, 6–7). The 1909 Act also required registration formalities that were inconsistent with the Berne Convention. In addition to these international problems, the Act provided insufficient protection for most unpublished work, resulting in the growth of a system of state law copyright protection for these works (Leaffer 1999, 39).

### The Copyright Act of 1976 and the 1988 Berne Convention Implementation Act

In 1955, the United States became a party to the Universal Copyright Convention, an alternative to the Berne Convention, and Congress embarked on what ultimately became a twenty-year project to review and revise U.S. copyright law to bring it into line with international norms. The Copyright Act of 1976, a sweeping revision of U.S. copyright law, marked a far more dramatic departure from the Statute of Anne than had the 1909 Act. The 1976 Act eliminated the renewable twenty-eight-year term of copyright, replacing it with the Berne Convention minimum of the lifetime of the author plus fifty years for individually authored works, and with a term of seventy-five years from publication or 100 years from creation, whichever was less, for most other works. It preempted state copyright law, eliminating the cumbersome dual system. And it provided far clearer definitions of the rights of copyright holders, and the limitations to which those rights were subject, than previous statutes. The 1976 Act and a subsequent 1988 statute finally made it possible for the United States to join the Berne Convention, creating a universal copyright regime.

## Changing the Rules: The Internet

Just as the United States and the last other major holdouts were joining the Berne Convention, a new information revolution, as dramatic as the invention of printing, was taking place: the advent of home computing and the Internet. Digital computing offered something no other copying technology had been able to offer: perfect copies, without any deterioration in quality, of any work already in digital form. And the Internet made it possible to disseminate these copies far more easily than any previous technology. In a few seconds and at no cost to the copier, a copied work could be made available to every user of the Internet anywhere on the planet.

This new technological revolution has brought a quicker response, in part because of the greater interconnectedness that the Internet itself makes possible. Internationally, treaties promulgated by the World Intellectual Property Organization (WIPO) and the World Trade Organization have addressed the problem of digital piracy. In the United States, additional copyright laws in the Internet era have included the No Electronic Theft Act of 1997, and the Digital Millennium Copyright Act (DMCA) and Sonny Bono Copyright Term Extension Act, both enacted in 1998.

The No Electronic Theft Act of 1997 was enacted to control warez trading. Warez are unauthorized copies of copyrighted computer software. Warez can be unlawfully traded or given away over the Internet or copied onto disks and given away or sold. Although commercial copying was illegal under previously existing law, before 1997 some noncommercial copying had been beyond the reach of criminal prosecution (*United States v. LaMacchia*, 871 F. Supp. 535). The No Electronic Theft Act greatly expanded the government's ability to impose criminal sanctions on noncommercial warez traders.

The DMCA, a multifaceted and complex revision of copyright law relating to digital works, had five distinct sections, called "titles," four of which addressed copyright in digital works. (The fifth created a new form of intellectual property protection for vessel hull designs [17 U.S.C. §§ 1301–1332].) Title I, the WIPO Copyright and Performances and Phonograms Treaties Implementation Act, was enacted to fulfill the obligations of the United States under two WIPO treaties. One aspect of Title I was especially controversial: the prohibition of the circumvention of technological measures designed to prevent digital copying (17 U.S.C. §§ 1201–1204). This provision, which makes it unlawful to circumvent the copy protection on DVDs, for example, is seen as unfair by many consumers. The prohibition has been extended not only to the sale or free distribution of software that enables copying of protected DVDs, but even to posting links on a website to other sites from which such software may be downloaded (*Universal City Studios, Inc. v. Corley*, 273 F.3d 429).

Title II, the Online Copyright Infringement Liability Limitation Act, addressed the concerns of Internet service providers (ISPs) that they might be held liable for copyright infringement committed on or over their networks. Title II provides a safe harbor from such liability for ISPs that comply with certain requirements (17 U.S.C. § 512). Without such a safe harbor, the ISPs might be unable to function, as policing their networks for copyright-infringing material would be a near-impossible task.

Title III, the Computer Maintenance Competition Assurance Act, provides that a person who activates a computer for purposes of maintenance or repair and makes a copy of a program by doing so is not liable for copyright infringement, provided that the new copy is not used for any other purpose or retained afterward (17 U.S.C. § 117(c)). While this may seem considerably less earthshaking than the safe harbor provisions of Title II or the anticircumvention provisions of Title I, Congress thought it necessary to prevent the creation of vendor monopolies on maintenance of computer equipment after the 1993 decision in *MAI Systems v. Peak Computer*, which had held that the creation of such copies during maintenance could provide a basis for liability for copyright infringement (991 F.2d 511). Title IV of the DMCA was

something of a catchall, addressing miscellaneous issues including ephemeral recordings and webcasting, copies made for
distance education, library and archival preservation and interli-
brary loan copies, the effect of transfer of rights in motion pictures on collective bargaining agreements, and certain functions
of the Copyright Office (17 U.S.C. §§ 106, 108–110, and 112).

The Sonny Bono Copyright Term Extension Act (sometimes
derisively called the Mickey Mouse Protection Act because one of
its most notable supporters and beneficiaries was the Walt Disney
Company) increased the duration of most copyright terms by
twenty years, bringing U.S. terms into line with European Union
norms (and exceeding the requirements of the Berne Convention). Under the Act, U.S. copyright law now protects most
individually authored works for the lifetime of the author plus
seventy years, and most other works for ninety-five years from
publication or 120 years from creation, whichever is less (17
U.S.C. §§ 302, 304; see "Duration of Copyright").

## Trademark: From Bakers' Marks to Metatags

A trademark is a mark that can be placed on goods to distinguish
them from other goods. Other marks distinguish other things in
commerce: service marks, for example, identify providers of services. The term "trademark" is often used to refer to the legal
regime governing all protected marks, and all such marks are
sometimes referred to as "trademarks." The law of trademark in
the Anglo-American tradition has more ancient roots than copyright.

The association of a maker's name or mark with his or her
work is probably as ancient as commerce itself. Many trade
names still in use today as marks date back more than a thousand
years. The Hoshi Ryokan, a Japanese inn, has operated under the
Hoshi family's name—and management—for 1,300 years; the
Japanese construction firm Kongo Gumi has been using that
name for more than 1,400 years (World's Oldest Companies
2004). In Europe, well-known beers Lowenbrau and Stella Artois
have been marketed under those names since the fourteenth century; the more obscure Weihenstephan dates back to AD 1040.

Modern Anglo-American trademark law, however, had its
origin in the Bakers Marking Law of 1266. As the name says, the

law required bakers to place a mark on loaves of bread that they sold, identifying the baker. Originally these marks were intended to protect the public, a rationale that continues to underlie much of modern trademark law. If a loaf of bread was defective or of insufficient weight, the incompetent or unscrupulous baker could easily be tracked down. Not surprisingly, however, these marks came to serve as marketing tools, as consumers sought out the marks of especially competent bakers.

By 1618 the urge to gain market share by counterfeiting a more popular mark had given rise to Britain's first reported decision in a case of trademark infringement: *Southern v. How,* in which a clothier brought an action for deceit against another clothier for using the first clothier's mark to cause potential purchasers to believe the cloth had been made by the first clothier. *Southern v. How* refers to a yet earlier, presumably unreported case involving a similar issue (Austin 2004, 840 n. 51).

Trademark had a rocky start in the United States. The Patent and Copyright Clause of the U.S. Constitution makes no mention of trademark. Although Thomas Jefferson, among others, favored a national law of trademark protection, it was not until 1870 that Congress passed a Trademark Act. Nine years later the Act was struck down as unconstitutional by the Supreme Court (*In re Trade-Mark Cases,* 100 U.S. 82).

In striking down the Trademark Act, the Supreme Court did not reject the idea of trademark protection. Rather, it endorsed the idea of protection of trademarks at the state level, whether through common law (law made by judges in deciding reported cases) or by state statute:

> The right to adopt and use a symbol or a device to distinguish the goods or property made or sold by the person whose mark it is, to the exclusion of use by all other persons, has been long recognized by the common law and the chancery courts of England and of this country, and by the statutes of some of the States. It is a property right for the violation of which damages may be recovered in an action at law, and the continued violation of it will be enjoined by a court of equity, with compensation for past infringement. This exclusive right was not created by the act of Congress, and does not now depend upon it for its enforcement. (*In re Trade-Mark Cases,* 100 U.S. at 92)

The prospect of a continuing regime of different and inconsistent trademark laws in each state, each with its own registration system, was a bit daunting. The Supreme Court did leave Congress an alternative, however. It pointed out that Congressional authority over trademarks could not be based on the Patent and Copyright Clause, because a trademark does not "depend upon novelty, invention, discovery, or any work of the brain. It requires no fancy or imagination, no genius, no laborious thought. It is simply founded on priority of appropriation" (*In re Trade-Mark Cases*, 100 U.S. at 94). Congress lacked all authority to regulate trademark between citizens of the same state. However, it might possess the authority under the Commerce Clause to regulate trademark insofar as it affected commerce between and among states, with foreign nations, and with Indian tribes (see *In re Trade-Mark Cases*, 100 U.S. at 94–95).

Congress missed the hint and, in 1881, enacted a tentative trademark act allowing national registration of marks used in commerce with foreign nations and Indian tribes, but somehow omitting interstate commerce. In 1905 Congress finally allowed national registration of "fanciful" and "arbitrary" marks (but not of merely "descriptive" marks) used in interstate commerce (Berger 2004, 394). Like copyright, however, trademark is necessarily international; companies need protection for their trademarks in all countries in which they do business. In 1910, the United States and several Latin American countries entered into the Inter-American Convention for the Protection of Industrial Property. In 1920, a new Trademark Act was enacted to carry out the obligations of the United States under the convention.

Federal trademark law as it now exists in the United States dates from the Lanham Trademark Act of 1946. Congress, in enacting the Lanham Act, attempted to modernize, simplify, and unify existing federal trademark law and to carry out the obligations of the United States under international law. The Lanham Act was also designed to create an incentive to register trademarks by attaching certain rights to registration (Robert 1996, 375). The Lanham Act itself has been amended several times, most dramatically by the Trademark Law Revision Act of 1988, the Federal Trademark Dilution Act of 1995, the Anticounterfeiting Consumer Protection Act of 1996, the Anticybersquatting Consumer Protection Act of 1999, and the Trademark Dilution Revision Act of 2006.

In the years following the Lanham Act, international trademark law continued to evolve, and the 1988 Revision Act, like the earlier 1920 Act, was aimed at bringing U.S. law into conformity with international law. The 1996 Acts were inspired in part by the increase in global trade. The Anticounterfeiting Act provided remedies for U.S. trademark holders threatened by "counterfeit" trademark-infringing goods originating outside the United States, while the controversial Dilution Act provided a remedy for holders of "famous" marks against those who used the same or similar marks in ways that might "dilute" the strength of the mark. This dilution can occur in two ways: through "blurring," which causes the mark to lose its distinctive quality, and "tarnishment," which associates undesirable qualities with the mark. Thus, the Dilution Act can impose liability for trademark dilution even when there is no likelihood that consumers would be confused by the diluting use. This grants a powerful weapon to the wealthiest (in intellectual property terms) trademark holders, which has the potential for misuse to quell legitimate criticism or innocent uses (Greene 2004). In a 2003 case, the Supreme Court questioned whether the federal statute covered dilution by tarnishment; however, in the Trademark Dilution Revision Act of 2006, Congress affirmed that dilution can occur by blurring or tarnishment (*Mosely,* 537 U.S. 418; PL 109-312, 120 Stat. 1730).

The advent of the Internet led to the Anticybersquatting Consumer Protection Act, which addressed the then-new problem of protecting trademark holders from other Internet users who might register the trademark holders' trademarks as domain names. The Act imposes liability on anyone who, with a bad-faith intent to profit, registers a domain name that creates a likelihood of confusion with or (in the case of "famous" marks) dilutes another's mark (15 U.S.C. § 1125(d)). This also has the potential for abuse; for example, in Los Angeles, the parents of a two-year-old girl, Veronica Sams, registered the name veronica.org to create a website about their daughter, and were sued by Archie Comics Publications, which holds a trademark in the name "Veronica" for one of its characters (Greene 2004, 637). The suit was eventually dropped. The idea that a company could entirely preempt all uses of a given name seems absurd, but many parents confronted with such a suit would be unwilling or unable to contest it and would simply have yielded the domain name.

The advent of the Internet has also given rise to the abuse of trademarks in metatags and other forms of search-engine spamming. Metatags are text inserted into an HTML document (such as a Web page) in a way that makes them invisible when the document is viewed in the usual way. (To view metatags, if any, on a Web page, select "View/Source" or the equivalent from your browser's menu bar.) Metatags are mostly used for legitimate purposes, but they can also include the use of a competitor's trademark to increase the page's chance of being located by search engines (and rank when located) when people search for the competitor. Search-engine spammers can also use trademarks in other ways to spam search engines (including Google) that do not rely on metatags.

## Patent

Patent, like copyright, has its origins in royal monopolies granted to certain businesses. In medieval Europe some of these monopolies may have been granted in response to innovation in particular fields; however, the first explicit linking of innovation to the grant of a monopoly—and thus the first patent statute in the modern sense—was the Venetian patent statute of 1474. The first known patent had been issued more than fifty years earlier, in 1421, by the city of Florence to Filippo Brunelleschi. Brunelleschi is remembered today as the architect of the Duomo di Firenze, the cathedral of Santa Maria del Fiore. To transport marble for his cathedral, Brunelleschi designed a new type of ship; it was for this that the patent was granted (Nard and Morriss 2004, 8)

The Venetian statute, however, was the first governmental act to systematize the granting of patents. (Some medieval guilds had already done so for their own members.) Although Venice may have granted patents as early as 1416, the 1474 statute provided inventors "who shall build any new and ingenious device in this City, not previously made in our Commonwealth" with the right to prevent all other persons from making the same device (Nard and Morriss 2004, 8 n. 39, 9 n. 47). The term of the patent was set at 10 years, and to receive the patent the inventor had to disclose the way in which the invention was made and operated, so that after the expiration of the ten-year period others could freely copy the invention.

The patent statute may have helped to make Venice a hub of technological innovation and development in the fifteenth and sixteenth centuries, or it may have arisen because Venice was already well on its way to becoming such a hub. At the same time, however, England was a relative technological backwater. Although a royal patent of monopoly was granted as early as 1449 (by King Henry VI to John of Utynam, for manufacturing stained glass), patent law as a systematic means of rewarding and encouraging invention developed there somewhat later. Throughout the late sixteenth century, patents were granted in England on an occasional basis, as they had been in Venice and Florence in the early and middle fourteenth century. The granting of patents was haphazard; while a patent for a water closet was denied, a patent for vinegar was granted (Nard and Morriss 2004, 33).

By the early 1600s the granting of patents had become a source of contention between Parliament and the Crown. Eventually this conflict led to the 1623 Statute of Monopolies, the Anglo-American legal system's first patent act. The 1623 Statute provided that "the true and first inventor" should have the right to exclude or prevent others from making an invention for a period of fourteen years from the date of the grant of the patent (Statute of Monopolies, reprinted in Dinwoodie 2002, 39–40). This was not a recognition of the rights of inventors outside England; it was restricted to inventions "within this realm," and a patent could be granted to an "inventor" in Britain who merely copied something that had already been done elsewhere (Kaufer 1989, 6–7).

Patent laws based on the Statute of Monopolies were adopted in the British North American colonies, beginning with Massachusetts in 1641. After independence, patent law, like copyright law, was specifically placed under the authority of Congress by the Patent and Copyright Clause of the U.S. Constitution, which gives Congress the power to make laws "To promote the Progress of Science and useful Arts, by securing for limited Times to Authors and Inventors the exclusive Right to their respective Writings and Discoveries" (Const. art. I, § 8, cl. 8). The first patent statute, in 1790, marked a departure from the Statute of Monopolies. The 1790 Act focused not on the right of the sovereign to grant monopolies, but on the right of the individual inventor to his (or, somewhat later, her) invention. The Act also required an official examination before a patent could be granted, although this requirement was eliminated in 1793 and not reinstituted until 1836 (Kaufer 1989, 8).

A patent, like a copyright or a trademark, is initially limited to the territory of the sovereign granting it, yet it may be infringed upon by persons outside that territory. Like copyrights and trademarks, patents require international protection if they are to be effective in a global economy. At the outset of the nineteenth century there was considerable international pressure against the adoption of patent laws. This antipatent movement attempted to repeal patent laws in the German states, successfully resisted six attempts to introduce a patent law in Switzerland, and succeeded (in 1869) in repealing the patent law of the Netherlands (Kaufer 1989, 8–10). By the end of the nineteenth century, however, the antipatent movement had been defeated, and the Paris Convention for the Protection of Industrial Property created the beginnings of a global patent regime that covered much of Latin America, North America, and Europe, including even Switzerland.

In the United States, the establishment of the U.S. Patent Office by the 1836 Patent Act marked the beginning of modern patent law. A subsequent Patent Act, in 1870, unified and simplified existing law but made little substantive change. Patent law, like copyright law, has continued to undergo modification to adapt to new technologies. Occasionally these adaptations prove controversial, as with the patenting of computer programs (discussed in detail in Chapter 2); living organisms (permitted since 1930 by the Plant Patent Act); or business methods (required under the Treaty on Trade Related Aspects of Intellectual Property Rights, or TRIPs, and permitted by the Federal Circuit's decision in *State Street Bank & Trust Co. v. Signature Financial Group*). The U.S. Patent and Trademark Office (as it has been called since 1975) has also been subject to domestic and international criticism for its perceived laxness in granting patents.

# Intellectual Property Law in the United States Today

## Copyright Overview

Copyright, as the name says, is the exclusive right to make copies of a work. The term "copyright" today also covers several other rights, including the right to perform or display a work, the right to publish or otherwise distribute a work, the right to digitally broadcast a work, and the right to create derivative works based on a work (17 U.S.C. § 106). These rights—the right to copy, distribute, perform, display, and make derivative works—can collectively be described as "economic rights." Another category of rights, called "moral rights," includes the right to be acknowledged as the author of a work, the right to decide when and in what form the work shall be presented to the public, and the right to prevent the work from being altered or distorted. Moral rights have not traditionally been protected in U.S. copyright law, although some moral rights in certain works, especially works of visual art, have been protected (17 U.S.C. § 106A).

### Copyrightable Subject Matter: What Can Be Copyrighted

Copyright protects "Original works of authorship fixed in any tangible medium of expression" (17 U.S.C. § 102). In other words, to be protected by copyright under U.S. law, a work must possess three qualities: It must be original, it must be a work of authorship, and it must be fixed in a tangible medium of expression.

The "originality" requirement for copyright protection is minimal. Compiling cases in a case reporter in a particular order, together with the resulting page numbering, may satisfy the requirement (*Oasis*, 924 F. Supp. 918). The requirement is not nonexistent, however. In the 1991 case of *Feist Publications v. Rural Telephone Service Co.*, the U.S. Supreme Court rejected the idea that copyright can be a reward for hard work in the absence of originality (499 U.S. 340). Copyright, the Supreme Court held, cannot be based on the "sweat of the brow" of the creator of a work. The "originality" in *Feist* consisted of arranging names in a telephone directory in alphabetical order; this was insufficiently original to support a claim of copyright.

A list of "works of authorship" can be found in the Copyright Act (17 U.S.C. § 102(a)), including

1. literary works;
2. musical works, including any accompanying words;
3. dramatic works, including any accompanying music;
4. pantomimes and choreographic works;
5. pictorial, graphic, and sculptural works;
6. motion pictures and other audiovisual works;
7. sound recordings; and
8. architectural works.

Computer programs have been protected as literary works, defined in 17 U.S.C. § 101 as "works, other than audiovisual works, expressed in words, numbers, or other verbal or numerical symbols or indicia" (17 U.S.C. § 101; *Williams Electronics,* 685 F.2d 870). This protection has been extended to operating systems as well as applications (*Apple Computer,* 714 F.2d 1240).

To be "fixed in a tangible medium of expression," a work must be recorded "by or under the authority of the author," in a form "sufficiently permanent or stable to permit it to be perceived, reproduced, or otherwise communicated for a period of more than transitory duration" (17 U.S.C. § 101). The fixed work need not be readable by the unaided human senses; a work is fixed in a tangible medium even if it can only be perceived with mechanical or electronic assistance (*Williams Electronics,* 685 F.2d 870; *Midway Manufacturing,* 704 F.2d 1009). Thus, computer programs and sound and video recordings on CDs, tape cassettes, DVDs, and other magnetic, optical, and electronic media are all "fixed" for copyright purposes. Live broadcast works can also be "fixed" for copyright purposes: "A work consisting of sounds, images, or both, that are being transmitted, is 'fixed' for purposes of this title if a fixation of the work is being made simultaneously with its transmission" (17 U.S.C. § 101).

Some subject matter is specifically made noncopyrightable even if it otherwise appears to meet the statutory requirements of originality, work of authorship, and fixation. Copyright will not protect "any idea, procedure, process, system, method of operation, concept, principle, or discovery," even if embodied within an otherwise copyrightable and copyrighted work (17 U.S.C. § 102(b)). Although a particular and original expression of an idea can be copyrightable, when an idea can be expressed in only a limited number of ways, the idea and the expression merge and the expression is uncopyrightable (*Baker,* 101 U.S. 99; *NEC,* 10 U.S.P.Q.2d 1177). Certain works may also be uncopyrightable under the *scènes a fàire* doctrine.

Procedures, processes, systems, and methods of operation, to the extent that they can be protected as intellectual property, are more properly the subjects of patent than of copyright—although the unavailability of copyright does not mean that a particular procedure, process, system, or method is eligible for patent protection. Concepts and principles may not be protectable at all, except perhaps as trade secrets, while "discovery" is used in the Patent Code as a synonym for "invention" (35 U.S.C. § 100). Uncopyrightable methods of operation include the menu command hierarchy of a computer program (*Lotus Development,* 140 F.3d 70).

Operating systems, however, are, as already noted, copyrightable. They are not mere methods of operation but are protected literary works (*Apple Computer*, 714 F.2d 1240).

*Scènes a faire* are works, or more often portions of works, that are dependent on basic, common ways of treating particular subject matter to such an extent as to render them uncopyrightable (*Hoehling*, 618 F.2d 972; *Data East USA*, 862 F.2d 204). A video game based on the sport of karate, for instance, must include certain types of kicks and punches; these moves are *scènes a faire* and cannot be copyrighted (*Data East USA*, 862 F.2d 204). Similarly, a book or movie about the Hindenburg airship disaster is likely to include images of German soldiers drinking in beer halls, saying "Heil Hitler" and singing the German national anthem. These images are *scènes a faire;* they are a standard part of any depiction of Germany in the Nazi era, and thus cannot be copyrighted (*Hoehling*, 618 F.2d 972).

### Copyright Formalities

Previously, U.S. law imposed notice and registration formalities as a prerequisite for copyright protection. To obtain a copyright under modern U.S. law, however, it is necessary to do nothing more than to fix one's original work of authorship in a tangible medium of expression. This will afford the author copyright protection not only in the United States but also, subject to local law, in all of the countries that are parties to the Berne Convention. However, copyrights may still be registered with the U.S. Copyright Office, a division of the Library of Congress. (Forms for various types of copyrightable works can be downloaded from the Copyright Office's website at http://www.copyright.gov/register/.) For most works, registration requires a completed application form, a fee of $45, and one copy (for unpublished works, works first published outside the United States, and collective works or contributions thereto) or two copies (for most other works first published in the United States) of the work to be registered (U.S. Copyright Office 2006a). Special rules apply to online publications, computer programs, and databases. Special provisions have been made to allow computer programs to be registered without disclosing all of the program's source code (U.S. Copyright Office 2006b). The fee, completed form, and copy or copies of the work must then be sent to the Copyright Office. Special fees apply to serial publications, newspapers, changes to existing registrations, and expedited requests.

The Berne Convention Implementation Act of 1988 eliminated the notice requirement for works fixed after 1 March 1989. For earlier works, notice was required, and works first fixed before that date may have fallen into the public domain if notice of a claim of copyright was not affixed. For these earlier works, the copyright notice should take the form of the word "Copyright" (or "Copr.") or the copyright symbol "©" along with the year of first publication (for most works) and the name of the copyright owner or other information sufficient to identify the owner (17 U.S.C. § 401(b)). For later works, even though notice is not required, it is generally a good idea to include a notice of a claim of copyright along with sufficient information to enable a reader to identify and contact the copyright holder. This warns potential copiers and facilitates licensing of the work.

### Exclusive Rights of the Copyright Holder

The copyright holder has economic rights in the work, including the right to control the copying, distribution, performance, or display of the work and the making of derivative works. For example, Acuff-Rose Music, Inc., which owns the copyright in the 1964 Roy Orbison song "Pretty Woman," has the right to prevent others from making copies of the song and selling those copies at flea markets or offering them for download over a file-sharing network. (Several sets of rights are actually involved here: the rights of the composer of the music, the rights of the writer of the lyrics, and the rights of the performing artist. Unraveling the complex sets of rights involved in music copyright is a daunting task, but an excellent book on the subject is *Kohn on Music Licensing* [see Chapter 8].) The holders of the copyright in "Pretty Woman" have the right to prevent other musicians from performing the song, unless those musicians first obtain permission, as Van Halen did when it covered the song in 1982. The copyright holders have the right to license the making of derivative works, including a movie drawing its title and general theme from the song, such as the 1990 movie *Pretty Woman,* starring Richard Gere and Julia Roberts. Visual artists also have limited moral rights in their works, including the rights of integrity and attribution under the Visual Artists Rights Act of 1990 (17 U.S.C. § 106A).

However, there are limitations on these exclusive rights. The right of first sale allows the purchaser or other lawful recipient of a licensed copy of a work to sell, give away, destroy, or otherwise dispose of that copy. A person who is dismayed to find a recording of Roy Orbison's "Pretty Woman" in his or her Christmas stocking may turn around and regift that copy to someone else (17 U.S.C. § 109(a)).

More worrisome to the content industry is the right of fair use. While the right of first sale is not a right to copy, the right of fair use permits the copying of a copyrighted work "for purposes such as criticism, comment, news reporting, teaching (including multiple copies for classroom use), scholarship, or research" (17 U.S.C. § 107). The statute provides that

> In determining whether the use made of a work in any particular case is a fair use the factors to be considered shall include—
>
> (1) the purpose and character of the use, including whether such use is of a commercial nature or is for non-profit educational purposes;
>
> (2) the nature of the copyrighted work;
>
> (3) the amount and substantiality of the portion used in relation to the copyrighted work as a whole; and
>
> (4) the effect of the use upon the potential market for or value of the copyrighted work.

These factors are a bit fuzzy, and determining the boundaries of fair use has been and continues to be the source of much work for the courts. Among the fair uses of the song "Pretty Woman," however, are space shifting, time shifting, and parody. If you have a lawfully obtained, licensed copy of "Pretty Woman" on CD, you may copy it onto a tape cassette to play in your 1983 Toyota Corolla, which lacks a CD player. You may also copy it onto your computer to play at work (but not to upload to a file-sharing service) or onto your MP3 player to listen to while you work out. These uses—transferring the licensed copy to another medium for use in another player—are space-shifting uses. When the copy will be used by the same person, space shifting has been held to be fair use (see *Recording Industry Association of America v. Diamond Multimedia Systems, Inc.*, 180 F.3d 1072).

Time-shifting is similar. If you know the movie *Pretty Woman* will be broadcast by a local television station at 1 p.m. on a workday, and you want to watch the movie, you may set your TiVo or VCR to record it, then watch the show when you return home from work. This is time shifting, and it has also been held to be fair use (see *Sony*, 464 U.S. 417).

Acuff-Rose Music also lacks the power to protect Roy Orbison's song from mockery. When the early rap group 2 Live Crew requested Acuff-Rose's permission to create a parody of the song, Acuff-Rose denied permission. Without permission, 2 Live Crew wrote, recorded, and distributed the parody, and Acuff-Rose, predictably, sued. The U.S. Supreme Court held that parody, within certain limits, can be fair use and is protected by the First Amendment's guarantee of freedom of expression (*Campbell*, 510 U.S. 569).

The disassembly of a computer program to reverse engineer for compatibility has also been found to fall within the parameters of fair use (*Sega Enterprises*, 977 F.2d 1510; *Sony Computer*, 203 F.3d 596). In addition to the fair-use exception in 17 U.S.C. § 107, the copyright code also provides exceptions to the exclusive rights of the copyright holder for copies of software made as backups or for diagnostic or maintenance purposes (17 U.S.C. § 117) and for copies made by ISPs in the routine course of information transmission, storage, caching, or location (17 U.S.C. § 512).

Recent court battles related to fair use have tended to fall into three categories: (1) attempts by content owners to restrict or prohibit the sale of copying devices; (2) the ongoing battle over file sharing; and (3) disputes arising from the DMCA's provisions on the circumvention of technological copy-protection measures (17 U.S.C. § 1201). Examples from each of these categories are discussed in Chapter 2.

### Copyright Infringement

A person who violates an exclusive right of the copyright owner has committed copyright infringement. In other words, the unauthorized copying, distribution, performance, or display of a copyrighted work, or the unauthorized making of a derivative work, is infringement unless it falls within a statutory exception such as those already described. Importing infringing copies of a work made outside the United States (even if made legally in some other country) into the United States is also infringement (17 U.S.C. § 501(a)). Infringement can give rise to a civil lawsuit by the copyright holder or a person authorized to enforce the copyright holder's rights (17 U.S.C. §§ 501–505) and to criminal prosecution in some cases (17 U.S.C. § 506).

The person committing the actual violation is a direct infringer. Indirect infringers may also be liable as contributory infringers or as inducing infringers. Contributory infringement requires that the contributory infringer have actual or constructive knowledge of an underlying direct infringement by some other person, and that the contributory infringer make a material contribution to the direct infringer's activities (*Fonovisa*, 76 F.3d 259). Contributory infringement may also be found where one person intentionally induces or encourages a direct infringement. This can be done by distributing a device (including a computer program) with the object of promoting its use to infringe copyright (*MGM v. Grokster*, 125 S.Ct. at 2776, 2780).

Vicarious infringement also requires an underlying direct infringement and further requires that the vicarious infringer have the right and ability to control the direct infringer's actions and receive a direct financial benefit from the infringing activity (*Fonovisa*, 76 F.3d 259). In recent years the content industry has used lawsuits for contributory and vicarious copyright infringement liability as its main weapon against peer-to-peer (P2P) file-sharing networks (discussed in Chapter 2).

A civil suit for infringement, whether direct or indirect, can lead to injunctive relief, the confiscation of infringing copies, and an award of money damages. Serious infringements may also lead to an action for criminal copyright infringement, which occurs when the infringement is committed

> (1) for purposes of commercial advantage or private financial gain, or (2) by the reproduction or distribution, including by electronic means, during any 180-day period, of 1 or more copies or phonorecords of 1 or more copyrighted works, which have a total retail value of more than $1,000. (17 U.S.C. § 506(a))

Penalties for criminal copyright infringement can include forfeiture and destruction of infringing copies and copying equipment, fines, and prison terms (18 U.S.C. § 2319).

## Duration of Copyright

The current duration of copyright terms under U.S. law is set by the Sonny Bono Copyright Term Extension Act of 1998. The Act sets the term for copyrighted works created after 1 January 1978 at the lifetime of the author plus an additional 70 years for most individually authored or coauthored works, and a term of 95 years from publication or 120 years from creation, whichever is shorter, for most other works, including anonymously and pseudonymously authored works and works for hire.

This term is much longer than that set in the first U.S. Copyright Act. Like the Statute of Anne before it, the first Copyright Act set the term of copyright at fourteen years, potentially renewable once for an additional fourteen years. The 1909 Copyright Act doubled this term, giving most works a copyright term of twenty-eight years, renewable once for an additional twenty-eight years. The 1976 Act replaced the renewable term with a single term for works created after 1 January 1978, measured by the life of the author plus an additional fifty years for most individually authored or coauthored works, and a term of seventy-five years for most other works, including anonymously and pseudonymously authored works and works for hire. The Sonny Bono Copyright Term Extension Act extended these terms to life plus seventy years and ninety-five years, respectively. It also extended to sixty-seven years the renewal term for works published before 1 January 1978 and copyrighted under the 1909 Act, which had previously been made automatic and extended to forty-seven years (see generally Leaffer 1999, 223–226).

What all of this means is that the copyright term is quite easy to determine for works published after 1 March 1989, fairly easy to determine for works published after 1 January 1978, and potentially quite difficult to determine for works published in 1977 or earlier. For works fixed in a tangible medium of expression after 1 March 1989, even if not formally published, the term is either the life of the author plus seventy years or ninety-five years. For works published between 1 January 1978, and 28 February 1989, the term is the same, provided that proper notice of a claim of copyright was affixed to the work. If proper notice was not affixed, the work may have fallen into the public domain, although several exceptions apply to allow the copyright holder to remedy the failure to affix notice.

The Copyright Renewal Act of 1992 retroactively made copyright renewal automatic for works published between 1964 and 1977 and otherwise eligible for copyright renewal. The length of this renewal term was subsequently extended to sixty-seven years, so that all such works are still in copyright. For works created in 1950 and earlier, it must first be determined whether the copyright was renewed. If it was not, and if it was not otherwise extended in some way, the copyright expired on 31 December of the twenty-eighth year of the copyright. If the copyright was renewed, the current sixty-seven-year extension applies automatically, so that, for example, the copyright on a work published in 1940 and renewed in 1968 will expire on 31 December 2035. Works originally copyrighted between 1 January 1951 and 31 December 1963, would still have been in their first copyright term on 1 January 1978, and renewal after that date was not automatic. These works still had to be renewed to gain the benefit of the sixty-seven-year renewal term (see generally U.S. Copyright Office 2004). In other words, for works published in 1963 and earlier, the copyright expired twenty-eight years after publication unless it was renewed. If copyright was renewed it expired or will expire ninety-five years after publication.

### The Public Domain

All works on which the copyright has expired, as well as all works that have never been copyrighted, are in the public domain. While some works fixed before 1 March 1989, were either deliberately or inadvertently placed in the public domain by failure to claim copyright, all newer works are copyrighted as soon as they are fixed, with one exception: Original U.S. government works are also in the public domain; they are never copyrighted (17 U.S.C. § 105). Works in the public domain may be freely copied, adapted, distributed, performed, and displayed without the consent of the creator of the work. State and local government works may be copyrighted, although many such works— statutes, ordinances, reported decisions, and the like—are non-copyrightable on the theory that the people must have free access to the laws governing them (see, for example, *Georgia v. The Harrison Co.,* 548 F. Supp. 110; Leaffer 1999, 93). This same logic applies even if the document was originally written by a private party and is later adopted as law by the government (*Building Officials,* 628 F.2d 730). The same logic should apply to international legal documents such as treaties or resolutions of the United Nations Security Council and, somewhat more tenuously, to official materials of foreign governments.

Much of the history of copyright law can be read as an attempt by content owners to fence off increasingly large portions of the public domain. In the twentieth century, the extensions of the copyright term in 1909, 1976, and 1998 took portions of the public domain and gave them to copyright holders. In the previous century, copyright holders had attempted, unsuccessfully, to use trademark law for the same purpose. In 1890, the publishers of the 1847 edition of *Webster's Dictionary*, on which the copyright had expired, brought suit against another publisher that had reproduced and distributed for sale the entire 1847 edition. The federal court hearing the case refused to allow trademark to be used in this way. To do so, it observed, would "continue that monopoly indefinitely," in effect granting a perpetual copyright (*Merriam*, 43 F. 450).

Six years later, the U.S. Supreme Court reached the same result in a patent case, refusing to allow the makers of Singer sewing machines to use trademark law to prevent others from manufacturing those machines after the patent had expired (*Singer*, 163 U.S. at 185–186). The *Singer* case also introduced the term "public domain" (as "the domain of things public") to U.S. law, giving it a definition somewhat different from that given to *domaine publique* in nineteenth-century French law and in the Berne Convention.

Because the Berne Convention Implementation Act of 1988 eliminated the requirements of registration and notice for copyright protection, all original works of authorship fixed in a tangible medium of expression are now copyrighted; U.S. copyright law contains no procedure by which copyright holders may choose to forgo copyright. Authors cannot place their works in the public domain; those who wish to do so must opt for the next best alternative, an open-source license. A wide variety of such licenses are available, including the well-known GNU General Public License (for software) and the various licenses available from Creative Commons for works of all types. The release of a work under a public license is sometimes referred to as "placing the work in the public domain," but in fact the work remains copyrighted, under the open-source license, for the full statutory term. The term "copyleft" is sometimes used as an alternative.

### Ownership, Transfer, and Licensing of Copyrights

Individual authors own the copyright in the works they create. Joint authors not working for hire own the copyright jointly (17 U.S.C. § 201(a)). A collective work is not the same thing as a joint work. The authors of a joint work intend that their work will form part of a unitary whole (such as a course textbook, even if entire chapters are written by a single author), while the pieces of a collective work (such as articles in an encyclopedia) are themselves independent works (17 U.S.C. § 101). When works are made for hire, the employer owns the copyright (17 U.S.C. §§ 101, 201(b)).

Once acquired, ownership of a copyright may be freely transferred in whole or in part. The transfer may include some or all of the copyright holder's exclusive rights (*Effects Associates*, 908 F.2d 555). Transfers must ordinarily be in writing:

> A transfer of copyright ownership, other than by operation of law, is not valid unless an instrument of conveyance, or a note or memorandum of the transfer, is in writing and signed by the owner of the rights conveyed or such owner's duly authorized agent. (17 U.S.C. § 204(a))

While a certificate of acknowledgment of the transfer is not required, it may serve as prima facie evidence that a transfer took place (17 U.S.C. § 204(b)). Transfers of copyright, like the copyrights themselves, can be (and, if there is any chance that the copyright might become valuable or that there might be conflicting claims to the copyright, should be) recorded with the Copyright Office (17 U.S.C. § 205).

In addition to a transfer of all or part of the copyright, the copyright holder may also license others to perform certain acts (such as making and distributing copies) that would otherwise be the exclusive right of the copyright holder. While exclusive licenses, like transfers, must be in writing, nonexclusive licenses may be granted orally. Nonexclusive licenses may even be granted by implication, in the absence of any explicit oral license, if the conduct or relationship between the parties shows an intent to grant the license (see Leaffer 1999, 219). Licenses, like transfers, can be recorded with the Copyright Office, and should be if there is any possibility that the copyright will become valuable or that conflict or uncertainty might arise.

Copyright may be transferred involuntarily when the author has placed the copyright as collateral for a debt or in bankruptcy. It may not, however, be taken by a foreign government to suppress opinions with which that government disagrees (Leaffer 1999, 222; 17 U.S.C. § 20(e)). Sound and video recordings, however, may be subject to a compulsory license in some situations. These compulsory licenses allow the licensee to use the work without the copyright holder's consent, so long as the licensee pays an appropriate royalty fee (see Leaffer 1999, 285). Most holders of performance rights in music recordings license those rights to a performing rights society such as ASCAP or BMI (in the

United States), or similar organizations outside the United States, such as Buma/Stemra in the Netherlands. These organizations then grant a blanket license to radio stations and similar entities wishing to play the recordings and divide the fees received among the performance right holders in proportion to the frequency with and the size of the markets in which they are played. While disputes inevitably arise concerning the allocation of licensing fees, the system persists because it is more workable than the alternative—separately licensing millions of music recordings to thousands of media outlets.

A similar logic underlies the open-source movement, although the motive is not pecuniary. To work around the impossibility of placing privately created works in the public domain, open-source programmers and authors use a voluntary collective license—a license under which the copyright owner relinquishes the right to choose the licensee. The copyright owner does not necessarily relinquish the right to be paid; much shareware, for instance, is distributed under licenses that do not restrict copying but do require the copier to pay the copyright holder. Voluntary collective licenses used for open-source works require no payment (or, sometimes, payment only for commercial uses), but may impose other conditions.

## Trademark Overview

A trademark is not, surprisingly, a mark used in trade. In the narrow sense, a trademark is a mark used in commerce "to identify and distinguish . . . goods . . . from those manufactured or sold by others and to indicate the source of the goods" (15 U.S.C. § 1127). Service marks are used "to identify and distinguish the services of one person . . . from the services of others and to indicate the source of the services"; collective marks "indicat[e] membership in a union, an association, or other organization"; and certification marks "certify regional or other origin, material, mode of manufacture, quality, accuracy, or other characteristics of . . . goods or services or that the work or labor on the goods or services was performed by members of a union or other organization" (15 U.S.C. § 1127). These four types of marks—trademarks, service marks, collective marks, and certification marks—are often, but inaccurately, collectively referred to as "trademarks." The body of law governing these types of marks and related concepts may, however, be properly referred to as "trademark law."

The rationale for trademark is to protect the public as well as the mark holder. Marks benefit consumers by providing an indication of quality. Infringement upon or dilution of the mark may harm the mark holder, unjustly enrich the infringer, and confuse the public.

## What Can Be Trademarked?

A letter, word, logo, slogan, motto, design, phrase, picture, shape, symbol, or some combination thereof can become a protected mark. A color, such as the pink color of a brand of fiberglass insulation, may become a trademark if it is sufficiently distinctive (see *Qualitex Co.*, 514 U.S. 159). Even a smell may become a trademark, provided that it is distinctive and not merely functional; thus, a particular scent for a brand of scented embroidery yarn may be registered as a trademark (*In re Clarke*, 17 U.S.P.Q.2d 1238).

Certain things may not be registered as marks under federal law, however. A mark that is immoral, deceptive, disparaging, or scandalous may not be registered (15 U.S.C. § 1052(a)), although this restriction is quite narrowly construed. While a logo showing, in silhouette, a dog defecating, is scandalous, an "Old Glory" condom, made to look like a U.S. flag, is not (*In re Old Glory Condom Corp.*, 26 U.S.P.Q.2d 1216). The flag itself, though, as well as other insignia and flags of the federal, state, and foreign governments, cannot be registered as a mark (15 U.S.C. § 1052(b)). The Washington Redskins' mark has been the subject of years of litigation by Native American activists seeking to cancel the mark's federal registration on the grounds that it disparages a particular ethnic group.

Marks that are confusingly similar to an existing mark cannot be registered. Nor can generic marks—for example, marks that are merely the names of the goods or services they are used to identify, such as "You have mail" as an e-mail service's announcement that a message has arrived—be registered (15 U.S.C. § 1052(e)(1); *America Online*, 64 F. Supp.2d 549). Marks that are deceptive cannot be registered, although marks that are deceptively misdescriptive may be registered if they have acquired a secondary meaning. A mark is deceptive if it leads the consumer to believe the product is something other than it actually is and influences the buying decision (see generally 15 U.S.C. § 1052(a)). It is deceptively misdescriptive if consumers might be misled as to the nature of the product, but their buying decisions would not be influenced. Thus, the name "Lovee Lamb" for car seat covers made of synthetic sheepskin is deceptive, because consumers might prefer seat covers made of lambskin or sheepskin to synthetic covers. And while the name "Glass Wax" for a glass and metal cleaner that contains no wax may lead consumers to believe the product contains wax, it is unlikely to affect their buying choices. Consumers are probably indifferent to whether the product contains wax (*In re Budge Manufacturing*, 857 F.2d 773; *Gold Seal Co.*, 129 F. Supp. 928).

Descriptive terms, geographic terms, and personal names can become trademarks if and only if they acquire a secondary meaning. This secondary meaning is acquired when the mark becomes established in the minds of the public, or at least in the minds of the audience at which the mark is aimed, as referring to the particular thing described and not to the broader class of things to which it belongs (*Abercrombie & Fitch*, 537 F.2d at 9). Terms that are suggestive, arbitrary, or fanciful are always eligible for registration as marks, provided they are not scandalous, deceptive, or otherwise ineligible. Suggestive terms suggest something about the goods or services to which they apply, without directly describing them: "Windex" used to describe a window cleaning fluid is suggestive. Arbitrary marks are words and images whose everyday use neither suggests nor describes the goods or services to which they are applied: "Element" used to describe an automobile is arbitrary. Fanciful marks are coined or created for no reason other than to serve as a mark: "Aptiva" used to describe a computer is fanciful.

The term "element" would not be arbitrary in all cases, however; the difficulty of placing terms within these categories is "compounded because a term that is in one category for a particular product may be in quite a different one for another" (*Abercrombie & Fitch*, 537 F.2d at 9). For example, the term "'ivory' would be generic when used to describe a product made from the tusks of elephants but arbitrary as applied to soap" (*Abercrombie & Fitch*, 537 F.2d at 9 fn. 6). In addition, "a term may shift from one category to another in light of differences in usage through time" (*Abercrombie & Fitch*, 537 F.2d at 9). This is what happened to "the coined word 'Escalator', originally fanciful, or at the very least suggestive," which by 1950 had become generic (*Abercrombie & Fitch*, 537 F.2d at 9 fn. 7). In addition, "a term may have one meaning to one group of users and a different one to others," and "the same term may be put to different uses with respect to a single product" (*Abercrombie & Fitch*, 537 F.2d at 9).

Abercrombie & Fitch involved several uses of the word "safari" to describe clothing, hats, and footwear. The court held that "A&F could not apply 'Safari' as a trademark for an expedition into the African wilderness. This would be a clear example of the use of 'Safari' as a generic term. What is perhaps less obvious is that a word may have more than one generic use" (*Abercrombie & Fitch*, 537 F.2d at 11). The use of "safari" to describe "a broad flat-brimmed hat with a single, large band" was generic; that type of hat had become known as a safari hat, and Abercrombie & Fitch could not claim a trademark in the name. Similarly, "a belted bush jacket with patch pockets and a buttoned shoulder loop" was generically known as a safari jacket, and "when the jacket is accompanied by pants, the combination is called the 'Safari suit'" (*Abercrombie & Fitch*, 537 F.2d at 11–12). A smaller version of the safari hat was a "minisafari," a term in which Abercrombie & Fitch could also claim no trademark. However, "there is no evidence that 'Safari' has become a generic term for boots." The defendant's use may have been protected by the fair use defense, because the defendant's boots were called "Camel Safari," "Hippo Safari," and "Chukka Safari," and the defendant actually operated safari tours to Africa.

### Trademark Formalities

Unlike patents and copyrights, marks are protected by a significant body of state law as well as by federal law. Thus, marks can be protected at the state level even in the absence of a federal trademark registration. The basic requirement for state common law trademark protection is that the mark be used in commerce; the first person to do so gains rights in the mark. Protection does not stem from the act of creating the mark, as it would in copyright, but from prior, open, bona fide use of and control over the mark. Registration of a mark may also ensure protection even before the mark is actually used: "A person who has a bona fide intention, under circumstances showing the good faith of such person, to use a trademark in commerce may request registration of its trademark . . ." (15 U.S.C. § 1051(b)). Although the registration will not actually issue until the use has occurred, the registrant will be able to use the filing date to establish priority over other claimants.

While unregistered marks may be suitable for very small or very new businesses, marks that have or are likely to have significant value should be registered. Federal registration is available for marks used in interstate commerce. The U.S. Patent and Trademark Office's website provides a useful tool for new registrants. The Trademark Electronic Search System (TESS) allows users to search a database of more than three million registered trademarks in order to avoid submitting applications that will be rejected because they are for marks identical or similar to marks already registered to someone else for the same or similar goods or services.

Once a mark has been selected, the applicant must draft a description of the goods or services to be covered by the mark. The applicant then submits this description to the U.S. Patent and Trademark Office, along with a clear depiction of the mark itself and an application fee ($325 for most applications if filed online or $375 for most applications if filed in hard copy) (U.S. Patent and Trademark Office website). Shortly after filing, the applicant will receive a notice that the application has been received, but a decision on the application may take six months to a year if no difficulties arise, or much longer in unusual, difficult, or contested cases. Registration in the United States does not, by itself, provide protection outside the United States. The global trademark protection regime (discussed in Chapter 3) is much less developed than that of copyright or even patent.

*Notice of trademark:* It is not necessary to give notice of a claim of trademark for common-law trademark protection, but it is advisable. Use of the superscripts "TM" (for trademark) and "SM" (for service mark) indicate a claim in an unregistered trademark. The trademark registration symbol "®" indicates a federally registered trademark, as do the words "Registered U.S. Patent and Trademark Office" or "Reg. U.S. Pat. & TM Off." The term "Marca Registrada" or the superscript "MR" is required in some countries.

### Trademark Infringement

Property rights in protected marks can be harmed in two ways: infringement and dilution. All marks are subject to infringement, which occurs when an unauthorized person uses the mark in a way that creates a likelihood of confusion. Not all marks are subject to dilution, however, which occurs when an unauthorized person tarnishes the mark or blurs its distinctiveness; only famous trademarks can be diluted (15 U.S.C. § 1125(c)(1)).

*Infringement:* Infringement occurs when an unauthorized person uses a mark belonging to another, or a similar mark, in a way that creates a likelihood of confusion in the minds of the public. The various federal circuits have adopted similar, but not identical, tests for determining whether a use creates a likelihood of confusion. The Ninth Circuit Court of Appeals' eight-factor test examines (1) the strength of the mark, (2) the proximity of the goods, (3) the similarity of the marks, (4) the evidence of actual confusion, (5) the marketing channels used, (6) the type of goods and the degree of care likely to be exercised by the purchaser, (7) the defendant's intent in selecting the mark, and (8) the likelihood of expansion of the product lines (*Playboy Enterprises*, 279 F.3d 796). These are factors, not elements. A court may find a likelihood of confusion if the balance of factors shows a likelihood of confusion, even if one or perhaps more factors seem to weigh against such a finding.

*Dilution:* The threshold question in any dilution action is whether the mark in question is "famous" within the meaning of the Trademark Dilution Act, which states:

> For purposes of paragraph (1), a mark is famous if it is widely recognized by the general consuming public of the United States as a designation of source of the goods or services of the mark's owner. In determining whether a mark possesses the requisite degree of recognition, the court may consider all relevant factors, including the following:
>
> (i) The duration, extent, and geographic reach of advertising and publicity of the mark, whether advertised or publicized by the owner or third parties.
>
> (ii) The amount, volume, and geographic extent of sales of goods or services offered under the mark.
>
> (iii) The extent of actual recognition of the mark.
>
> (iv) Whether the mark was registered under the Act of March 3, 1881, or the Act of February 20, 1905, or on the principal register. (15 U.S.C. § 1125(c)(2)(A), as amended by 120 Stat. 1730)

It is not necessary for all of the listed factors to be present in order for a mark to be famous. Even if some factors weigh against a finding that the mark is famous, those factors may be outweighed by others (McCarthy 2004, 175–176).

If the mark is famous, it has been diluted if an unauthorized person has blurred or tarnished it. The diluting use must be a commercial use, and it must have arisen after the mark became famous. In addition to noncommercial uses, commercial uses for purposes of parody, criticism, comment, news reporting, or comparative advertising are protected from liability for dilution (120 Stat. 1730).

Blurring occurs when a mark similar to the famous mark is used on some other product, resulting in a diminution in the distinctiveness of the famous mark. Congress has defined blurring as "association arising from the similarity between a mark or trade name and a famous mark that impairs the distinctiveness of the famous mark" (15 U.S.C. § 1125(c)(2)(B), as amended by 120 Stat. 1730). To determine the likelihood of blurring, "the court may consider all relevant factors, including" the degree of similarity between the marks, the distinctiveness and degree of recognition of the famous mark, the extent to which the use of that mark is exclusive, whether the user intends to create an association with the secondary mark, and any actual association between them.

Claims for blurring give somewhat broader protection to the owners of famous marks than "likelihood of confusion" infringement claims give to the holders of all marks. However, when the consumers at whom the marks are aimed are sophisticated and there is no bad intent on the part of the second user, courts are unlikely to find blurring. For example, the name "Lexus" for luxury automobiles, although similar to the name "Lexis" already in use for an online legal research service, does not blur the Lexis trademark. The products are different, the Lexis name is famous only among attorneys and virtually unknown elsewhere, and attorneys are sophisticated consumers who are not likely to be misled as to the source of either the cars or the research service (*Mead Data Central*, 875 F.2d at 1031–1032).

Tarnishment occurs when a famous mark is used in a way that casts disrepute upon it or otherwise interferes with positive mental associations attached to the mark. Congress has defined "dilution by tarnishment" as "association arising from the similarity between a mark or trade name and a famous mark that harms the reputation of the famous mark" (15 U.S.C. § 1125(c)(2)(C), as amended by 120 Stat. 1730). For example, a reproduction of the red and white Coca-Cola logo, substituting the words "Enjoy Cocaine" for "Enjoy Coca-Cola," tarnishes Coca-Cola's mark by associating dangerous and illegal drug use with the product (*Coca-Cola,* 346 F. Supp. 1183; although this case pre-dates the Federal Trademark Dilution Act, the court discussed a state trademark dilution statute).

*Third-party liability:* As with copyright and patent, third parties may be liable for trademark infringement by others. A party who "intentionally induces another to infringe a trademark, or . . . continues to supply its product to one whom it knows or has reason to know is engaging in trademark infringement . . . is contributorily responsible for any harm done as a result of the deceit" (*Inwood Labs,* 456 U.S. at 854). This has potentially serious repercussions for ISPs.

*Fair use:* As with copyright, a defendant in a trademark action may claim that his or her infringing or diluting use is protected as a fair use. Trademark fair use may be either traditional or nominative. Traditional or classic fair use occurs when a trademark is also a descriptive term and is used by a person other than the trademark holder in its descriptive sense. For example, the use of "sweet-tart" to describe Ocean Spray cranberry juice does not infringe on the trademark "SweeTarts" for candy. Ocean Spray is using "sweet-tart" as a description of the taste of its cranberry juice, not as a trademark, and the description is accurate (*Sunmark,* 64 F.3d 1055).

Nominative fair use occurs when one person uses another's trademark not, or not exclusively, to identify his or her own product or service, but to identify the trademark holder's product or service. Thus, a mechanic repairing Toyota automobiles may use the name "Toyota" in advertisements, because there is no other simple way for the mechanic to identify his or her services. Similarly, a temporary agency offering to place workers skilled in the use of Microsoft Office may use the name "Microsoft Office" in its advertisements, rather than some unwieldy circumlocution such as "the principal business-oriented suite of software distributed by a large software company headquartered in Redmond, Washington." Nominative fair use has played a significant role in legal disputes over search-engine spamming and related techniques and is discussed in Chapter 2.

### Transfer, Duration, and Termination of Trademark

Marks are alienable interests in property. They may be licensed or assigned, provided the requirement of actual use of the mark continues to be met. While patents and copyrights are constitutionally required to be of limited duration, trademarks are not.

Trademarks may last forever, but trademark registrations must be renewed periodically. Registrations issued after 16 November 1989 must be renewed every ten years (15 U.S.C. §§ 1058–1059). Lapse of registration by itself does not terminate a trademark, but a trademark that remains unused for three years may be abandoned, in which case it can be claimed by another person. (See *Silverman*, 870 F.2d 40, which discusses whether trademarks in "Amos 'n' Andy" radio characters had been abandoned after twenty-one years of nonuse.) Trademarks may also fall into the public domain by becoming generic; everyday words such as "escalator" and "aspirin" were once trademarks. The owners of trademarks such as Coca-Cola, Xerox, Magic Marker, and Frigidaire have waged successful campaigns to keep their trademarks from becoming generic.

## Patent Overview

A patent is an intellectual property right that allows the holder to exclude others from making, selling, using, or offering to sell an invention, as well as from importing the invention or a device incorporating it into the United States, even if it was legally manufactured elsewhere (McCarthy 2004, 433–435). Unlike copyrights and trademarks, patents do not arise automatically from the creative process; they must be affirmatively applied for. The U.S. Patent and Trademark Office grants utility patents, design patents, and plant patents.

### Patentable Subject Matter: What Can Be Patented?

Utility patents may be granted under U.S. law for "any new and useful process, machine, manufacture, or composition of matter, or any new and useful improvement thereof" (35 U.S.C. § 101). Inventions can be patented if they are useful, novel, and nonobvious (35 U.S.C. §§ 101 [useful], 102 [novel], 103 [nonobvious]). Novelty and nonobviousness are assessed in relation to the prior art—the existing body of inventions and technical knowledge in the area. Patents cannot be obtained for natural phenomena, abstract ideas, or laws of nature. They may, however, be obtained for a wide variety of things not traditionally thought of as inventions, such as plants or business methods.

Design patents may be granted under U.S. law for "any new, original, and ornamental design for an article of manufacture"

(35 U.S.C. § 171), while plant patents may be granted for the invention or discovery and asexual reproduction (such as reproduction by grafting) of "any distinct and new variety of plant, including cultivated sports, mutants, hybrids, and newly found seedlings, other than a tuber propagated plant or a plant found in an uncultivated state" (35 U.S.C. § 161), as well as for sexually reproduced plants and plants propagated from tubers (7 U.S.C. § 2402).

## Patent Formalities

While the formalities for a grant of copyright were never onerous and are now *de minimis,* and the formalities for a grant of trademark are fairly straightforward, the formalities of the patent application process are complex. The application form initially filed must include the title of the invention (37 C.F.R. 1.72(a)), a specification, a drawing, and the applicant's oath (35 U.S.C. § 111). The specification contains the claims and is the heart of the patent application.

> The specification shall contain a written description of the invention, and of the manner and process of making and using it, in such full, clear, concise, and exact terms as to enable any person skilled in the art to which it pertains, or with which it is most nearly connected, to make and use the same, and shall set forth the best mode contemplated by the inventor of carrying out his invention.
>
> The specification shall conclude with one or more claims particularly pointing out and distinctly claiming the subject matter which the applicant regards as his invention. (35 U.S.C. § 112)

With regard to the drawing, the code provides that:

> The applicant shall furnish a drawing where necessary for the understanding of the subject matter sought to be patented. When the nature of such subject matter admits of illustration by a drawing and the applicant has not furnished such a drawing, the Director may require its submission within a time period of not less than two months from the sending of a notice thereof. (35 U.S.C. § 113)

In the oath, the applicant must state "that he [or she] believes himself [or herself] to be the original and first inventor of the process, machine, manufacture, or composition of matter, or improvement thereof, for which he [or she] solicits a patent; and shall state of what country he [or she] is a citizen" (35 U.S.C. § 115).

The application must also be accompanied by the appropriate fee. Figuring out the fee is itself a complex task, requiring the applicant (or his or her patent agent or attorney) to consult a ten-page fee schedule published by the U.S. Patent and Trademark Office. For utility patent applications filed on or after 8 December 2004, the basic filing fee is $300, with "small entities" (small businesses, nonprofit organizations, and individual inventors) receiving a 50 percent discount. Small entities filing electronic rather than hard-copy applications receive an additional discount, paying only $75. If the application contains more than twenty claims or more than three independent claims, additional per-claim fees apply. Applications longer than 100 sheets also pay a surcharge. The basic filing fee for design, plant, and provisional patents filed on or after 8 December 2004 is $200; again, small entities receive a 50 percent discount, and surcharges may apply (U.S. Patent and Trademark Office website, FY 2006 Fee Schedule).

With copyrights, the applicant's role in the registration process usually ends when the initial application is completed. With registration of marks, too, there is little left for the applicant to do, unless the registration is contested or unusual in some way. The patent application process, however, typically takes two to three years, during which there may be considerable communication and give and take between the applicant and the U.S. Patent and Trademark Office. If, at any time, the applicant fails to respond to any action by the U.S. Patent and Trademark Office within six months of the action, the office will consider the application abandoned, unless the applicant can show that the delay was unavoidable.

During this process a number of dates may be important. The first, chronologically, is the invention date, also called the conception date. This is the date upon which the inventor first thinks of the invention. In most of the world the invention date has no legal significance; the United States, however, is a "first-to-invent" jurisdiction. In the United States, when there is a dispute between two inventors who invented the same thing at more or less the same time, the inventor who first thought of the invention wins, provided that the inventor can prove the date on which he or she first thought of the invention and show that he or she subsequently exercised diligence in reducing the invention to practice. In the rest of the world, the conflict is resolved more simply, if perhaps less fairly: The first inventor to file a sufficiently complete application wins. In effect, under U.S. law the invention date may replace the priority date in some cases.

The next legally significant date in the application process is the filing date—the date upon which the application papers are received by the U.S. Patent and Trademark Office. This is followed by the priority date—the date upon which the technical disclosure that fully describes the invention covered by that claim was first filed with some patent office. The patent office with which the disclosure was first filed need not be the U.S. Patent and Trademark Office; it could be a patent office outside the United States. If the elements of a claim have been published elsewhere before the priority date, the claim is invalid in most of the world. In the United States, as already noted, an inventor may substitute the invention date for the priority date in such a case, provided that the invention date is less than one year earlier than the priority date and, as noted, that the inventor can provide sufficient proof (through notes, workbooks, or the like) of the invention date.

After the priority date—usually about eighteen months after, although the time span may vary—comes the publication date. This is the date on which a patent application is published and the correspondence between the U.S. Patent and Trademark Office and the applicant is made public. This is a somewhat tense time for the patent applicant, because at that point all of the information necessary to duplicate the applicant's invention or discovery will be available to the whole world, including the applicant's business competitors—but the applicant will not yet have a patent. The applicant will be anxiously waiting for the issue date—the date on which the patent application is granted and matures into a patent. The issue date is the earliest date on which the patent holder may sue for infringement.

The relationship between the U.S. Patent and Trademark Office and the applicant does not end there, however. Patents may be adjusted; errors may be corrected, resulting in a reissue of the patent. Additional fees must be paid at various stages in the application process and must continue to be paid during the life of the patent. These fees include, among others, search fees, examination fees, and maintenance fees. The maintenance fees, in particular, can be quite hefty, with fees of $900, $2,300, and $3,800 due at 3.5, 7.5, and 11.5 years, respectively (U.S. Patent and Trademark Office website, FY 2006 Fee Schedule; maintenance fees apply only to utility patents).

To be protected against patent infringement in other countries, the inventor must apply for and be granted a patent in each. This application process is greatly simplified by the Patent Cooperation Treaty (discussed in Chapter 3).

### Exclusive Rights of the Patent Holder and Patent Infringement

Once the patent is granted, the patent holder has the right to exclude others from using the patented invention or discovery. This does not necessarily mean that the patent holder has a right to make or use the invention or discovery; doing so may in turn require the use of inventions or discoveries patented by others.

Under the doctrine of equivalents, patent infringement can occur even when the infringing conduct or device does not exactly duplicate the description in the patent claims. Conduct or devices not literally within the scope of the patent are still covered by the patent if they differ only insubstantially. The breadth or narrowness with which the doctrine of equivalents will be applied depends on the degree of innovation inherent in the patent. Pioneer patents will be interpreted as covering a broad range of equivalents, while minor patents in an already crowded field will cover a narrower range. The doctrine of equivalents is also subject to three limitations. First, it can never be extended to cover prior art; anything already known or obvious to a person having ordinary skill in the prior art cannot be covered by the patent. Second, the doctrine is limited by the colorfully named "nose of wax rule": the claims may not be treated "like a nose of wax, which may be turned and twisted in any direction . . . so as to make it include something more than, or something different from, what its words express" (*White,* 119 U.S. at 51). Finally, the doctrine of equivalents is limited by prosecution history estoppel, also called file wrapper estoppel.

The file wrapper that gives the doctrine one of its names is the folder in which the U.S. Patent and Trademark Office keeps the papers filed during the process of a patent application. The patent application process is called the prosecution of the patent, and the papers in the file wrapper form the prosecution history that gives the doctrine its other name. During the course of prosecuting a patent, an applicant may concede in writing that certain things are not covered by the claims in the patent. The documents containing these concessions will be placed within the file wrapper and will form part of the prosecution history. By either name, the doctrine prevents a patent holder from asserting the doctrine of equivalents against an alleged infringer if the conduct complained of falls within these concessions. Patent holders may not use the doctrine of equivalents to reclaim processes or products that have been given up during the prosecution of the patent, even though they might otherwise be covered by the doctrine. They are "estopped" (legalese for prevented or prohibited) from maintaining a suit for patent infringement based on those conceded areas.

A patent holder who is able to prove infringement may obtain injunctive relief and damages against the infringer, which may include seizing and blocking importation of infringing goods (35 U.S.C. §§ 281–284). An accused infringer may, as an affirmative defense, attack the validity of the patent. Although the patent is presumed valid, an alleged infringer who establishes that the patent is invalid is, of course, not an infringer (35 U.S.C. § 282). Other persons may also challenge the validity of a patent.

As with copyright and trademark, third parties may be liable for patent infringement under certain circumstances. Third-party liability may be imposed for contributory patent infringement or for induced infringement. Contributory infringement occurs when a third party

> offers to sell or sells within the United States or imports into the United States a component of a patented machine, manufacture, combination or composition, or a material or apparatus for use in practicing a patented process, constituting a material part of the invention, knowing the same to be especially made or especially adapted for use in an infringement of such patent, and not a staple article or commodity of commerce suitable for substantial noninfringing use, shall be liable as a contributory infringer. (35 U.S.C. § 271(c))

Thus, a claim of contributory patent infringement has four elements: (1) someone must have sold, offered, or imported some component of a patented device or something for use in a patented process; (2) the component must be material—that is, not inessential; (3) the person must know that the component is made or adapted for use in that patented device or process; and (4) the component must not be a staple article of commerce (i.e., it must not be capable of a substantial noninfringing use).

The statutory definition of induced infringement provides only that "Whoever actively induces infringement of a patent shall be liable as an infringer" (35 U.S.C. § 271(b)). Courts have interpreted this as requiring that the inducer has knowledge of the underlying direct infringement and provides active and knowing assistance to the direct infringer (see *Manville Sales*, 917 F.2d at 553). In contrast to direct or contributory infringement, induced infringement can occur even when the defendant's conduct takes place outside the United States.

### Duration of Patent

A valuable patent, such as a new pharmaceutical patent, may cost ten times as much to bring to market as a valuable Hollywood movie. The Hollywood movie studio will have little effort and expense obtaining a copyright, and once it has done so any who violate the copyright may be subject not only to civil penalties, but also to criminal penalties, possibly including prison time. Most dramatic is the difference in the length of the monopoly granted: The movie studio's copyright will last for ninety-five years, but the pharmaceutical firm's patent will last for less than twenty years. The duration of utility patents is twenty years from the filing date—typically two to three years before the date on which the patent is granted (35 U.S.C. § 154(a)(2)). If obtaining the patent takes more than three years, the term may be extended by the amount over three years (35 U.S.C. § 154(b)(1)(B); see also 35 U.S.C. § 154(b)(1)(C)). The twenty-year term is set by TRIPs and was adopted by the United States in fulfillment of its TRIPs obligations; patents granted before 8 June 1995 may be governed by the earlier term of seventeen years from the date of issue (rather than a term measured from the filing date), if doing so would be beneficial to the patent holder. Such patents are valid for a term of seventeen years from the issue date or twenty years from the earliest regular patent filing date, whichever is longer (35 U.S.C. § 154(c)(1)). Plant patents are also valid for twenty years from the filing date, but design patents have an even shorter duration. Design patents are valid for fourteen years from the issue date (not filing date) (35 U.S.C. § 173). Patents that have expired, as well as those that have been abandoned, are in the public domain. They may be used freely but may not be recaptured by repatenting (35 U.S.C. § 102).

While the duration of copyright has increased dramatically since the founding of the United States, the duration of patents has not. The copyright term has increased from a maximum of twenty-eight years to life plus seventy years, so that a work by a twenty-year-old who lives to be ninety would remain in copyright for 140 years, or five times the original maximum term. The first Patent Act, in contrast, set a term of fourteen years, measured from the issue date. The current term of twenty years from the filing date—in effect, seventeen years and perhaps a few months from the issue date—represents no significant increase, and may in part explain why so much creative energy in the United States has been channeled away from the sciences and toward the creation of copyrightable works.

### Ownership, Transfer, and Licensing of Patents

The ownership of a patent arises from the act of creation, as with copyright. The inventor is the initial owner of the patent interest, but this interest may be assigned. A great many inventions are created by employees of companies in the course of their employment, and these inventions are typically assigned to the company. This may be done before the application is filed, but no assignment is valid unless it is recorded with the U.S. Patent and Trademark Office (35 U.S.C. § 261). An inventor or the inventor's assignee may also issue a license allowing another person or persons to make, use, or sell the invention.

# Summary

This chapter provides an overview of the development of intellectual property law in the United States and elsewhere, from the invention of printing through the advent of the Internet. It looks at the legal treatment of the three main forms of intellectual property—copyright, trademark, and patent—in U.S. law and introduces the tensions and international issues that will be addressed in Chapters 2 and 3.

The history of intellectual property law is closely connected to the history of technology. As information technology has advanced, copyright law has been forced to adapt in response.

Trademark law has grown as trade has grown, and patents have followed technical innovation. They came into being in the Italian Renaissance, and after the Industrial Revolution became the subject of a government agency within the United States—the U.S. Patent and Trademark Office.

We are now in the midst of a new wave of changes in intellectual property law, made necessary by the Internet information revolution. Computers and the Internet offer new scope for inventions and discoveries, requiring changes to patent law. Internet domain names provide a new category of things to be trademarked, while search engines provide new incentives for trademark infringement. And the area under greatest stress is copyright: The Internet provides enormously enhanced opportunities for content creation and for copyright infringement, resulting in the passage of laws that would have seemed shockingly harsh just a quarter of a century ago.

# Treaties

"Agreement on Trade-Related Aspects of Intellectual Property Rights (TRIPS), Marrakesh Agreement Establishing the World Trade Organization, Annex 1C." April 15, 1994. 33 I.L.M. 81.

"Buenos Aires Convention." August 20, 1910. 38 Stat. 1785, 155 L.N.T.S. 179.

"Convention Concerning the Creation of an International Union for the Protection of Literary and Artistic Works (Berne Convention)." September 9, 1886, as last revised at Paris, July 24, 1971 (amended 1979). 25 U.S.T. 1341, 828 U.N.T.S. 221.

"Convention Establishing the World Intellectual Property Organization." July 14, 1967, as amended on September 28, 1979 (WIPO Convention). 21 U.S.T. 1749, 828 U.N.T.S. 3.

"Convention on the Grant of European Patents." October 5, 1973. 13 I.L.M. 276. Text as amended through December 10, 1998, available at http://www.european-patent-office.org/legal/epc/e/ma1.html.

"Inter-American Convention for the Protection of Industrial Property." August 20, 1910. 39 Stat. 1675; TS 626; 1 Bevans 772. Replaced by General Inter-American Convention for Trademark and Commercial Protection. February 20, 1929. 46 Stat. 2907, TS 833, 2 Bevans 751, 124 L.N.T.S. 357.

"Madrid Agreement Concerning the International Registration of Marks." April 14, 1891. As revised at Brussels on December 14, 1900, at

Washington on June 2, 1911, at The Hague on November 6, 1925, at London on June 2, 1934, at Nice on June 15, 1957, and at Stockholm on July 14, 1967, and as amended on September 28, 1979. 828 U.N.T.S. 389.

"Paris Convention for the Protection of Industrial Property." March 20, 1883. As revised at Brussels on December 14, 1900, at Washington on June 2, 1911, at The Hague on November 6, 1925, at London on June 2, 1934, at Lisbon on October 31, 1958, and at Stockholm on July 14, 1967, and as amended on September 28, 1979. 21 U.S.T. 1583, 828 U.N.T.S. 305.

"Patent Cooperation Treaty." Washington. June 19, 1970. As amended on September 28, 1979, and as modified on February 3, 1984, and October 3, 2001. 28 U.S.T. 7645, 9 I.L.M. 978.

"Patent Law Treaty." June 1, 2000. 39 I.L.M. 1047.

"Protocol Relating to the Madrid Agreement Concerning the International Registration of Marks." June 27, 1989. Available from http://www.wipo.int/madrid/en/legal_texts/.

"Trademark Law Treaty." October 27, 1994. Available at http://www.wipo.int/clea/docs/en/wo/wo027en.htm.

"Universal Copyright Convention." September 6, 1952. 6 U.S.T. 2731. Revised at Paris, July 24, 1971. 25 U.S.T. 1341.

"WIPO Copyright Treaty." December 20, 1996. 36 I.L.M. 65 (1997).

"WIPO Performance and Phonograms Treaty." December 20, 1996. 36 I.L.M. 76 (1997).

# Regulations

Code of Federal Regulations, Title 37.

# Statutes and Legislative Materials

Anticybersquatting Consumer Protection Act, 15 U.S.C. § 1125(d).

Copyright Act of 1976 (as amended), §§ 101–1331.

Digital Millennium Copyright Act, 17 U.S.C. §§ 512, 1201–1205.

Lanham Trademark Act, 15 U.S.C. §§ 1052, 1058, 1059, 1125–1127.

No Electronic Theft Act, amending and codified at 17 U.S.C. §§ 101, 506 & 507 and 18 U.S.C. §§ 2319–2320.

Patent Act, 35 U.S.C. §§ 100 et seq.

Penalties for Criminal Infringement of a Copyright, 18 U.S.C. § 2319.

Plant Variety Protection Act of 1970 (part), 7 U.S.C. §§ 2401–2404.

Semiconductor Chip Protection Act, 17 U.S.C. §§ 901–914.

Statute of Monopolies (1623), 21 James I ch. 3.

Trademark Act of July 8, 1870, ch. 530, §§ 77–84, 26 Stat. 198.

Trademark Dilution Revision Act of 2006, PL 109-312, Oct. 6, 2006, 120 Stat. 1730.

Vessel Hull Design Protection Act, codified at 17 U.S.C. §§ 1301–1332.

Visual Artists Rights Act of 1990, 17 U.S.C. § 106A.

# Cases

*A & M Records, Inc. v. Napster, Inc.*, 239 F.3d 1004 (9th Cir. 2001), *on remand*, 2001 WL 227083 (N.D. Cal. 2001), *affirmed*, 284 F.3d 1091 (9th Cir. 2002).

*Abercrombie & Fitch Co. v. Hunting World, Inc.*, 537 F.2d 4 (2d Cir. 1976).

*America Online Inc. v. AT&T Corp.*, 64 F. Supp.2d 549 (E.D. Va. 1999).

*AMF Inc. v. Sleekcraft Boats*, 599 F.2d 341, 348–349 (9th Cir. 1979).

*Apple Computer v. Franklin Computer*, 714 F.2d 1240 (3d Cir. 1983).

*Baker v. Selden*, 101 U.S. 99 (1880).

*Building Officials & Code Administration v. Code Technology, Inc.*, 628 F.2d 730 (1st Cir. 1980).

*Campbell v. Acuff-Rose Music, Inc.*, 510 U.S. 569 (1994).

*Coca-Cola Co. v. Gemini Rising, Inc.*, 346 F. Supp. 1183 (E.D. N.Y. 1972).

*Data East USA v. Epyx*, 862 F.2d 204 (9th Cir. 1988).

*Diamond v. Diehr*, 450 U.S. 175 (1981).

*Donaldson v. Beckett*, (1774) 1 Eng. Rep. 837 (H.L.).

*Effects Associates v. Cohen*, 908 F. 2d 555 (9th Cir. 1990).

*Eldred v. Ashcroft*, 123 S.Ct. 769 (2003).

*Feist Publications v. Rural Telephone Service Co.*, 499 U.S. 340 (1991).

*Fonovisa, Inc. v. Cherry Auction, Inc.*, 76 F.3d 259 (9th Cir. 1976).

*Georgia v. The Harrison Co.*, 548 F. Supp. 110, *vacated by agreement between the parties*, 559 F. Supp. 37 (N.D. Ga. 1983).

*Gold Seal Co. v. Weeks*, 129 F. Supp. 928 (D.C. Cir. 1956), *affirmed*, 230 F.2d 832, *certiorari denied*, 328 U.S. 829 (1956).

*Goodis v. United Artists Television, Inc.*, 425 F.2d 397 (2d Cir. 1970).

*Gottschalk v. Benson*, 409 U.S. 63 (1972).

*Hoehling v. Universal City Studios, Inc.*, 618 F.2d 972 (2d Cir. 1980).

*In re Alappat*, 33 F.3d 1526 (Fed. Cir. 1994).

*In re Budge Manufacturing Co.*, 857 F.2d 773 (Fed. Cir. 1988).

*In re Clarke*, 17 U.S.P.Q.2d 1238 (T.T.A.B. 1990).

*In re Old Glory Condom Corp.*, 26 U.S.P.Q.2d 1216 (T.T.A.B. 1993).

*In re Prater*, 415 F.2d 1393 (C.C.P.A. 1969).

*In re Trade-Mark Cases*, 100 U.S. 82 (1879).

*International Business Machines Corporation*, Technical Board of Appeal of the European Patent Office, Case No. T 0935/97–3.5.1 (1999).

*Inwood Labs, Inc. v. Ives Labs, Inc.*, 456 U.S. 844 (1982).

*Lotus Development Corp. v. Borland International*, 140 F.3d 70 (1st Cir. 1998).

*MAI Systems Corp. v. Peak Computer*, 991 F.2d 511 (9th Cir. 1993).

*Manville Sales Co. v. Paramount Systems, Inc.*, 917 F.2d 544 (Fed. Cir. 1990).

*Mead Data Central, Inc. v. Toyota Motor Sales, Inc.*, 875 F.2d 1026 (2d Cir. 1989).

*Merriam v. Holloway Publishing Co.*, 43 F. 450 (C.C.E.D. Mo. 1890)

*MGM Studios, Inc. v. Grokster, Ltd.*, 125 S.Ct. 2764 (2005).

*Midway Manufacturing Co. v. Arctic International*, 704 F.2d 1009 (7th Cir. 1982).

*Mosely v. V Secret Catalog Inc.*, 537 U.S. 418 (2003).

*NEC v. Intel*, 10 U.S.P.Q.2d 1177 (N.D. Cal. 1989).

*Oasis Publishing Co. v. West Publishing Co.*, 924 F. Supp. 918 (D. Minn. 1996).

*Playboy Enterprises, Inc. v. Welles*, 279 F.3d 796 (9th Cir. 2002).

*Polaroid Corp. v. Polarad Electronics Corp.*, 287 F.2d 492 (2d Cir. 1961).

*Qualitex Co. v. Jacobson Products Co.*, 514 U.S. 159 (1995).

*Recording Industry Association of America v. Diamond Multimedia Systems, Inc.*, 180 F.3d 1072 (9th Cir. 1999).

*Sega Enterprises v. Accolade*, 977 F.2d 1510 (9th Cir. 1992).

*Silverman v. CBS Inc.*, 870 F.2d 40 (2d Cir. 1989).

*Singer Manufacturing Co. v. June Manufacturing Co.*, 163 U.S. 169 (1896).

*Sony Computer Entertainment, Inc. v. Connectix Corp.*, 203 F.3d 596 (9th Cir. 2000).

*Sony Corp. of America v. Universal City Studios, Inc.*, 464 U.S. 417 (1984).

*Southern v. How,* (1618) Popham 143.

*State Street Bank & Trust Co. v. Signature Financial Group,* 149 F.3d 1368 (Fed. Cir. 1998); *certiorari denied,* 525 U.S. 1093.

*Sunmark, Inc. v. Ocean Spray Cranberries, Inc.,* 64 F.3d 1055 (7th Cir. 1995).

*UMG Recordings, Inc. v. MP3.Com, Inc.,* 92 F. Supp.2d 349 (S.D. N.Y. 2000).

*United States v. LaMacchia,* 871 F. Supp. 535 (D. Mass. 1994).

*Universal City Studios, Inc. v. Corley,* 273 F.3d 429 (2nd Cir. 2001), affirming *Universal City Studios, Inc. v. Reimerdes,* 111 F. Supp.2d 294 (S.D. N.Y. 2000).

*Vault Corp. v. Quaid Software,* 847 F.2d 255 (5th Cir. 1988).

*White v. Dunbar,* 119 U.S. 47 (1886).

*Williams Electronics v. Arctic International,* 685 F.2d 870 (3d Cir. 1982).

# Sources and Further Reading

Austin, Graeme W. 2004. "Trademarks and the Burdened Imagination." *Brooklyn Law Review* 69: 827.

Berger, Eric. 2004. "*Traffix Devices, Inc. v. Marketing Displays, Inc.:* Intellectual Property in Crisis: Rubbernecking the Aftermath of the United States Supreme Court's Traffix Wreck." *Arkansas Law Review* 57: 383.

Bibliothèque Nationale de France. *Histoire: Sept Siècles.* http://www .bnf.fr/pages/connaitr/siecle.htm (in French).

British Library website. http://www.bl.uk.

Choi, Yunjeong. 2003. "Development of Copyright Protection in Korea: Its History, Inherent Limits, and Suggested Solutions." *Brooklyn Journal of International Law* 28: 643.

Dinwoodie, Graeme B., William O. Hennessey, and Shira Perlmutter. 2002. *International and Comparative Patent Law.* Newark, NJ: Matthew Bender.

Fishman, Stephen. 2001. *Copyright Your Software.* 3rd ed. Berkeley, CA: Nolo Press.

Ginsburg, Jane C. 1990. "A Tale of Two Copyrights: Literary Property in Revolutionary France and America." *Tulane Law Review* 64: 991.

Greene, Kevin J. 2004. "Abusive Trademark Litigation and the Incredible Shrinking Confusion Doctrine—Trademark Abuse in the Context of Entertainment Media and Cyberspace." *Harvard Journal of Law and Public Policy* 27: 609.

History/Timeline: Lowenbrau Yesterday & Today. http://www.lowen braubeer.com/b_history.html.

International Trademark Association. *The Lanham Act: Alive and Well After 50 Years.* http://www.inta.org/about/lanham.html.

Kaufer, Erich. 1989. *The Economics of the Patent System.* Chur, Switzerland: Harwood Academic Publishers.

Leaffer, Marshall. 1999. *Understanding Copyright Law.* 3rd ed. New York: Matthew Bender.

Lee, Ilhyung. 2001. "Culturally-Based Copyright Systems? The U.S. and Korea in Conflict." *Washington University Law Quarterly* 79: 1103.

*Leuven, City of Beer.* http://www.leuven.be/showpage.asp?iPageID =1677.

McCarthy, J. Thomas, Roger Schechter, and David J. Franklyn. 2004. *McCarthy's Desk Encyclopedia of Intellectual Property.* 3rd ed. Washington, DC: Bureau of National Affairs.

Nard, Craig Allen, and Andrew P. Morriss. 2004. *Constitutionalizing Patents: From Venice to Philadelphia.* Case Research Paper Series in Legal Studies. Working Paper 04-12. http://www.law.nyu.edu/journals/lib erty/Images/Morriss_Patents.pdf and at http://ssrn.com/abstract =585661.

Nimmer, David. 2004. *Copyright: Sacred Text, Technology, and the DMCA.* The Hague: Kluwer Academic/Plenum Publishers.

Robert, Daphne. 1996. "Commentary on the Lanham Trade-Mark Act." *Trademark Reporter* 6: 373.

Samuelson, Pamela. 1997. "The U.S. Digital Agenda at WIPO." *Virginia Journal of International Law* 37: 369.

Samuelson, Pamela, Randall Davis, Mitchell D. Kapor, and J. H. Reichman. 1994. "A Manifesto Concerning the Legal Protection of Computer Programs." *Columbia Law Review* 94: 2308.

Schechter, Frank I. 1925. *Historical Foundations of the Law Relating to Trademarks.* New York: Columbia University Press.

Sunder, Madhavi. 1996. "Authorship and Autonomy as Rites of Exclusion: The Intellectual Propertization of Free Speech in *Hurley v. Irish-American Gay, Lesbian, and Bisexual Group of Boston*." *Stanford Law Review* 49: 143.

Staatliche Brauerei Weihenstephan. http://www.weihenstephan.de/ weihenstephan/plan/brauerei.html.

United States Copyright Office. 2004. "Duration of Copyright: Provisions of the Law Dealing with the Length of Copyright Protection." Circular 15a. December. http://www.copyright.gov/circs/circ15a.html.

United States Copyright Office. 2006a. "Copyright Registration: Literary Works." July 11, 2006. http://www.copyright.gov/register/literary .html.

United States Copyright Office. 2006b. "Copyright Registration: Literary Works—Deposit Requirements." July 11, 2006. http://www.copyright .gov/register/literary.html.

U.S. Patent and Trademark Office. 2006. "FY 2006 Fee Schedule, Oct. 14, 2006." http://www.uspto.gov/web/offices/ac/qs/ope/fee2006october 14.htm.

U.S. Patent and Trademark Office. "TEAS Important Notice." http://www.uspto.gov/teas/eTEASimportantnotice.htm#NoRefund.

U.S. Patent and Trademark Office. "Trademark Electronic Search System (TESS)." http://tess2.uspto.gov/.

"The World's Oldest Companies: The Business of Survival." 2004. *The Economist*, December 16.

# 2

# Problems, Controversies, and Solutions

The revolution in information technology in the last part of the twentieth century imposed great stresses on information law. Disputes arose as to whether computer programs were copyrightable or patentable, and whether the look and feel of those programs could be copyrighted. The Internet has created new methods of doing business, just as those methods have become patentable. Computers have made it possible to compile enormous electronic databases, and debate continues to rage about how, or whether, the work that goes into creating those databases should be protected.

Copyright owners have tried to reduce the impact of the new technology with lawsuits aimed at prohibiting the sale of copying devices; with lobbying to outlaw the circumvention of copy-control measures; and most spectacularly in the pitched three-way battle between content owners, consumers, and equipment manufacturers over online file sharing. Trademark, too, has been affected, as the Web creates new forms of trademark infringement—cybersquatting and search-engine spamming.

# Patent, Copyright, and Computer Programs

Patent law is also under stress, as it has been since the beginning of the computer era. In addition to the recent controversy over business method patents already discussed, patent law has also dealt poorly at times with the challenges posed by computer technology. In the 1960s, when computers were enormous machines, filling entire buildings and orders of magnitude less powerful than the average cell phone today, the U.S. Patent and Trademark Office considered itself overwhelmed by applications for computer hardware patents and strongly opposed the idea that software could also be patented. Then-president Lyndon Johnson created a Commission on the Patent System that investigated, among other things, the patentability of computer programs. In 1966 this commission issued a report opposing the grant of computer program patents. Despite a 1969 case in the Federal Court of Customs and Patent Appeals holding that software for an analog computer was patentable, the report of the President's Commission and the stand of the U.S. Patent and Trademark Office helped influence the Supreme Court in its 1972 decision in *Gottschalk v. Benson*. In *Gottschalk*, the Court held that a mathematical algorithm used in a computer program was not patentable (*Gottschalk*, 409 U.S. 63). The decision came at a time when most people, the justices of the Supreme Court included, had little or no experience with computers, and it had a significant and possibly harmful effect on the subsequent development of intellectual property rights in computer programs.

Computer programs are composed of information, and they can be protected as literary works because of their expressive content. Few people read the code of a program for this content, however; computer programs differ from books, movies, films, photographs, and other literary works in that they are valued more (much more) for their function than for their expressive content.

Yet if in 1972 computer programs did not precisely fit within the traditional categories of works protected by copyright, they fit even more awkwardly within the boundaries of patent law at the time. In *Gottschalk,* the court's opinion, although addressing only algorithms used in programs, was widely interpreted as holding that computer programs themselves were unpatentable. After *Gottschalk*, the U.S. Patent and Trademark Office suspended all pending computer program patent applications. Other countries, perhaps incorrectly assuming that the United States had carefully considered all of the consequences and ramifications of its actions, followed the U.S. lead. In Europe, for example, the European Patent Convention to this day provides that computer programs are not patentable subject matter (European Patent Convention, art. 52(2)(c)). To grant such patents, the European Patent Office (itself authorized by art. 4(2)(a) of the same convention) has had to go through awkward legal contortions (see *International Business Machines*, Technical Board of Appeal of the European Patent Office, Case No. T 0935/97—3.5.1).

As a result of *Gottschalk*, copyright rather than patent became the main form of intellectual property protection for computer programs. Copyright protection is far easier to obtain than patent protection, and provides a far longer term of protection. The current ninety-five-year term for works for hire is longer than the entire history of digital computing, so far. As a practical matter, this means that no computer program ever written, other than original programs created by the United States or some other governments, is in the public domain—or is likely to be at any point in the near future. (Open-source software, as discussed in Chapter 1, is not in the public domain.) In other words, aside from a few government-created programs, there is no software public domain. Many see this lack of a public domain as stifling creativity and encouraging monopolies; the open-source movement is one response to this perceived problem.

The problem might easily have been avoided, however. Presented with a new type of content, not fitting comfortably under either "copyright" or "patent," Congress could have created a new form of intellectual property protection, as some scholars have urged (Samuelson et al. 1994). The creation of a special category of "software patent" or "software copyright" or "computer program registration" would have been within the authority granted Congress under the Patent and Copyright Clause "To promote the Progress of Science and useful Arts, by securing for limited Times to Authors and Inventors the exclusive Right to their respective Writings and Discoveries" (U.S. Constitution, art. 1, § 8, cl. 8). Indeed, Congress has created new forms of intellectual property rights for "Authors and Inventors" of other types of Writings and Discoveries," such as vessel hull designs (17 U.S.C. §§ 1301–1332) and semiconductor manufacturing mask work registrations (17 U.S.C. §§ 901–914).

However, Congress has not chosen to do this, and computer programs remain somewhat awkwardly protected by copyright and patent, although subsequent changes in patent law have smoothed out some of the difficulties that led to *Gottschalk*. In the 1981 case of *Diamond v. Diehr*, nine years after *Gottschalk*, the Supreme Court backed down a bit, holding that a computer program incorporating a mathematical formula and controlling a rubber-curing press was patentable (*Diamond*, 450 U.S. 175). After *Diamond*, the U.S. Patent and Trademark Office began to accept applications for, and issue, patents for computer programs, but it was not until a later case that the U.S. Patent and Trademark Office accepted the idea to the extent of actually publishing guidelines on the patentability of computer programs as a general category.

The case that finally established the patentability of computer programs as a general category was *In re Alappat*, a 1994 case from the Federal Circuit Court of Appeals. The Federal Circuit had been created in 1982, transferring some functions from earlier courts to a new court with special expertise in certain areas, including patents; its creation may have been in part the result of a wish to avoid missteps such as *Gottschalk*. In *In re Alappat*, the court upheld the patentability of a computer program incorporating a mathematical algorithm. The program, an anti-aliasing program for oscilloscopes, smoothed the edges of the image in a digital display; the court held that the program was not an unpatentable attempt to monopolize all possible uses of a mathematical algorithm, but a patentable practical application (*In re Alappat*, 33 F.3d 1526).

In 1995, a year after *Alappat*, the U.S. Patent and Trademark Office finally issued guidelines for software patents. But although the controversy over patentability of computer programs appears to have been resolved in the United States, it is still very much alive in Europe. In 2005 the European Parliament threw out a bill that would have permitted the European Union to issue such patents ("EU Software Patent Law Faces Axe" 2005). A wide variety of groups continues to oppose software patents, while some industry interests support them.

## Is the Look and Feel of a Computer Program or a Website Copyrightable?

In the early days of personal computing, look-and-feel infringement was one of the first copyright battlegrounds. The "look" of a program is the combined visual effect of its graphics, fonts, color scheme, and on-screen layout. The "feel" is determined by the way in which the various on-screen and off-screen components—such as buttons, menus, keyboard and mouse commands, links, and dialog boxes—are used to control and navigate the program. The concept of menu command hierarchy is closely related to look and feel. The menu command hierarchy consists of the commands by which a user tells the program to do certain things and the order in which those commands are arranged.

Computer users invest considerable time and effort in learning to use new programs. Once they have learned to use one, they will be reluctant to switch to another, even if the new program is better, because of the time and effort involved in learning the new program. Thus, the first program of a particular type to hit the market has an advantage. This advantage can be overcome, to some extent, if new programs are able to mimic the menu command hierarchy and the look and feel of existing programs. The ability to mimic these characteristics thus benefits late entrants in a field, but harms early entrants. These early entrants invoked copyright theories in defense of their market share; more recently, trademark theories have been proposed for the same purpose.

Copyright, as we saw in Chapter 1, protects the expression of ideas rather than the ideas themselves. The late entrants, opposed to the idea that a program's menu command hierarchy or look and feel could be copyrighted, insisted that these things, to the extent that they were expressions and not ideas, were expressions of ideas that could only be expressed in a very limited number of ways. Thus, under the merger doctrine, the idea and the expression merged and the result could not be copyrighted.

One of the most closely watched battles over look and feel pitted two industry leaders against each other. In 1985, sales of personal computers (PCs) running Microsoft's MS-DOS operating system still accounted for less than half of all PC sales (Reimer 2005). Apple, whose command-prompt interface Apple II accounted for 12 percent of computer sales that year, had just introduced the Macintosh, a computer with a graphical user interface (GUI) that was easier for technically unsophisticated users to navigate. Although the Macintosh GUI has evolved over time, the 1985 version would be recognizable to any Mac user today— or to any Windows user. Microsoft's Windows GUI looks and feels a lot like the Macintosh GUI.

In that year (1985) Apple and Microsoft reached an agreement regarding the development of Windows. In the agreement, Microsoft acknowledged "that the visual displays in Windows 1.0 are derivative works of the visual displays generated by Apple's Lisa and Macintosh graphical user interface programs" (Rosenoer 1994). (The Lisa was a bulky, expensive precursor to the Macintosh.) The deal fell apart, though, when subsequent versions of Windows came to resemble the Macintosh GUI more closely than Windows 1.0 had, especially after Microsoft licensed Windows to Hewlett-Packard to develop Hewlett-Packard's NewWave software desktop. The Macintosh-like Windows 2.03 and NewWave were released in 1988, and the parties wound up in court for the next six years.

In 1994, after many intermediate skirmishes, the battle ended in the federal Ninth Circuit Court of Appeals (*Apple Computer*, 35 F.3d 1435). The Ninth Circuit affirmed a decision of the federal district court for the Northern District of California two years earlier. Apple lost against Microsoft, although it did prevail in two claims against Hewlett-Packard: The district court had found that NewWave's trash can and file folder icons were infringing, and NewWave was consigned to the trash can of software history (*Apple Computer*, 799 F. Supp. at 1034–1036). Apple petitioned for certiorari to the U.S. Supreme Court, but the Court refused to hear the case, denying certiorari in 1995. The reasoning of the district court, as adopted and affirmed by the Ninth Circuit, remains one of the most important sources of information about look and feel infringement.

In its opinion, later affirmed by the Ninth Circuit, the district court used the Ninth Circuit's two-step analysis for finding copyright infringement in a case of this nature.

> The Ninth Circuit employs a two-part test to determine whether a work infringes the copyright in another work. First, the "ideas" of the works in suit are compared for substantial similarity, using an "extrinsic test" or "objective analysis of expression.". . . Analytic dissection, em-

ploying a list of criteria of comparison informed by expert testimony, is a part of this exercise, which makes this well-suited for determination as a matter of law. . . . If the ideas are substantially similar, then an "intrinsic test" or "subjective analysis of expression" is used. (*Apple Computer,* 799 F. Supp. at 1020)

The district court found most of Apple's claims barred because Apple had consented to the use in the 1985 agreement, because the expression lacked sufficient originality to be protected by copyright, or because the expression in question was uncopyrightable under the merger and *scènes a fàire* doctrines. For example, the use of overlapping windows on the screen had been used in twenty-six other computer interfaces in the previous decade. It was evidently a standard treatment in the industry, and thus uncopyrightable under the *scènes a fàire* doctrine (*Apple Computer,* 799 F. Supp. at 1027). The court rejected the idea that the rectangular shape of the window could be protected, apparently because it lacked originality. Similarly, the use of a muted background behind the active window "hardly can be said to represent the sort of creative achievement or expression which the law should exert itself to protect" (*Apple Computer,* 799 F. Supp. at 1028). The display of the active window as the top-most window in a set of overlapping windows was not protected by copyright "due to merger of idea and expression" as well as under the *scènes a fàire* doctrine. The court pointed out that "it is hard to imagine the usefulness of an obscured window being the active window" (*Apple Computer,* 799 F. Supp. at 1032). Where one of the three grounds for uncopyrightability applied, two or often all three did; the court observed that it had "on an earlier occasion in this case expressed its belief that the various doctrines that limit copyright protection are often barely distinguishable from one another" (*Apple Computer,* 799 F. Supp. at 1022, citing *Apple Computer, Inc. v. Microsoft Corp.,* 779 F. Supp. at 134 (N.D. Cal. 1991)).

A year after the Ninth Circuit's decision in *Apple Computer,* the federal court of appeals for the First Circuit declared in *Lotus Development v. Borland* that the menu command hierarchy of a computer program was not copyrightable (*Lotus Development,* 49 F.3d 807). The First Circuit's decision, later affirmed by the Supreme Court (516 U.S. 233), followed more or less the same line of reasoning as the Ninth Circuit's decision in *Apple Computer.*

In order to tell a computer program to do things, the user typically selects certain commands from a preset menu. These commands are arranged under headings; the commands, the headings under which they are arranged, and the order in which they appear under those headings form the menu command hierarchy. The plaintiff and defendant in *Lotus Development Corp. v. Borland* made spreadsheet programs, Lotus 1-2-3 and Quattro Pro, respectively. Borland copied the menu command hierarchy of Lotus 1-2-3 into Quattro Pro (and another version, Quattro) "so that spreadsheet users who were already familiar with Lotus 1-2-3 would be able to switch to the Borland programs without having to learn new commands or rewrite their Lotus macros" (*Lotus Development*, 49 F.3d at 810). Borland did not copy Lotus 1-2-3's code.

While the copying was undeniable, Borland maintained that the menu command hierarchy was a mere method of operation and thus not copyrightable under 17 U.S.C. § 102. The Ninth Circuit agreed:

> In many ways, the Lotus menu command hierarchy is like the buttons used to control, say, a video cassette recorder ("VCR"). A VCR is a machine that enables one to watch and record video tapes. Users operate VCRs by pressing a series of buttons that are typically labelled [sic] "Record, Play, Reverse, Fast Forward, Pause, Stop/Eject." That the buttons are arranged and labeled does not make them a "literary work," nor does it make them an "expression" of the abstract "method of operating" a VCR via a set of labeled buttons. Instead, the buttons are themselves the "method of operating" the VCR.
>
> When a Lotus 1-2-3 user chooses a command, either by highlighting it on the screen or by typing its first letter, he or she effectively pushes a button. Highlighting the "Print" command on the screen, or typing the letter "P," is analogous to pressing a VCR button labeled "Play." (*Lotus Development*, 49 F.3d at 817)

Clicking "Print" is no more an expressive act than is pressing "Play" on the remote control of a VCR or, these days, a DVD player. The purpose of the act is to print a document or play a video, not to express an idea. The court went on to explain that the menu command hierarchy was an indispensable functional component of the program rather than an expressive one.

Just as one could not operate a buttonless VCR, it would be impossible to operate Lotus 1-2-3 without employing its menu command hierarchy. Thus the Lotus command terms are not equivalent to the labels on the VCR's buttons, but are instead equivalent to the buttons themselves. Unlike the labels on a VCR's buttons, which merely make operating a VCR easier by indicating the buttons' functions, the Lotus menu commands are essential to operating Lotus 1-2-3. Without the menu commands, there would be no way to "push" the Lotus buttons, as one could push unlabeled VCR buttons. While Lotus could probably have designed a user interface for which the command terms were mere labels, it did not do so here. Lotus 1-2-3 depends for its operation on use of the precise command terms that make up the Lotus menu command hierarchy. (ibid.)

The decision in *Lotus* has been criticized as failing to acknowledge, or to acknowledge sufficiently, that "user interfaces, including menu commands," may be expressive, original works and thus "should receive at least narrow protection under copyright law" (Stagnone 1997, 948). The combined effect of *Apple* and *Lotus*, however, seems to have been to put an end to copyright suits based on menu command hierarchies and look and feel. Although this might suggest that the law in this area is settled, some scholars have suggested an alternative way to attack programs— and websites—that imitate the look and feel of other programs and websites.

The World Wide Web did not exist at the time Apple and Microsoft reached their 1985 agreement. It was still in its infancy at the time *Apple* and *Lotus* were decided. Today, however, Web pages number in the billions; some of those pages are valuable commercial sites, with a distinctive look and feel created by their graphics, layout, and even menu command hierarchies. If this look and feel cannot be protected by copyright, perhaps it can be protected by the trademark theory of trade dress.

Trade dress protects the "total image and overall appearance" of a product (*Two Pesos*, 505 U.S. at 764 n. 1, citing *Blue Bell Bio-Medical v. Cin-Bad Inc.*, 864 F.2d 1253, 1256 (5th Cir. 1989); see also Restatement (Third) of Unfair Competition § 16, comment a). It is the "manner in which . . . goods or services are presented to prospective purchasers[.]" (Restatement (Third) of Unfair

Competition § 16, comment a). Once this manner of presentation, or image and appearance, has become an identifier of the source of goods or services, it can function as a trademark (Restatement (Third) of Unfair Competition § 16, comment a). Many websites, such as Amazon.com or RottenTomatoes.com, have appearances—a look and feel, in other words—that may sufficiently identify the source of the goods or services offered through the website, and may thus be protectable as trade dress.

To date, trade dress look-and-feel litigation has been more anticipated than actual. There has been scholarly speculation, and attorneys may advise clients on the possibility (see Nguyen 2000, 1244). But there are obstacles to the use of trade dress law to protect the appearance of websites. First, to the extent that the elements of a website are functional rather than expressive, they are not protected as trade dress; purely functional elements are no more eligible for trademark protection than they are for copyright protection. Second, the appearance of many websites is constantly changing. The text and images of the BBC's home page (http://news.bbc.co.uk) are different from one hour to the next, although the look and feel of the site may remain the same because headers, layout, menu command hierarchy, and graphics remain more or less the same over time. Finally, the appearance of a website on a screen is the result not of the Web design alone, but also of the interaction between the site and the user's computer and browser. Different computers and browsers will display the same site differently; even two identical computers—running the same browser and connecting through the same Internet service provider (ISP) at the same connection speed—may display the site differently, because users can choose different display settings. Whether such an interactive display, even at default settings, can constitute trade dress infringement is a question the courts have yet to address.

## Is a Method of Doing Business Patentable?

A computer program's menu command hierarchy, as we have just seen, is a mere method of operation and thus not copyrightable (*Lotus Development*, 49 F.3d 807). If a method of operating a computer program or website is not copyrightable, is it patentable? At one time, the answer would certainly have been "no." The Supreme Court that decided *Gottschalk* seemed unwilling to grant any patents for software, let alone for something as intangible as a method of doing business. That has changed, however, not only as a result of the Court's later willingness to accept the idea of software patents, but also because of the entry into force of the World Trade Organization's intellectual property treaty, the Marrakesh Agreement on Trade-Related Aspects of Intellectual Property Rights (TRIPs). TRIPs provides that "patents shall be available for any inventions, whether products or processes, in all fields of technology," with certain exceptions (TRIPs art. 27). Article 27 was generally understood as requiring World Trade Organization members to issue business methods patents.

In the United States, courts had historically rejected the patentability of business methods, or so it appeared (*Hotel Security Checking*, 160 F. at 469). After TRIPs entered into force on 1 January 1995, the United States was under an international legal obligation to grant patents for methods of doing business; whether there was a domestic statutory obligation to do so was, at the time, unclear. The test came in 1996, with the decision in *State Street Bank & Trust v. Signature Financial Group*. In 1993 Signature had obtained U.S. Patent No. 5,193,056, titled "Data Processing System for Hub and Spoke Financial Services Configuration," which, the patent explained, "provides a data processing system and method for monitoring and recording the information flow and data, and making all calculations, necessary for maintaining a partnership portfolio and partner fund (Hub and Spoke) financial services configuration." The patent was for a method of managing complex investments, allowing mutual funds to pool their assets. The full patent can be read on the U.S. Patent and Trademark Office's website by entering the patent number into the patent Quick Search engine, although it makes excruciatingly dull reading for all but the most dedicated aficionados of investment method patents.

In *State Street Bank & Trust* the Federal Circuit held that business methods were not unpatentable subject matter. A business method could be patented if it met the statutory requirements of usefulness, novelty, and nonobviousness (149 F.3d at 1375). In the years following *State Street Bank & Trust*, a great many business method patents have been granted amid considerable controversy. Much of the public ridicule heaped upon business method patents focuses on those patents that seem at best minimally innovative; the scorn might better be directed at the U.S. Patent and Trademark Office's willingness to grant patents for almost everything than at the idea of business method patents. U.S. Patent No. 5,993,336 may be laughable (and is only a "business method" for professional tennis players):

> A method of executing a tennis stroke includes covering a knee of a tennis player with a knee pad during tennis play. The covered knee of the player is placed on a tennis court surface with the knee pad positioned between the knee and the surface. The tennis racket is swung toward a tennis ball so as to hit the tennis ball with the racket either while the covered knee is on the tennis court surface, or just prior to the knee contacting the tennis court surface.

But it is not any more ridiculous than the infamous peanut butter and jelly sandwich patent, U.S. Patent No. 6,004,596, which, among its innovations, includes a method—independently discovered by every parent who has ever packed peanut butter and jelly sandwiches in a child's lunchbox—for preventing the jelly from making the bread soggy:

> The upper and lower fillings are preferably comprised of *peanut butter* and the center filling is comprised of at least *jelly*. The center filling is prevented from radiating outwardly into and through the bread portions from the surrounding *peanut butter*. [Italics in original.]

This patent is more traditional in its subject matter, but no less absurd. Yet it has already withstood at least one challenge (*Albie's Foods,* 170 F. Supp.2d 736).

Perhaps the most celebrated and controversial business methods patent is U.S. Patent No. 5,960,411—Amazon.com's patent on one-click ordering. The patent was issued on 28 September 1999, in the early years of near-universal World Wide Web use in the United States. The 1999 Christmas season came at the end of the Internet bubble; it was heralded as the first true test of online retailing as a business model, and no online retailer was watched more closely than Amazon.

Less than a month after the patent was issued, Amazon (then still almost entirely a bookseller) obtained an injunction against another online bookseller, Barnes & Noble. Barnes & Noble, the country's largest bricks-and-mortar bookseller, also sold books online through its Barnesandnoble.com website. Amazon's injunction prevented Barnes & Noble from using its own one-click ordering system (*Amazon.com*, 239 F.3d 1343). Barnes & Noble responded by challenging the patent; it pointed out that similar ordering methods had been described in print and used by online retailers long before Amazon filed its patent application (*Amazon.com*, 239 F.3d at 1360–1366). The federal District Court for the Western District of Washington (the district that includes Seattle, where Amazon has its real-world headquarters) rejected Barnes & Noble's arguments. On appeal, the Court of Appeals for the Federal Circuit reversed, saying that Barnes & Noble had "raised substantial questions as to the validity of the '411 patent" and that "we must conclude that the necessary prerequisites for entry of a preliminary injunction are presently lacking" (*Amazon.com*, 239 F. 3d at 1366). In other words, Barnes & Noble won; the injunction should not have been issued. But Barnes & Noble's victory was a Pyrrhic one; the Federal Circuit's decision came on 14 February 2001, after the end of the 2000 Christmas shopping season and a month before the Internet bubble began to burst. The injunction had lasted long enough to allow Amazon to secure its position as the leading online bookseller in the United States. In fact, Amazon's media sales now not only exceed Barnes & Noble's online sales by an order of magnitude, but also exceed Barnes & Noble's total sales. The October 1999 injunction is not, of course, the sole factor in Amazon's victory, but it did help.

In 2006, the U.S. Supreme Court greatly limited the hitherto nearly automatic right of patent holders to permanent injunctive relief; patent holders are now required to make showings equivalent to those made by parties seeking injunctive relief in areas other than patent law (*eBay*, 126 S.Ct. 1837). In addition, Congress has taken action to protect businesses, especially small businesses, from having to defend themselves against "inventors" obtaining patents on methods that the small businesses had already been using: In 1999 Congress responded to *State Street Bank* with the First Inventor Defense Act. The Act provides that:

> It shall be a defense to an action for [patent] infringement . . . with respect to any subject matter that would otherwise infringe one or more claims for a method in the patent being asserted against a person, if such person

had, acting in good faith, actually reduced the subject matter to practice at least 1 year before the effective filing date of such patent, and commercially used the subject matter before the effective filing date of such patent. (35 U.S.C. § 273)

Under the First Inventor Defense Act, in other words, a business that can show that it reduced a method to practice a year before the filing date and began to use the method at any time before the filing date is protected from liability for patent infringement. While "reduction to practice" in patent law is a term of art that can refer either to filing a patent application (constructive reduction to practice) or to constructing an apparatus or carrying out the steps necessary for the invention, in this case it is unlikely to be the former. The First Inventor Defense Act will protect not only any business actually using a method for over a year before the filing date, but also those who have used the method for less than a year, provided that they reduced the idea to practice in some way—perhaps by testing a business plan or carrying out other necessary steps—over a year before the filing date.

As with software patents, the European Patent Convention remains at odds with actual national and international practice; it still provides that "schemes, rules and methods for . . . doing business" are not patentable subject matter, even though the countries that are parties to the Convention are also parties to TRIPs (European Patent Convention, art. 52(2)(c)).

## Is an Electronic Database Copyrightable?

As we saw in Chapter 1, the Supreme Court in *Feist* held that collecting names in a telephone directory and arranging those names in alphabetical order—in other words, the creation of a database of names and phone numbers—cannot be protected by copyright, no matter how much work goes into its creation, because it lacks the requisite originality (*Feist*, 499 U.S. 340). Yet creating databases is a valuable service; so to encourage people to create databases, intellectual property law has struggled to find some way to protect databases from unauthorized copying. U.S. copyright law allows compilations of data to be protected under certain conditions. In U.S. copyright law, a "compilation" is defined as "a work formed by the collection and assembling of preexisting materials or of data that are selected, coordinated, or arranged in such a way that the resulting work as a whole constitutes an original work of authorship" (17 U.S.C. § 101). However, this protection does not extend to the underlying data itself:

> The copyright in a compilation or derivative work extends only to the material contributed by the author of such work, as distinguished from the preexisting material employed in the work, and does not imply any exclusive right in the preexisting material. (17 U.S.C. § 103(b))

There also remains the problem that *Feist* and Section 101 provide no protection for databases, like telephone directories, that are not original but do require hard work to create. One way in which database creators have tried to protect their work under U.S. law is through contract rather than intellectual property law: The creator of the database distributes or allows use of the database only to those who agree beforehand to certain conditions, typically restricting the use of the database to form new databases, the copying of more than a set amount of material from the database, or the sharing of the database with persons not covered by the contract. (The telephone directory in *Feist* was prepared pursuant to a statutory duty, which might have precluded the plaintiff from attempting to restrict the use of its database in this way.) These restrictions can then be enforced under state contract law.

Such attempts to create a quasi-copyright in databases through contractual provisions run into difficulty because of the preemption clause of the Copyright Act of 1976, which provides that

> . . . all legal or equitable rights that are equivalent to any of the exclusive rights within the general scope of copyright . . . in works of authorship that are fixed in a tangible medium of expression and come within the subject matter of copyright . . . are governed exclusively by this title. Thereafter, no person is entitled to any such right or equivalent right in any such work under the common law or statutes of any State. (17 U.S.C. § 301)

Interestingly, Section 301 omits the word "original" before works of authorship.

Section 301 has been interpreted as prohibiting state law from enforcing contractual clauses that conflict with federal copyright law. *Vault Corporation v. Quaid Software,* for example, dealt with a Louisiana state contract statute. Vault made copy-protection software, ProLok, that it placed on disks and sold to other software makers. The software makers, in turn, placed their own programs on the disks and sold them to the public. Vault's licensing agreement provided that the end users, by using the disks containing the copy-protection software, agreed not to copy, decompile, or disassemble that software. Quaid violated this agreement to produce a program, RamKey, which enabled users to copy programs protected with ProLok. (Today this would probably be illegal under § 1201 of the Digital Millennium Copyright Act, a federal copyright statute.)

This type of agreement, which the end user sees only after removing the shrink-wrap from a software package, is called a shrink-wrap agreement; the online equivalent is a click-wrap agreement. The federal Court of Appeals for the Fifth Circuit held that Vault's shrink-wrap agreement was an adhesion contract (a "take it or leave it" contract between parties with unequal bargaining power) that could only be permissible if authorized by state law. In Louisiana there was such a law: the Louisiana Software License Enforcement Act (La. Rev. Stat. Ann. § 51:1961 et seq.). The Louisiana statute allowed "a software producer to impose a number of contractual terms upon software purchasers. . . . Enforceable terms include the prohibition of: (1) any copying of the program for any purpose; and (2) modifying and/or adapting the program in any way, including adaptation by reverse engineering, decompilation or disassembly" (*Vault Corp.*, 847 F.2d at 268–269, citing La. Rev. Stat. Ann. § 51:1964).

The Fifth Circuit found that the Louisiana statute could not be enforced against Quaid because it was preempted by the Copyright Act; it impermissibly went beyond the scope of the federal Copyright Act in protecting the interests of copyright holders. (Among its flaws, the Louisiana statute set no time limit to its protection and was thus unconstitutional as well as preempted; copyrights, like patents, are to be granted only for limited times.)

A decade later the Ohio Supreme Court reached a similar result, striking down an Ohio statute as preempted by section 301. Perry, the defendant, had been convicted of violating an Ohio statute forbidding unauthorized use of software (Ohio Rev. Code

§ 2913.04). Perry was factually guilty; he had traded copies of software over an online bulletin board. However, the court held that he could not be convicted under the Ohio statute, because everything prohibited by the Ohio law was already prohibited by federal law, and the Ohio law was thus preempted. The Ohio court pointed out that "allowing state claims where the core of the complaint centers on wrongful copying would render the preemption provisions of the Copyright Act useless" (*Ohio v. Perry*, 697 N.E.2d at 627).

Although these cases might seem to bode ill for state law protection of databases, the computer programs in each case were already the subjects of federal copyright law. Nonoriginal databases are not, and they can still be protected to some extent by state contract law, as they were in the 1996 Seventh Circuit case of *ProCD, Inc. v. Zeidenberg*. The facts were similar to the facts in *Feist*: ProCD made a computer database incorporating the contents of 3,000 telephone directories. This was made available subject to a shrink-wrap license with the usual prohibitions against copying and other unauthorized use. ProCD invested more than $10 million in creating the database and had ongoing maintenance and updating costs. It offered different versions of the database at different prices; those who wished to make more sophisticated uses of the database, such as compiling and exporting lists of potential customers, paid a higher price and received a license to do these things. Zeidenberg bought the cheapest license but exceeded its terms by selling information copied from the database over the Web. When ProCD sued to enforce the shrink-wrap agreement under Wisconsin state contracts law, Zeidenberg claimed, among other defenses, that to the extent state law would enforce the shrink-wrap agreement against copying, it was preempted by Section 301.

The Seventh Circuit disagreed. The contract and the Wisconsin statute permitting its enforcement, the court pointed out, did not create rights equivalent to copyright, as the Louisiana and Ohio statutes discussed above had. Rather, the contract created a private obligation between two parties, not binding on others outside the contract, and the statute permitted the enforcement of that contract in the same way as it permitted the enforcement of other contracts. Therefore, neither the statute nor the contract was preempted by Section 301 (*ProCD*, 86 F.3d at 1454–1455).

Thus, the default setting in U.S. law appears to be that databases lacking the requisite originality are not copyrightable;

however, copying and other uses may be specifically restricted by contract. The European Union, in contrast, has gone much farther in protecting databases. In March 1996 the European Union adopted its Database Directive, providing protection for databases for a fifteen-year term even in the absence of originality (EU Database Directive arts. 3, 7–8, 10). After the Database Directive was adopted, the member states of the European Union pushed for an international treaty requiring other countries to adopt similar laws; the treaty was proposed and discussed in the World Intellectual Property Organization later in the same year, but was opposed by the United States and developing countries and was not adopted (Schneider 1998, 562–563). The United States has a history of somewhat reluctantly following Europe's lead in copyright matters, however, so a change in U.S. law on database protection remains possible, although efforts in that direction have been unsuccessful (see, for example, Schneider 1998, 563–564).

# Can Content Owners Restrict or Prohibit the Sale of Copying Devices?

Copyright law was largely unnecessary in the days before mechanical copying devices existed, although even manual copying could excite fierce passions. According to legend, in the sixth century the Irish monk, later saint, Columba left Ireland as the result of a dispute over copying. Columba had copied a psalter belonging to Finnian, the abbot of Columba's monastery (and also later a saint). Finnian discovered the copy and claimed that it belonged to him; the dispute was submitted to King Diarmait, who decided that just as a cow's calf belongs to the owner of the cow, the copy of a book belonged to the owner of the book. Columba then went to war against Diarmait, and 3,000 of Diarmait's men were killed. In penance, Columba left Ireland, never to see it again (see St. Columba in *Catholic Encyclopedia* 1908).

A photocopier would have made St. Columba's task far easier. The content industry has been alarmed at each new development in copying technology and has tried to suppress it in various ways, although it has stopped short of actual war. Photocopiers and audio- and videocassette recorders were threatening enough, and inspired lawsuits (see *Sony Corp. of America*, 464 U.S.

417). But digital copying was a threat of a different order: Digital copies, unlike the analog copies made by VCRs, for example, can be reproduced repeatedly with no deterioration in quality; if the original from which the copies are made is also digital, each copy will be an exact replica of the original.

The first digital recording technology to become available to individual consumers was digital audio tape (DAT). The music content industry, still smarting from its defeat in the war against analog tape recorders, lobbied for protection from DAT recorders. The content industry's efforts were successful; in 1992 Congress enacted the Audio Home Recording Act (AHRA), which attempted to control recording in two ways: through copy-control technology and through a royalty on recorders and tapes.

The AHRA requires that "any digital audio recording device or digital audio interface device" imported into, manufactured in, or distributed in the United States include a primitive form of electronic rights management technology called the Serial Copy Management System (SCMS) (17 U.S.C. § 1002(a)). SCMS-equipped recorders place an inaudible identifying code on copies they make and will not make copies of originals bearing the identifying code. This makes second-generation copying (making copies of copies) impossible, although it does nothing to prevent the making of multiple copies of a single original master copy. The SCMS requirement, by its terms, applies to digital audio recording devices, not merely DAT recorders, that are "designed or marketed for the primary purpose of, and that [are] capable of, making a digital audio copied recording for private use" (17 U.S.C. § 1001(3)). This requirement remains in effect today, but it does not apply to computers; this may have prevented the growth of a market for stand-alone digital recording devices and may be one reason that computers have become the most commonly used devices for copying music.

The royalty provisions, on the other hand, were aimed specifically at the DAT format. The AHRA imposes a royalty on digital audio recording equipment and media (17 U.S.C. § 1003). From the consumer's point of view this royalty, paid in advance, looks like a tax; it is collected by the Copyright Office and distributed to existing music industry copyright owners. Digital audio recorders are taxed at 2 percent, with a maximum royalty of eight dollars and a minimum of one dollar; digital recording media are taxed at 3 percent (17 U.S.C. § 1004). This DAT tax may have done more than anything else to kill off the DAT format and encourage the use of computers for digital copying: The only media taxed are those "primarily marketed or most commonly used by consumers for the purpose of making digital audio copied recordings by use of a digital audio recording device" (17 U.S.C. 1001(4)(A)). This neatly excludes most CDs and other computer media; media for recording "motion pictures or other audiovisual works" as well as "nonmusical literary works, including computer programs or data bases," is not covered (17 U.S.C. 1001(4)(B)(ii)). These royalty provisions were unpopular in part because they presumed the consumer's guilt: "We're going to charge you a royalty up front because we know you're going to use this to make unauthorized copies."

The AHRA was the opening skirmish in the content industry's war on digital copying; while it may have seemed a victory at the time, the effect was to move digital copying to a far more powerful device, the home computer. In 1984 the content industry was able to win a battle against a device allowing users to make copies of game cartridges (*Atari, Inc.*, 747 F.2d 1422). It was much less successful against the first MP3 player, the Diamond Rio.

The MP3 file format (actually an abbreviated form of MPEG-1/2 Audio Layer 3; "MPEG" stands for "Motion Picture Experts Group") revolutionized digital music copying. MP3 files are compressed versions of audio files; because they are much smaller than the uncompressed files, hundreds of files can be stored in the same amount of space in which dozens of uncompressed files can be stored on a single CD. The compressed files can also be traded easily over the Internet.

Before Diamond Multimedia manufactured the Rio, MP3 files were of limited appeal. Technically unsophisticated users could only play the files on a computer. The Rio made it possible for users to transfer their MP3 files from the computer, after which they could be played anywhere. The Ninth Circuit Court of Appeals determined that this space shifting was a fair use analogous to the time shifting in *Sony*. Because the Rio could be used to play music already owned, it was capable of a substantial noninfringing use (*Recording Industry Association of America*, 180 F.3d 1072).

By the time the Rio case was decided, however, the main battle had already moved on; the biggest threat to the content industry's interests was not mechanical copying devices but software. While users might trade dozens of physical copies of a song with their friends and acquaintances, it was far easier to trade millions of files with total strangers over the Internet.

# Copyright's Front Line: File Sharing

No area of copyright law has been more hotly contested in recent years than file sharing—the sharing of files on one computer with other computers to which the computer is linked through some sort of network. While most file sharing is routine and perfectly legal, file-sharing networks can also be used by large numbers of people who do not know each other to exchange copyrighted information—books, movies, photographs, computer programs, and most of all music—over the Internet. In discussions of copyright law, the term "file sharing" is generally used not to refer to routine, unquestionably legal file sharing but to this particular type of file sharing.

The MP3 file format that made widespread Internet sharing of popular music feasible also gave its name to a file-sharing pioneer. MP3.com, a company based in San Diego, California, purchased CDs containing tens of thousands of copyrighted songs, converted the songs to MP3 format, and placed them, as MP3 files, on its servers. MP3.com offered a service, MyMP3.com, which allowed subscribers to access these songs. As a protection against copyright infringement, subscribers had to place an authorized recorded CD in their computer to demonstrate that they owned (or had access to) an authorized copy of the song they wished to download. This seems absurdly cumbersome today, when any user with a copy of the CD can easily make his or her own MP3, but at the time MyMP3.com provided a means of space shifting. It also provided an opportunity for piracy; after verifying their ownership of particular CDs, users could share passwords and user names—and thus CD collections—with each other. To the content industry, MyMP3.com was a menace that had to be stopped.

And it was. The federal district court for the Southern District of New York held that MP3.com's copying and posting of its CDs exceeded the limits of fair use (*UMG Recordings, Inc.*, 92 F. Supp. 2d 349). By this point the content industry had reluctantly acknowledged, without becoming reconciled to, the idea that copying licensed recordings from one medium to another for individual use was fair use. Copying to share with a family member or a friend was fair use, too, although the content industry was not very happy with that idea either. An individual who bought 45,000 CDs and copied every song on each disk to his or her own hard drive for personal use was probably committing no copyright violation. But copying the music files to share them with the whole world—with anyone with Internet access, a user name, and a password—was not fair use.

In retrospect, it seems that the content industry's litigation strategy was more reactive than strategic. The lawsuit against MP3.com achieved its immediate objective—the defeat of MyMP3.com. But it, and subsequent lawsuits, served as lessons for file sharers, showing the ways in which the technology would have to evolve to remain legal. The rapid pace of the lawsuits also forced correspondingly rapid innovation and evolution in file-sharing technology. By 2000, when the decision in *UMG Recordings v. MP3.com* was published, Napster was already up and running, with the music content industry in pursuit.

MP3.com lost its court battle because it was a direct infringer; the act that violated the copyrights was the copying of the songs onto MP3.com's own servers. This was the first lesson file sharers learned: An online file-sharing company is vulnerable if it copies any music onto its own system. Napster avoided this by having the users share the files directly with each other; at no point did any MP3 files pass through any servers or equipment belonging to or controlled by Napster. Napster did, however, maintain and constantly update a searchable directory of music files available for downloading on users' computers. Napster and the networks that followed it were peer-to-peer (P2P) networks; they functioned not within the World Wide Web, but as a separate network on the Internet created by the software they distributed—although they did use the Web to advertise and distribute that software.

Because Napster made no copies, it could not be held liable as a direct copyright infringer. For the music content industry to prevail against Napster, it would have to prove that Napster was liable as a third-party infringer. Third-party or indirect infringement, as discussed in Chapter 1, can occur in two ways: contributory infringement and vicarious infringement. In the Ninth Circuit at the time of *Napster*, a contributory infringer was one who had actual or constructive knowledge of an underlying direct infringement by some other person and made a material contribution to that direct infringer's activities (*Fonovisa*, 76 F.3d 259). One who has the right and ability to control a direct infringer's actions and receives a direct financial benefit from the infringing activity is a vicarious infringer (*Fonovisa*, 76 F.3d 259). Napster, it turned out, was both a contributory infringer and a vicarious infringer.

There was no serious question as to whether there was an underlying direct infringement; Napster's users were exchanging copyrighted files by the millions, far outside the fuzzy boundaries of fair use. Napster was a contributory infringer because it had actual or constructive knowledge of this direct infringement, and because it made a material contribution to the direct infringers' activities. The Ninth Circuit in *A&M Records v. Napster* interpreted the knowledge requirement as leniently as possible; it was willing to regard Napster's service as "capable of a substantial noninfringing use," which according to the Ninth Circuit's interpretation of *Sony* meant that *actual* knowledge of *specific* acts of infringement was required. Even this requirement was met, though; Napster had actual knowledge. An e-mail from Napster cofounder Sean Parker referred to the fact that Napster users were "exchanging pirated music," and Napster used screen shots showing copyrighted material to promote its service (*A&M Records*, 239 F.3d at 1020 n. 5). The material contribution was even simpler to establish: Without the software and the searchable directory of downloadable files, maintained on Napster's system, the users would have been unable to share files with each other. The Ninth Circuit stated that "Napster has *actual* knowledge that *specific* infringing material is available using its system, [it can] block access to the system by suppliers of the infringing material, and . . . it failed to remove the material" (*A&M Records*, 239 F.3d at 1022; italics in original).

Napster was also a vicarious infringer, because it had the right and ability to control the direct infringers' actions and because it received a direct financial benefit from the infringing activity. It had the right and ability to control the users' actions because in its user agreement (a click-wrap agreement—users had to click "I agree" to download and install the Napster software), Napster reserved the right to block any user's access to the Napster website at its discretion. And it received a direct financial benefit in the form of an increased customer base; more customers meant a more valuable company and more potential income in the future, even if that potential was not yet realized (*A&M Records*, 239 F.3d 1004).

To the makers of file-sharing software, *A&M Records v. Napster* was just another decision to design around. File sharers learned valuable lessons from *Napster*: First, try not to know what users are sharing. Second, if just distributing the software is enough to satisfy the "material contribution" requirement, not much can be done—but try not to have anything at all on your own servers. Third, don't retain the right and ability to control the users' actions. About the fourth problem, there's nothing much that a for-profit enterprise can, or at least would want to, do to avoid receiving a direct financial benefit.

The next generation of P2P networks that appeared in the wake of *A&M Records v. Napster* was considerably more technically advanced. Two strategies were tried to avoid the problems Napster had encountered: encryption and decentralization.

Aimster was an encrypted file-sharing service. It used encrypted communications over America Online's instant messaging system, AIM (from which it took its name), to prevent anyone other than the users from monitoring or discovering the contents of traded files. Encrypted communications networks of this sort, piggybacking on existing networks, are called virtual private networks (VPNs). VPNs have many legitimate uses; they are far cheaper and easier to set up than actual, dedicated private networks, making them especially well-suited for confidential business communications.

Aimster distributed software to its users; when an Aimster user connected to AIM, the software identified all other Aimster users logged on to AIM as "buddies" and therefore members of the VPN. Using the software, Aimster users could then send encrypted files to each other. There was no way for Aimster to identify the content of the encrypted files that were being exchanged. For a monthly fee, Aimster offered a premium version of its software, Club Aimster, that included a tutorial, a website listing the forty most popular downloads, and a one-click download option.

Predictably, content industry parties quickly sued Aimster. At trial, Aimster did not argue that there had been no underlying direct infringement; because Aimster itself had copied no files, however, it—like Napster before it—could only be held liable as a third-party infringer. The federal district court for the Northern District of Illinois found that Aimster was, in fact, contributorily and vicariously liable (*In re Aimster Copyright Litigation*, 252 F. Supp.2d 634).

Aimster was contributorily liable because it had actual or constructive knowledge of and materially contributed to its users' direct infringement. The knowledge could be presumed from several facts. First, the content industry plaintiffs had written letters from the plaintiffs giving notice of direct infringements. (This probably would not have met the Ninth Circuit's more stringent test in *Napster,* but the Northern District of Illinois is located in the Seventh Circuit, which applied a different test.) Second, the Club Aimster website identified and commented on copyrighted material, and the tutorial used copyrighted titles as examples. Third, although it was true that the encryption made it impossible for Aimster to know what was being traded, the court found this self-induced unawareness insufficient to negate the knowledge requirement. The court reasoned that Aimster itself had made the encryption available, and that "there is absolutely no indication in the precedential authority that such specificity of knowledge is required in the contributory infringement context." It pointed out that "Plaintiffs have provided defendants with screen shots of the Aimster system showing the availability of Plaintiffs' copyrighted sound recordings on those users' hard drives. . . . The screen shots unequivocally identify the individual users ('buddies') who possess the offending files" (*In re Aimster Copyright Litigation*, 252 F. Supp.2d at 651).

The material contribution element was met, as in *Napster,* by providing the software and services that enabled users to connect with each other, as well as by ranking the songs, enticing potential infringers, and providing a one-click download option and tutorial.

According to the district court, Aimster was also a vicarious infringer. The district court found that Aimster had the right and ability to control the infringers' actions because it reserved the right to bar users and required a user name and password for the Club Aimster site. In addition, Aimster received a direct financial benefit from the directly infringing activity, not least because of the fee paid by Club Aimster users. On appeal the Seventh Circuit was not so sure; it neither affirmed nor reversed the trial court's decision on this issue, saying only that it was "less confident" that the plaintiffs would prevail on the merits of the vicarious liability claim than on the merits of the contributory liability claim (*In re Aimster Copyright Litigation*, 334 F.3d at 654).

The Aimster approach, despite the encryption, was too much like the Napster approach; the Club Aimster website, like Napster's directory, tied the company distributing the software too closely to the file-sharing process. Decentralized P2P networks were a better, if not perfect, solution to the legal and technical problems encountered by earlier file-sharing networks. In the wake of *Napster* and *Aimster,* the best-known P2P network was

KaZaA (later Kazaa). KaZaA Media Desktop was originally distributed by Consumer Empowerment, a company founded by Swedish and Dutch citizens in the Netherlands. It used a new technology to avoid a problem of earlier file-sharing networks: Rather than placing the directory on a central server controlled by the company, the file-sharing software placed and maintained directories on some users' computers, knows as supernodes. All of the computers running KaZaA Media Desktop could connect to each other, view directories of available files on the supernodes, and share files with each other, without Consumer Empowerment being involved in any way. In theory, this made Consumer Empowerment less like Napster than like a seller of cassette recorders, who has no ongoing connection with the purchaser and no way to control what the purchaser does after the sale.

After a lawsuit in the Netherlands, Consumer Empowerment applied its decentralization strategy to its corporate structure as well as its software. Sharman Networks, a company incorporated in the Pacific island nation of Vanuatu and headquartered in Australia, is now the principal owner, although the original Dutch and Swedish owners retain some influence. FastTrack software, upon which KaZaA Media Desktop is based, is now apparently the intellectual property of the founders and Bluemoon Interactive, an Estonian company. FastTrack has been licensed to many companies to create other P2P networks on the KaZaA model; it has also been pirated to produce KaZaA clones, capable of sharing with KaZaA Media Desktop.

KaZaA's dispersion has made it a difficult target. On appeal, Consumer Empowerment prevailed in the Netherlands; Sharman Networks has also been involved in litigation in Australia. In the United States, twenty-eight content-industry plaintiffs sued Sharman Networks, Consumer Empowerment, another FastTrack P2P network called Grokster, and others in the district court for the Central District of California. Both the trial court (in 2003) and the federal Court of Appeals for the Ninth Circuit (in 2004) found that Grokster was neither a contributory infringer nor a vicarious infringer. (Sharman Networks, as a Vanuatuan company doing business in Australia, had been dropped from the suit after the trial stage.) Grokster did not have "actual knowledge of infringement at a time when [it could] use that knowledge to stop the particular infringement" (*MGM v. Grokster,* 259 F. Supp.2d at 1037). Although the plaintiffs had notified Grokster of infringing conduct, Grokster could do nothing either to facilitate or prevent that conduct. Thus, in the district and circuit courts' view, the knowledge requirement for contributory infringement was not met for the same reason that the "right and ability to control" element of vicarious liability was not met.

The district and circuit courts also found that the "material contribution" element of contributory liability was not met, seeming to tie this element to the "right and ability to control" element as well. By the time of the litigation, Grokster no longer had control over a root supernode; the P2P network was operating without any information passing through any computer controlled by Grokster, and Grokster could not have shut down the P2P network had it wished to. Grokster was more like a seller of photocopy machines or cassette recorders than like Napster (see *MGM v. Grokster*, 259 F. Supp.2d at 1042–1043).

Nor was Grokster vicariously liable. As noted, the element of right and ability to control the direct infringers' actions was not met, although Grokster did receive a financial benefit from the infringing activity, or at least from the distribution of its software.

The district court's and Ninth Circuit's decisions in *Grokster* were good news for file sharers, but they contained a weakness. All of the elements of third-party liability that were not met came down to a single fact—Grokster's lack of ongoing control over the users of its software. To Grokster's allies, this made Grokster less like Napster and more like Sony, which was not liable for infringements committed with its VCRs. To Grokster's opponents, the better comparison—although they may not have used this specific case—was to *Atari v. JS & A*, the case lost by the distributors of a device for copying Atari game cartridges. JS & A's advertisements seemed to encourage illegal copying; so did Grokster's. To allow Grokster to avoid liability, the content industry claimed, would leave it defenseless. The Ninth Circuit was not unaware of the problem; it was "not blind to the possibility that Defendants may have intentionally structured their businesses to avoid secondary liability for copyright infringement, while benefiting financially from the illicit draw of their wares." But the Ninth Circuit declined to create a new form of third-party liability to cover the situation; the remedy, it said, lay with Congress rather than with the judiciary (*MGM v. Grokster*, 259 F. Supp.2d at 1046).

The content industry did not have to wait for Congress to act, however. In 2005 the Supreme Court vacated and remanded, in a plurality opinion, in a way that probably left none of the parties, even the winners, completely satisfied.

The Court declined to address vicarious infringement. "Because we resolve the case based on an inducement theory, there is no need to analyze separately MGM's vicarious liability theory" (*MGM v. Grokster*, 125 S.Ct. at 2776 n. 9). It conflated contributory infringement with the patent law doctrine of induced infringement; rather than the rule for contributory infringement applied by the lower courts—knowledge of plus material contribution to a direct infringement—it stated that "One infringes contributorily by intentionally inducing or encouraging direct infringement" (*MGM v. Grokster*, 125 S.Ct. at 2776). For this surprising rule the Court cited *Gershwin Publishing Corp. v. Columbia Artists Management*, a 1971 case from the Second Circuit. What the *Gershwin* court actually said, though, was "Similarly, one who, with knowledge of the infringing activity, induces, causes or materially contributes to the infringing conduct of another, may be held liable as a 'contributory' infringer" (*Gershwin Publishing Corp.*, 443 F.2d at 1162). The familiar elements of knowledge and material contribution are still there, with inducement as an alternative to—perhaps even intended as a synonym or subset of—material contribution.

The Supreme Court then continued its analysis on an inducement theory, explaining that just as it had made sense in *Sony* to borrow the staple article of commerce doctrine from patent law, it made sense here to borrow the inducement theory of third-party liability:

> For the same reasons that Sony took the staple-article doctrine of patent law as a model for its copyright safe-harbor rule, the inducement rule, too, is a sensible one for copyright. We adopt it here, holding that one who distributes a device with the object of promoting its use to infringe copyright, as shown by clear expression or other affirmative steps taken to foster infringement, is liable for the resulting acts of infringement by third parties. (*MGM v. Grokster*, 125 S.Ct. at 2780)

Once the new rule was adopted, it was a simple matter to find that Grokster had violated it:

> Grokster's name is apparently derived from Napster, it too initially offered an OpenNap program, its software's function is likewise comparable to Napster's, and it attempted to divert queries for Napster onto its own web-

site. Grokster and StreamCast's efforts to supply services to former Napster users, deprived of a mechanism
to copy and distribute what were overwhelmingly infringing files, indicate a principal, if not exclusive, intent
on the part of each to bring about infringement. (*MGM
v. Grokster*, 125 S.Ct. at 2781)

The Court, while having declined to address the issue of vicarious liability, took time to reject the Ninth Circuit's finding on
contributory liability. The Court's wording here is not as clear as
it could be; it is not entirely clear that the Court is presenting the
inducement rule as an alternative rule of contributory liability,
rather than adopting an entirely new form of third-party liability
for copyright infringement. The Court explained that the Ninth
Circuit had misread *Sony* "as holding that distribution of a commercial product capable of substantial noninfringing uses could
not give rise to contributory liability for infringement unless the
distributor had actual knowledge of specific instances of infringement and failed to act on that knowledge" (*MGM v.
Grokster*, 125 S.Ct. at 2775). The Ninth Circuit had also found that
Grokster "did not materially contribute to their users' infringement because it was the users themselves who searched for, retrieved, and stored the infringing files, with no involvement by
the defendants beyond providing the software in the first place"
(*MGM v. Grokster*, 125 S.Ct. at 2775). Nonetheless, the Supreme
Court found contributory liability.

The Supreme Court's decision in *MGM v. Grokster* did not
spell the end of file sharing. It did, however, preempt one possible alternative; while some had speculated that the Court might
focus on the fact that Grokster profited from the use of its product for copyright infringement, the Court's inducement rule applies to nonprofit P2P networks as well. Other alternatives
remain, though. A file-sharing network that is a staple article of
commerce—capable of a substantial noninfringing use—might
not be covered. As Justice Breyer pointed out in his separate concurring opinion, about 10 percent of the files traded over Grokster
at the time of the litigation were noninfringing (*MGM v. Grokster*,
125 S.Ct. at 2778, 2786 n. 3, 2789–2790). This was more than the
percentage of time-shifting uses in *Sony* (9 percent; see *ibid.* at
2788–2789). Even accepting that times and circumstances have
changed since *Sony*, it seems unlikely that the Court would have
been willing to decide against Grokster had more than half of the

files traded with its software been noninfringing—however much the content industry might wish it. And one obvious lesson is that file-sharing networks should not advertise themselves as useful tools for copyright infringement.

Another, slightly more subtle, lesson is that there is no need for a P2P network to base itself in the United States. While many other countries—Sweden, France, the United Kingdom—have been as harsh or harsher in their treatment of file sharing, others have not, and businesses based entirely on distributing software are extremely mobile. Ultimately, international treaties and the copyright laws of those foreign countries may provide remedies for the content industry, but the process will be delayed.

The content industry is not willing to bet everything on the eventual worldwide adoption and enforcement of a complete ban on P2P networks. Although suits for third-party infringement are simpler, because they offer a few large targets, the content industry has chosen to go after the more numerous smaller targets as well: the direct infringers.

The Recording Industry Association of America (RIAA) has filed thousands of suits against individual users of P2P file-sharing networks. Although these lawsuits seem to have had the desired deterrent effect, they have also brought a considerable amount of negative publicity and may have inspired or encouraged the creation of nonprofit P2P software for ideological reasons (hatred of the content industry) rather than pecuniary ones.

One of the first persons sued by the RIAA, often held up as a symbol of all that is wrong about the content industry, was twelve-year-old Brianna LaHara. Brianna was unaware that she had been doing anything wrong; her mother paid a monthly fee to KaZaA, and not surprisingly Brianna "thought it was OK to download music because my mom paid a service fee for it" (Younge 2003). A Dickensian "poor widows and orphans" flair was added to Brianna's tale by the fact that she lived with her mother, a single parent, in public housing in New York City.

Many perceived Brianna, and others like her, as victims, and consequently perceived the RIAA as a bully. Although the content industry's figures for its losses from music piracy were overstated, it may have been a measure of the industry's desperation at the time that it was willing to be seen as a bully in order to reduce file sharing.

The music content industry, in particular, was slower to respond to one of the main reasons for file sharing: dissatisfaction with the music industry's business model. At the time, the only legal way to buy most songs was on albums—CDs containing several songs. Singles were rarely available, and overpriced when they were. Customers who wanted to buy one song would have to buy the entire album; customers might end up paying $16 for one song they wanted and ten they didn't want. If the song was obscure, they might have had to search in several stores or online shops before finding an album that contained it; in 1999, for example, people looking for the 1960 United Kingdom alternate version of the Connie Francis song "Robot Man" would have had to buy either an antique vinyl record, perhaps available on eBay, or a five-disc set with 148 songs on it, costing more than $100. Or, in the alternative, they could have searched for it online, found some other Connie Francis completist who already had the song, and downloaded it for free.

What the music companies were slow to realize was that these file sharers weren't thieves trying to rob them of a $100 sale. They would gladly have paid a fair price for the song; they just weren't willing to pay a $100 or more to have 147 songs that they didn't want (or, perhaps, already had) bundled together with the one that they did. When the music companies finally began to offer their own individual-song download sites, the sites were laughable and were understandably ignored. The songs were often unplayable anywhere except on the computer that played them; the catalogs were small and shallow. What consumers wanted was not necessarily music for free; in fact, many of them were already paying money for premium P2P software. What they wanted was a single location at which they could find any song they might want.

Finally, in April 2003, Apple's iTunes opened for business. At ninety-nine cents per song and with a deep catalog, iTunes was the first service to offer most of the convenience of P2P networks. It wasn't quite as good; ninety-nine cents was still more than zero cents, although as compensation there was no monthly fee, no adware, and no spyware. Some obscure songs were not in the catalog, although Apple has continued to expand it; and as compensation, the quality of iTunes downloads was ensured. And an .aap file is not quite as useful as an .mp3 file; it comes with some, though nondraconian, restrictions on copying. And, of course, iTunes offers the benefit of not subjecting the user to a potential lawsuit from the RIAA—the carrot to the RIAA's stick.

The music industry also seems to be willing to make other concessions to adapt to P2P file sharing, perhaps anticipating the day when a P2P network will withstand the Supreme Court's new inducement test. One possible solution is the Voluntary Collective License proposed by the Electronic Frontier Foundation, an activist group. The Voluntary Collective License would set up a system similar to that currently in place for radio, allowing the industry to collect royalties and apportion them among artists according to the frequency with which particular works were downloaded:

> [T]he music industry forms a collecting society, which then offers file-sharing music fans the opportunity to "get legit" in exchange for a reasonable regular payment, say $5 per month. So long as they pay, the fans are free to keep doing what they are going to do anyway—share the music they love using whatever software they like on whatever computer platform they prefer—without fear of lawsuits. The money collected gets divided among rights-holders based on the popularity of their music. (Electronic Frontier Foundation 2004)

Some record labels have reportedly already entered into negotiations with P2P networks ("I Want My P2P" 2004).

Other sectors of the content industry, particularly the movie content industry, are also concerned about file sharing, although for several reasons it does not pose as great a threat to them. Sales of most books (other than some reference works, perhaps, which are rarely read in their entirety) are unlikely to be seriously affected by file sharing. Part of the appeal of a book is that it can be read without mechanical assistance; it can be carried anywhere, it never runs out of power, and it can still be read even after being dropped on the floor or in a puddle. At some point e-paper or some other new technology may offer these advantages, but for the time being books, the oldest form of mass-produced information storage, seem fairly secure in their market niche.

Movies are more at risk, partly because the savings from copying a movie and recording it on a DVD are greater than the savings from copying a book and printing it on paper—although still much less than the savings from copying songs and recording them on a CD. Perhaps most importantly, movies, like books, are not bundled; they are sold as individual works, and consumers are not forced to buy several works they do not want in order to get the one they do. In addition, movies on DVD are already compressed; they cannot be compressed much further without a significant loss of quality, so the space-saving advantage is considerably less than with CDs (or, for that matter, books).

Consumers and the content industry are not the only parties in the file-sharing battle. Equipment manufacturers and ISPs are also concerned. Equipment manufacturers worry about potential liability and the possible chilling effect of copyright lawsuits on the development of new technology; they are also irritated by the statutory imposition of requirements, at the insistence of the content industry, that equipment be manufactured in particular ways. It was this tension that led Les Vadasz, then senior vice president of Intel Corporation, to describe the content industry as "a pimple on the elephant's rear end." (The elephant, of course, was the equipment manufacturing industry.)

While Napster and Grokster were ISPs, their services were specifically aimed at file sharing. ISPs such as America Online and Verizon are not file-sharing networks, but file-sharing and other copyright-infringing activities take place over their networks. These ISPs are also threatened by the content industry's pursuit of file sharers, and several (including AT&T, BellSouth, MCI, SBC, and Verizon) filed an amicus curiae brief in the Grokster case urging that the decision of the Ninth Circuit (favoring Grokster) be affirmed. ISPs have also stood between their subscribers and the RIAA's individual user lawsuits. In December 2003 Verizon Internet Services won an important victory for online privacy as well as for ISPs when the federal appellate court for the District of Columbia agreed that Verizon, as a conduit ISP, did not have to turn over the name of a subscriber who had allegedly shared copyrighted music files, even though the RIAA had previously obtained a subpoena issued pursuant to the streamlined procedure provided in Title I of the Digital Millennium Copyright Act (*Recording Industry Association of America v. Verizon*, 351 F.3d 1229). As a result, the RIAA must now bring "John Doe" lawsuits against file-sharing defendants, and then obtain a subpoena; this procedure is more difficult and provides some protection for the subscribers through judicial oversight.

# Copy Protection and Copyright

Although file sharing has been perhaps the most furiously liti-gated copyright battle in recent years, one other aspect of copy-right law has inspired the same degree of emotional intensity: copy protection. Fair use, discussed in Chapter 1, allows those who legitimately obtain, say, a music CD or a movie on DVD to make copies of part or all of that work under certain circum-stances, notably for space shifting. A publisher who does not want the work copied can include some form of technological protection against copying, so that consumers will be unable to copy the work even though it might otherwise be legal for them to do so. And sufficiently motivated and technically sophisticated consumers could overcome this copy protection and make fair-use copies anyway. At least, that was the way things were until the passage of the Digital Millennium Copyright Act of 1998 (DMCA).

The DMCA is a complex law that does a great many things, but mention the abbreviation "DMCA" to an information rights activist and the response—probably quite heated—that you receive will probably focus on the law's anticircumvention provisions. The anticircumvention provisions prohibit circum-venting "a technological measure that effectively controls ac-cess" to a copyrighted work (17 U.S.C. § 1201 (a)(1)(A)) as well as trafficking in any "technology, product, service, device, com-ponent or part" that "is primarily designed or produced for the purpose of circumventing" such a technological protection measure (17 U.S.C. § 1201(a)(2)). In other words, even if the copying would otherwise be fair use, it is unlawful if the work is copy protected.

"Circumvention" includes "to descramble a scrambled work, to decrypt an encrypted work, or otherwise to avoid, bypass, re-move, deactivate, or impair a technological measure, without the authority of the copyright owner" (17 U.S.C. § 1201(a)(3)(A)). Although there are some exceptions, the space-shifting copying practiced by most consumers would be prohibited.

The DMCA's use of the word "effectively" has also been used by information rights activists to argue that easily broken copy protection is not covered by the statute, because it is not "ef-fective." Some forms of "technological protection measures" can be circumvented with a black marker or a piece of tape, or by holding down the "Shift" key. The statute anticipates this, however, and provides that "a technological measure 'effectively controls access to a work' if the measure, in the ordinary course of its operation, requires the application of information, or a process or a treatment, with the authority of the copyright owner, to gain access to the work" (17 U.S.C. § 1201(a)(3)(B)). The copy-protection measure is like a locked door; in other words, even though it may be easy to force the door open, anyone doing so without authorization is breaking the law—and the fact that the door is locked provides notice of the illegality.

Fair use is a statutory, not a constitutional, right; there's no question that Congress can alter the scope of fair use if it chooses to do so, as it evidently did by enacting Section 1201. Nonetheless, many people felt deeply wronged by this diminution of fair use, and not only information pirates but also ideologues and ordinary consumers began to examine ways to circumvent copy protection.

At the time, few music CDs were copy protected; the main form of protected works were movies on VHS and DVD. Movies on VHS tape are often protected by a form of copy protection known, after the company that makes it, as Macrovision. Macrovision's copy protection exploits the automatic gain and tracking control features on VCRs to prevent analog copying of analog or digital recordings. In a video recording, several lines of information can be recorded in an area that is never displayed on the screen during playback; repeatedly changing the brightness of these lines from light to dark and back again will fool the VCR into adjusting the brightness of the recording to compensate, causing the "VCRs to make distorted copies, devoid of entertainment value" (Macrovision 2003, 2). The Macrovision copy protection has no effect on users watching an authorized VHS cassette or DVD incorporating the protection, as the affected lines are never displayed on the screen.

Macrovision's copy protection can be circumvented, of course, by using a VCR without automatic gain control. Some very old VCRs lack these features, but the DMCA ensures that no new ones will by providing that VCRs made in or imported to the United States after 26 April 2002 must contain automatic gain control (17 U.S.C. § 1201(k)). While the automatic gain control on existing VCRs can be disabled, most users will lack the technical skills to do so. To prevent technically skilled users from performing this service for others or offering devices to do so, Macrovision Corporation has obtained patents on many of the ways in which this might be done. When devices or services for disabling automatic gain control appear on the market, Macrovision can suppress them through suits for patent infringement (see, for example, "Macrovision Wins Preliminary Injunction" 2004).

Faced with such obstacles, and with VCRs and VHS a moribund technology, opponents of the anticircumvention provisions focused instead on the Content Scramble System (CSS) copy-protection technology for DVDs. On 6 October 1999, a fifteen-year-old Norwegian citizen, Jon Lech Johansen (see Chapter 5), posted DeCSS, a method for decrypting CSS-encrypted disks, to a mailing list. At the time, CSS-encrypted disks could not be played on Linux systems; DeCSS offered a way for Linux users to play DVDs on their computers—a use that, prior to Section 1201, would have been a space-shifting fair use in the United States. Norway's statute on circumvention of technological measures was similar to Section 1201, and Johansen was prosecuted. His arrest instantly became a cause célèbre among information rights activists worldwide. U.S. and international content-industry groups had urged his arrest; the Electronic Frontier Foundation, probably the best-known information rights advocacy group, assisted in his defense. In January 2003 he was acquitted, but the prosecution appealed the verdict. (In the United States this would have been impossible, but in many countries the prosecution can appeal a verdict of acquittal.) The appellate court agreed that decrypting disks to play the movies they contained on Linux systems was not a crime and upheld the acquittal in December 2003; the prosecution then dropped the case (*Sunde (for Norway) v. Johansen*).

Johansen's trial was only one chapter, however. The battle over DeCSS was to become for Section 1201 what the battle over file sharing was for third-party infringement. Johansen himself, then a Norwegian citizen living in Norway, was effectively outside the reach of the U.S. justice system. (He now lives in the United States.) In November 1999, however, activists Shawn Reimerdes, Roman Kazan, and Eric Corley posted DeCSS on their websites—inside the United States. They also encouraged others to post DeCSS as an act of civil disobedience. All three were immediately sued by a group of eight movie studios. The federal district court for the Southern District of New York held that CSS was a technological measure that effectively controlled access to copyrighted works and that DeCSS was a means of circumventing that control. Thus, DeCSS was within the scope of the statute and, by distributing it, the defendants had violated Section 1201(a)(2)(A).

The defendants made no copies of movies with DeCSS; the only thing they copied was DeCSS itself, for which they presumably had at least the author's tacit permission. It seems highly unlikely that the defendants could have been held liable for any third-party infringement committed with DeCSS. Although DeCSS may have materially contributed to some infringements, they did not know of any infringements committed with it. They did not have the right and ability to control the actions of those who downloaded DeCSS, nor did they profit from distributing the code. Even under the Supreme Court's new inducement standard from *MGM v. Grokster,* they would be unlikely to be held liable; nothing about their words or conduct suggested that they had the object of promoting the use of DeCSS to infringe copyright.

Nonetheless, they were liable. Section 1201 did not require that any copyright infringement actually be committed; simply trafficking in—in this case, distributing for free—something capable of breaking the copy protection on a protected work was sufficient. Somewhat surprisingly, even providing links to other sites from which DeCSS could be downloaded was sufficient to constitute "trafficking" under Section 1201.

Reimerdes, Kazan, and Corley raised several arguments in defense, including arguments based on statutory exceptions to Section 1201 and on the First Amendment. The district court rejected the defendants' contention that their conduct was protected under the reverse engineering, encryption research, or security testing exceptions (17 U.S.C. § 1201(f), (g), and (j), respectively). It also rejected the defendants' First Amendment arguments, although it accepted the underlying idea that computer code can be expressive speech. The anticircumvention provisions were not an unconstitutional restraint on this expressive speech, because they were not aimed at the expression but at the function of the program. Under the intermediate standard of review appropriate to a content-neutral restriction of this sort, the interest in freely expressing the expressive content was outweighed by the interest in protecting copyrights and reducing video piracy (*Universal v. Reimerdes,* 111 F. Supp.2d 294).

According to the court, section 1201 did not unconstitutionally limit access to the information contained in the DVDs themselves either. Other, lawful methods of making fair-use copies existed, although the quality of such copies would have been lower than the quality of copies made with DeCSS (*Universal v. Reimerdes*, 111 F. Supp.2d 294). Considering that a watchable copy of a movie protected by both CSS and Macrovision could not legally be made, the alternative would seem to have been to point a camcorder at the screen while the movie was playing, resulting in a copy of very poor quality indeed.

Corley appealed the district court's decision to the Second Circuit Court of Appeals, which for the most part agreed with the trial court. Pointing a camcorder at the screen was apparently exactly the fair use the court had in mind. Section 1201, the court stated,

> does not impose even an arguable limitation on the opportunity to make a variety of traditional fair uses of DVD movies, such as commenting on their content, quoting excerpts from their screenplays, and even recording portions of the video images and sounds on film or tape by pointing a camera, a camcorder, or a microphone at a monitor as it displays the DVD movie. The fact that the resulting copy will not be as perfect or as manipulable as a digital copy obtained by having direct access to the DVD movie in its digital form, provides no basis for a claim of unconstitutional limitation of fair use. (*Universal Studios*, 273 F.3d at 459)

In addition to a federal action under Section 1201, the movie industry pursued those who posted DeCSS under state laws. One of these was Andrew Bunner; the DVD Copy Control Association, which owns CSS, sued Bunner and many other defendants (including "Emmanuel Goldstein," an Internet alias drawn from George Orwell's *1984* and used by Eric Corley) under California's trade secrets law. CSS, the DVD Copy Control Association argued, was a trade secret, and Bunner had violated state laws protecting that secret. The California Supreme Court ultimately agreed (*DVD Copy Control Association*, 4 Cal.Rptr.3d 69).

Although both state and federal courts in the United States had ordered that it not be distributed, DeCSS refused to go away. Free speech advocates, including many who had little interest in the narrower copyright issues, picked up the cause. Artists, hackers, and others expressed the code as a series of haiku, as a T-shirt, as a work of graphic art, and even as a 1,401-digit prime number.

These works obviously have little or no functional value and seem designed entirely as statements of protests—political expression, in other words—and thus entitled to the highest level of First Amendment protection. (This did not stop the DVD Copy Control Association from naming the T-shirt company as a codefendant in *Bunner,* however.) And for those who actually wish to make copies of DVDs, programs far more sophisticated than DeCSS have become widely available; DeCSS itself, now more of a historical curiosity, can easily be downloaded from many websites outside the United States.

As means of circumventing copy protection have grown more sophisticated, however, so has copy protection. The content industry, in addition to its lobbying efforts, has continued to work on ways to make copying more difficult. Digital rights management technology can be used to make all copies traceable. Trusted computing can limit users' abilities to make copies of recordings played on their computers. Sometimes the content industry's protective measures go too far and excite a furious public response, as with Sony's inclusion on some audio CDs of the First4Internet rootkit. The rootkit, a dangerous piece of software that could allow malicious users to take control of CD-buyers' computers, attracted the unfavorable notice not only of consumers but also of the U.S. Department of Homeland Security (McMillan 2006). The content industry is apparently not trusting to Section 1201 alone to prevent copying of technologically protected works.

# Trademarks and the Web: Infringement and Fair Use Online

Like copyright and patent law, trademark law has been placed under stress by the development of computers and the Internet. Two areas of difficulty have been the use of trademarks to direct search-engine traffic to a particular website and the use of trademarks as domain names. Unlawful uses of the first type fall under the general category of search-engine spamming, while unlawful uses of the second type are cybersquatting. Not all such uses are unlawful, though.

Search-engine spammers can use a variety of techniques to direct search-engine traffic to a particular website. One such technique is to direct searches for a competitor's business name or other trademark to one's own site. In the days before Google became the most-used search engine, one way to do this was with metatags (discussed in Chapter 1). While metatags are now obsolete (Google does not use metatags to rank search results), other search-engine spamming techniques, such as splogging, cloaking, and link farming, have arisen to take the place of metatag abuse, and search-engine providers now maintain constant vigilance against such spamming (see "Dancing with Google's Spiders" 2006).

Use of a competitor's trademark in a way that influences search-engine results is trademark infringement unless an exception applies. In *New Kids on the Block v. News America Publishing*, the Ninth Circuit Court of Appeals recognized a nominative fair use defense; later, in a case involving a former model for *Playboy* magazine, Terri Welles (see Chapter 5), the Ninth Circuit explained the fair use of trademarked terms as metatags. Welles had used the trademarked terms "playboy" and "playmate" as metatags on her site, and Playboy Enterprises, the owner of the trademarks, had sued. The Ninth Circuit explained that Welles' use of the terms met the requirements of nominative fair use:

> First, the product or service in question must be one not readily identifiable without use of the trademark; second, only so much of the mark or marks may be used as is reasonably necessary to identify the product or service; and third, the user must do nothing that would, in conjunction with the mark, suggest sponsorship or endorsement by the trademark holder. (*Playboy Enterprises, Inc. v. Welles*, 279 F.3d at 801, citing *New Kids on the Block v. News America Publishing, Inc.*, 971 F.2d 302, 308 (9th Cir. 1992))

The first element, the court explained, was met because "Welles has no practical way of describing herself without using trademarked terms" (*Playboy Enterprises*, 279 F.3d at 803). The second element was met because "[t]he metatags use only so much of the marks as reasonably necessary" and the third element was met because "nothing is done in conjunction with them to suggest sponsorship or endorsement by the trademark holder" (*Playboy Enterprises*, 279 F.3d at 804).

The Ninth Circuit's approach was not universally accepted, however (see, for example, *PACAAR v. TeleScan Technologies*, 319 F.3d 243 (6th Cir. 2003)), and a 2004 Supreme Court decision has called the Ninth Circuit's three-part nominative fair-use test into question (*KP Permanent Make-Up, Inc v. Lasting Impression I*, 543 U.S. 111). In the wake of *KP Permanent Make-Up*, another federal appellate court, the Third Circuit, has adopted a new test. In contrast to the Ninth Circuit's approach, the Third Circuit requires the plaintiff (that is, the mark owner) to first establish a likelihood of confusion.  If the likelihood of confusion is established, the Third Circuit applies a slightly different three-factor test:

> a defendant must show: (1) that the use of plaintiff's mark is necessary to describe both the plaintiff's product or service and the defendant's product or service; (2) that the defendant uses only so much of the plaintiff's mark as is necessary to describe plaintiff's product; and (3) that the defendant's conduct or language reflect the true and accurate relationship between plaintiff and defendant's products or services. (*Century 21 Real Estate Corp. v. LendingTree*, 425 F.3d at 222)

Regardless of the test applied, nominative fair use has strict limits. In the early days of search-engine spamming, unsophisticated search engines could be fooled, by repetition of a single term dozens or hundreds of times, into giving the site repeating that term a higher rank on searches for the term than other sites using the term fewer times. The Ninth Circuit pointed out that it was not giving its approval to such a use: "We note that our decision might differ if the metatags listed the trademarked term so repeatedly that Welles' site would regularly appear above [Playboy's] in searches for one of the trademarked terms" (*Playboy Enterprises*, 279 F.3d at 804).

Even a single use of a trademark is not necessarily a nominative fair use. A company called Radiation Monitoring Devices, Inc. included a metatag on its Web page that said "The Home Page of Niton Corporation, makers of the finest lead, radon and multi-element detectors." The statement was completely untrue; Niton was a competitor, and Radiation Monitoring Devices was enjoined from using the metatag (*Niton Corp.*, 27 F. Supp.2d at 104–105).

# Trademarks and the Web: Cybersquatting

In the early days of the World Wide Web, many established businesses were slow to realize the new medium's importance and potential, and many failed to register their business names and other trademarks as domain names. Many independent entrepreneurs, known as cybersquatters, registered these domain names, hoping to sell them to the owners. Many owners paid; others took legal action to gain control of the domain name. For owners of famous marks, an action for trademark dilution was a possibility, especially because some cybersquatters placed pornographic content on the sites they registered in order to pressure the trademark owner. In such cases, an action for dilution by tarnishment was easy to maintain; even absent such conduct, the use of the domain name for some other purpose might constitute dilution by blurring.

Owners of marks that were not famous, but were merely distinctive, had a much more difficult time. If the registrant chose to use the site to compete with the mark owner in the line of business for which the mark was protected, the mark owner might be able to maintain an infringement action. If the registrant did nothing with the domain name other than register it, the mark owner's options were limited.

To address the perceived problem of cybersquatting, Congress enacted the Anticybersquatting Consumer Protection Act (ACPA) in 1999. The ACPA provides that a person who, with a bad faith intent to profit, registers, traffics in, or uses a domain name that at the time of registration is either identical to or confusingly similar to a distinctive mark, or that is identical to or confusingly similar to or dilutive of a famous mark, is liable in a civil action by the owner of the mark. If the mark owner prevails in an ACPA action, the court can transfer the offending domain name (15 U.S.C. § 1125(d)).

Most of the text of the ACPA is taken up with an attempt to define "bad faith intent to profit." The Act provides nine factors to be weighed in assessing this intent, and one exception that, if present, will negate the bad faith intent regardless of the other nine factors. The nine factors are

(I) the trademark or other intellectual property rights of the person, if any, in the domain name;

(II) the extent to which the domain name consists of the legal name of the person or a name that is otherwise commonly used to identify that person;

(III) the person's prior use, if any, of the domain name in connection with the bona fide offering of any goods or services;

(IV) the person's bona fide noncommercial or fair use of the mark in a site accessible under the domain name;

(V) the person's intent to divert consumers from the mark owner's online location to a site accessible under the domain name that could harm the goodwill represented by the mark, either for commercial gain or with the intent to tarnish or disparage the mark, by creating a likelihood of confusion as to the source, sponsorship, affiliation, or endorsement of the site;

(VI) the person's offer to transfer, sell, or otherwise assign the domain name to the mark owner or any third party for financial gain without having used, or having an intent to use, the domain name in the bona fide offering of any goods or services, or the person's prior conduct indicating a pattern of such conduct;

(VII) the person's provision of material and misleading false contact information when applying for the registration of the domain name, the person's intentional failure to maintain accurate contact information, or the person's prior conduct indicating a pattern of such conduct;

(VIII) the person's registration or acquisition of multiple domain names which the person knows are identical or confusingly similar to marks of others that are distinctive at the time of registration of such domain names, or dilutive of famous marks of others that are famous at the time of registration of such domain names, without regard to the goods or services of the parties; and

(IX) the extent to which the mark incorporated in the person's domain name registration is or is not distinctive and famous. . . . (15 U.S.C. § 1125(d)(1)(B)(i))

The exception provides that "[b]ad faith intent . . . shall not be found in any case in which . . . the person believed and had reasonable grounds to believe that the use of the domain name was a fair use or otherwise lawful."

In cases where the registrant cannot be located or jurisdiction over the registrant cannot be obtained (for example, because the registrant is outside the United States), the mark owner may bring an action in rem—that is, may proceed against the domain name itself (15 U.S.C. § 1125(d)(2)(A)(ii)). Before proceeding in rem, the mark owner must send notice of the alleged violation and intent to proceed to the registrant at the postal and e-mail address provided when registering the domain name and must then wait a reasonable time for a response.

Cybergriping, especially when the suffix "sucks" is used in a site name (as in Lucentsucks.com), presents a slightly different problem. While it is clearly intended to harm and tarnish the mark—the point of a cybergriping site is to criticize someone or something—it does not fit clearly within the nine "bad faith" factors of the ACPA. Cybergriping may also be protected by the First Amendment (see Sorgen 2001; *Bosley Medical Institute*, 403 F.3d 672).

Cybersquatting outside the United States may be resolved by an in rem proceeding under the ACPA, if a U.S. court has jurisdiction. If not, it may be resolved under the domestic law of some other country, or under the Uniform Domain Name Dispute Resolution Policy of the Internet Corporation for Assigned Names and Numbers. The anticybersquatting rule of the policy is similar, but not identical, to the ACPA. It provides that a complaining party must prove (1) that the domain name is identical or confusingly similar to its trademark, (2) that the defendant has no rights or legitimate interests in respect of the domain name, and (3) that the domain name has been registered in bad faith and is being used in bad faith (Uniform Domain Name Dispute Resolution Policy, art. 4(a)).

# Summary

This chapter examines several recent intellectual property controversies, many of which reflect the ongoing tensions between consumers, content owners, and equipment makers. In the controversy over the patentability of computer software, an early misstep led to copyright rather than patent becoming the main vehicle for protection of software. While the mistake was eventually remedied and computer programs are now patentable in the United States (although not in Europe), the damage could not be completely undone. It remains to be seen which current resolutions of intellectual property decisions will later turn out to have been mistakes.

Although the "look and feel" of software seems not to be copyrightable, questions remain about whether look and feel can be protected as trade dress under trademark law. The protection, if any, to be given to nonoriginal databases is similarly uncertain, but the patentability of business methods is now firmly established.

The content industry has had mixed results in its attempts to prohibit the sale of copying devices; devices that meet the standard article of commerce test of *Sony* may still be sold. It has had better luck in the battle over file sharing; the industry's recent victory in *Grokster* puts the law on its side, for the moment, at least in the United States. The anticircumvention provisions of Section 1201 and the content industry's subsequent court victories in battles over the statute have restricted fair use—a loss for consumers, a victory for the content industry, and a headache for equipment manufacturers. Meanwhile trademark owners have more or less successfully addressed the problems of cybersquatting and the use of trademarks in cybersquatting, with courts crafting solutions that nonetheless preserve trademark fair use.

# Treaties

"Agreement on Trade-Related Aspects of Intellectual Property Rights, Marrakesh Agreement Establishing the World Trade Organization, Annex 1C." April 15, 1994. 33 I.L.M. 81.

"Convention on the Grant of European Patents." October 5, 1973. 13 I.L.M. 276. Text as amended through December 10, 1998. http://www.european-patent-office.org/legal/epc/e/ma1.html.

# Statutes and Other Governmental Materials

Audio Home Recording Act, 17 U.S.C. §§ 1001–1003, 1008.

Copyright Act of 1976, 17 U.S.C. §§ 101–105.

Digital Millennium Copyright Act, 17 U.S.C. §§ 512, 1201.

Digital Performance Right in Sound Recordings Act, 17 U.S.C. § 106(6).

Directive 96/9/EC of the European Parliament and of the Council of 11 March 1996 on the Legal Protection of Databases, 1996 O.J. (L 77) 20 ("EU Database Directive").

First Inventor Defense Act, 35 U.S.C. § 273.

Lanham Trademark Act, 15 U.S.C. § 1125.

Louisiana Software License Enforcement Act, La. Rev. Stat. Ann. § 51:1961 et seq. (West 1987).

Ohio Rev. Code § 2913.04.

# Cases

*A&M Records, Inc. v. Napster, Inc.*, 239 F.3d 1004 (9th Cir. 2001).

*Albie's Foods, Inc. v. Menusaver, Inc.*, 170 F. Supp.2d 736 (E.D. Mich. 2001).

*Amazon.com, Inc. v. Barnesandnoble.com, Inc.*, 239 F.3d 1343 (Fed. Cir. 2001).

*Apple Computer, Inc. v. Microsoft Corp.*, 35 F.3d 1435 (9th Cir. 1994).

*Apple Computer, Inc. v. Microsoft Corp.*, 799 F. Supp. 1006 (N.D. Cal. 1992).

*Apple Computer, Inc. v. Microsoft Corp.*, 779 F. Supp. 133 (N.D. Cal. 1991).

*Atari, Inc. v. JS & A Group, Inc.*, 747 F.2d 1422 (Fed. Cir. 1984).

*Bihari v. Gross*, 119 F. Supp.2d 309 (S.D. N.Y. 2000).

*Bosley Medical Institute, Inc. v. Kremer*, 403 F.3d 672 (9th Cir. 2005).

*Buma/Stemra v. KaZaA*, Amsterdam Court of Appeal (2002). Unofficial English translation. www.eff.org/IP/P2P/BUMA_v_Kazaa/20020328 _kazaa_appeal_judgment.html.

*Century 21 Real Estate Corp. v. LendingTree, Inc.*, 425 F.3d 211 (3d Cir. 2005).

*Diamond v. Diehr*, 450 U.S. 175 (1981).

*DVD Copy Control Association, Inc. v. Bunner*, 113 Cal. Rptr.2d 338 (2001), rev'd, 4 Cal.Rptr.3d 69 (2003).

*eBay v. MercExchange*, 126 S.Ct. 1837 (2006).

*Feist Publications v. Rural Telephone Service Co.,* 499 U.S. 340 (1991).

*Fonovisa, Inc. v. Cherry Auction, Inc.,* 76 F.3d 259 (9th Cir. 1996).

*Gershwin Publishing Corporation v. Columbia Artists Management, Inc.,* 443 F.2d 1159 (2d Cir. 1971).

*Gottschalk v. Benson,* 409 U.S. 63 (1972).

*Hotel Security Checking Co. v. Lorraine Co.,* 160 F. 467 (2d Cir. 1908).

*In re Aimster Copyright Litigation (Aimster II),* 252 F. Supp.2d 634 (N.D. Ill. 2002); *affirmed in part,* 334 F.3d 643 (7th Cir. 2003); *certiorari denied sub nom Deep v. Recording Industry Association of America, Inc.,* 124 S.Ct. 1069 (2004).

*In re Alappat,* 33 F.3d 1526 (Fed. Cir. 1994).

*International Business Machines Corporation,* Technical Board of Appeal of the European Patent Office, Case No. T 0935/97—3.5.1 (1999).

*KP Permanent Make-Up, Inc. v. Lasting Impression I, Inc.,* 543 U.S. 111 (2004).

*Lotus Development Corporation v. Borland International, Inc.,* 49 F.3d 807 (1st Cir. 1995); *affirmed,* 516 U.S. 233 (1996).

*Lucent Technologies, Inc. v. Lucentsucks.com,* 95 F. Supp.2d 528 (E.D. Va. 2000).

*MGM Studios, Inc. v. Grokster, Ltd.,* 259 F. Supp.2d 1029 (C.D. Cal. 2003); *affirmed,* 380 F.3d 1154 (9th Cir. 2004); *vacated & remanded,* 125 S.Ct. 2764 (2005).

*New Kids on the Block v. News America Publishing, Inc.,* 971 F.2d 302 (9th Cir. 1992).

*Niton Corp. v. Radiation Monitoring Devices, Inc.,* 27 F. Supp.2d 102 (D. Mass. 1998).

*Ohio v. Perry,* 83 Ohio St. 3d 41, 697 N.E. 2d 624 (1998).

*PACAAR Inc. v. TeleScan Technologies LLC,* 319 F.3d 243 (6th Cir. 2003).

*Playboy Enterprises, Inc. v. Welles,* 279 F.3d 796 (9th Cir. 2002).

*ProCD, Inc. v. Zeidenberg,* 86 F.3d 1447 (7th Cir. 1996).

*Recording Industry Association of America v. Diamond Multimedia Systems, Inc.,* 180 F.3d 1072 (9th Cir. 1999).

*Recording Industry Association of America, Inc. v. Verizon Internet Services,* 351 F.3d 1229 (D.C. Cir. 2003); certiorari denied, 125 S.Ct. 309, 125 S.Ct 347 (2004).

*Religious Technology Center v. Netcom On-Line Communication Services, Inc.,* 907 F. Supp. 1361 (N.D. Cal. 1995).

*Sony Corp. of America v. Universal City Studios, Inc.,* 464 U.S. 417 (1984).

*Sporty's Farm L.L.C. v. Sportsman's Market, Inc.*, 202 F.3d 489 (2nd Cir. 2000).

*State of Ohio v. Perry*, 83 Ohio St. 3d 41, 697 N.E.2d 624 (1998).

*State Street Bank & Trust v. Signature Financial Group, Inc.*, 149 F.3d 1368 (Fed. Cir. 1999).

*Sunde (for Norway) v. Johansen*, Oslo First Instance Trial Court, January 7, 2003, No. 02-507 M/94, English translation by Professor Jon Bing. http://www.eff.org/IP/Video/Johansen_DeCSS_case/20030109 _johansen _decision.html; *on appeal*, Borgarting Appellate Court, December 22, 2003, No. LB-2003-00731, English translation by Professor Jon Bing. http://www.efn.no/DVD-dom-20031222-en.html.

*Two Pesos, Inc. v. Taco Cabana, Inc.*, 505 U.S. 763 (1992).

*UMG Recordings, Inc. v. MP3.com, Inc.*, 92 F. Supp.2d 349 (S.D. N.Y. 2000).

*Universal City Studios, Inc. v. Reimerdes*, 111 F. Supp.2d 294 (S.D. N.Y. 2000); *affirmed by Universal City Studios, Inc. v. Corley*, 273 F.3d 429 (2nd Cir. 2001).

*Vault Corporation v. Quaid Software Ltd.*, 847 F.2d 255 (5th Cir. 1988).

*Volkswagenwerk Aktiengesellschaft v. Church*, 411 F.2d 350 (9th Cir. 1969).

# Sources and Further Reading

Byerly, Lisa M. 1998. "Look and Feel Protection of Web Site User Interfaces: Copyright or Trade Dress?" *Santa Clara Computer and High Technology Law Journal* 14: 221.

Cole, Rodger R. 1995. "Substantial Similarity in the Ninth Circuit: A 'Virtually Identical' 'Look and Feel?'" *Santa Clara Computer and High Technology Law Journal* 11: 417.

"Dancing with Google's Spiders." 2006. *Economist Technology Quarterly* March 11, 14–15.

Electronic Frontier Foundation. 2004. *A Better Way Forward: Voluntary Collective Licensing of Music File Sharing.* "Let the Music Play" White Paper. February. http://www.eff.org/share/collective_lic_wp.php.

"EU Software Patent Law Faces Axe." 2005. BBC.com. February 17. http://news.bbc.co.uk/1/hi/technology/4274811.stm.

"Face Value: The Quiet Iconoclast—With KaZaA, Niklas Zennstrom Undermined the Music Industry." 2004. *The Economist*, July 3, 54.

Hasan, Amar A. 2005. "Sweating in Europe: The European Union Database Directive." *Computer Law Review and Technology Journal* 9: 479.

"I Want My P2P: Record Labels Are Trying to Do Deals with File-Sharing Networks." 2004. *The Economist*, November 20, 65.

"Internet Corporation for Assigned Names and Numbers. Uniform Domain Name Dispute Resolution Policy." August 26, 1999. http://www.icann.org/udrp/udrp-policy-24oct99.htm.

Kellner, Lauren Fisher. 1994. "Trade Dress Protection for Computer User Interface 'Look and Feel.'" *University of Chicago Law Review* 61: 1011.

Likourezos, George. 1995. "Trademark Law in the Computer Age: Applying Trademark Principles to the 'Look and Feel' of Software." *Journal of the Patent and Trademark Office Society* 77: 451.

Macrovision Corporation. 2003. "Preserving an Effective DVD Copy Protection System." March 3. http://www.macrovision.com/pdfs/Preserving-an-effective-DVD-Copying-System_0303.pdf.

"Macrovision Wins Preliminary Injunction Against 321 Studios In Patent and Copyright Infringement Lawsuit." 2004. Macrovision Press Release. May 20. http://www.macrovision.com/company/news/press/news detail.jsp?id=Thu%20May%2020%2010:28:39%20PDT%202004.

McMillan, Robert. 2006. "DHS: Sony Rootkit May Lead to Regulation: U.S. Officials Aim to Avoid Future Security Threats Caused by Copy Protection." *ComputerWorld*, February 16. softwarehttp://www.computer world.com/governmenttopics/government/policy/story/0,10801,1087 93,00.html.

Menn, Joseph. 2003. *All the Rave: The Rise and Fall of Shawn Fanning's Napster*. New York: Crown Business.

Nguyen, Xuan-Thao N. 2000. "Should It Be a Free for All? The Challenge of Extending Trade Dress Protection to the Look and Feel of Web Sites in the Evolving Internet." *American University Law Review* 49: 1233.

Reimer, Jeremy. No date. *Personal Computer Market Share: 1975-2004*. http://www.pegasus3d.com/total_share.html.

Reimer, Jeremy. 2005. "Total Share: 30 Years of Personal Computer Market Share Figures." *Ars Technica*, December 14. http://arstechnica .com/articles/culture/total-share.ars/1.

Rosenoer, Jonathan. 1994. "Apple Loses." *Cyberlaw*. http://www.cyberlaw .com/cylw994.html.

"St. Columba." 1908. In *The Catholic Encyclopedia*. New York: Robert Appleton Co. http://www.newadvent.org/cathen/04136a.htm.

Samuelson, Pamela, Randall Davis, Mitchell D. Kapor, and J. H. Reichman. 1994. "A Manifesto Concerning the Legal Protection of Computer Programs." *Columbia Law Review* 94: 2308.

Schneider, Mark. 1998. "The European Union Database Directive." *Berkeley Technology Law Journal* 13: 551.

Schortgen, Steven. 1994. "'Dressing' up Software Interface Protection: The Application of Two Pesos to 'Look and Feel.'" *Cornell Law Review* 80: 158.

Smith, Seagrumn. 2003. "From Napster to KaZaA: The Battle Over Peer-to-Peer Filesharing Goes International." 2003. *Duke Law & Technology Review* 2003: 8.

Sorgen, Rebecca S. 2001. "Trademark Confronts Free Speech on the Information Superhighway: 'Cybergripers' Face a Constitutional Collision." *Loyola of Los Angeles Entertainment Law Review* 22: 115.

Stagnone, Lauren A. 1997. "Copyright Law—Computer Program Menu Command Hierarchy: An Uncopyrightable Method of Operation? *Lotus Development Corporation v. Borland International, Inc.*, 49 F.3d 807 (1995), aff'd, 116 S. Ct. 804 (1996)." *Suffolk University Law Review* 30: 939.

Terry, Nicolas P. 1994. "GUI Wars: The Windows Litigation and the Continuing Decline of 'Look and Feel.'" *Arkansas Law Review* 47: 93.

Thompson, Bill. 2005. "Patents: Gone but not Forgotten." July 15. http://news.bbc.co.uk/2/hi/technology/4685731.stm.

"Unexpected Harmony: The Music and Computer Industries Make Peace, but Differences Remain." 2003. *The Economist,* January 23.

Wells, Matthew G. 2001. "Internet Business Method Patent Policy." *Virginia Law Review* 87: 729.

Woodford, Chad. 2004. "Trusted Computing or Big Brother? Putting the Rights Back in Digital Rights Management." *University of Colorado Law Review* 75: 253.

Younge, Gary. 2003. "US Music Industry Sues 261 for Online Song Copying." *The Guardian,* September 10. http://www.guardian.co.uk/online/news/0,12597,1038979,00.html.

# 3

# Worldwide Perspective

## Intellectual Property and International Law

Intellectual property rights are granted by national governments, which can only grant rights having effect within the territory under the authority of those governments. Yet intellectual property rights can easily be harmed by actions beyond the limits of the granting government's jurisdiction. To protect against such harm, and to further international trade in intellectual property, a system of global protection of intellectual property rights is needed. This system must contain elements of international law as well as effective intellectual property laws in every country at the national level.

Public international law is law that governs interactions between states and other international actors. A traditional starting point for examining the sources of international law can be found in Article 38(1) of the Statute of the International Court of Justice:

> The Court, whose function is to decide in accordance with international law such disputes as are submitted to it, shall apply:
>     a. international conventions, whether general or particular, establishing rules expressly recognized by the contesting states;
>     b. international custom, as evidence of a general practice accepted as law;

c. the general principles of law recognized by civilized nations;

d. subject to the provisions of Article 59, judicial decisions and the teachings of the most highly qualified publicists of the various nations, as subsidiary means for the determination of rules of law.

The Statute's list is far from complete, of course, and contains a quaint vestige of the twentieth-century colonialist outlook of many of the original parties to the Statute ("civilized nations"). But for purposes of determining the sources of the regime of international intellectual property law, it is safe to divide the sources listed in the Statute into two categories: conventional international law, which is defined by "international conventions, whether general or particular, establishing rules expressly recognized"; and customary international law, which is a set of normative expectations about the behavior of nations undertaken out of a sense of legal obligation, sources of which can be found in the other items listed in the Statute. To some extent this is an oversimplification of nonconventional international law, but all or nearly all international intellectual property law is conventional.

The treaties and other international agreements to which the United States is a party are a part of U.S. law under Article VI, clause 2 of the U.S. Constitution. These agreements become part of U.S. law after they are ratified by the president upon receipt of the advice and consent of the Senate. In practice this means that treaties supersede all prior federal law, but may later be modified or deprived of effect by Congress. State law, however, may not conflict with treaty law (Buergenthal 2002; Trimble 2002).

The ratification of an international agreement confers rights and obligations on the United States with respect to other countries under international law. In most cases, though, ratification alone does not confer any rights or obligations on U.S. citizens under U.S. law. Most treaties are non-self-executing and have no effect within U.S. law until Congress enacts legislation to implement them.

Specific treaty regimes govern each category of international intellectual property law; these are examined in detail below. This section addresses the overall administrative regime set up by the various intellectual properties. Two bodies administer almost all of the important multilateral intellectual property treaties now in force: the World Intellectual Property Organization (WIPO) and the World Trade Organization (WTO).

The WIPO administers most of the treaties discussed in this chapter, with one significant exception—the Treaty on Trade Related Aspects of Intellectual Property Rights (TRIPs), which is the intellectual property agreement of the WTO. Many of the treaty regimes governing patent, copyright, and trademark, especially the Berne Union (copyright) and the Paris Union (patent and trademark), predate WIPO by many decades; however, these regimes have now been brought within the WIPO framework. This has greatly simplified the administration of international intellectual property law. The Paris Union was the oldest international intellectual property treaty organization, dating from the 1883 Paris Convention; the Berne Convention created the Berne Union three years later, in 1886. Seven years later, the two combined to form the Bureaux Internationaux Réunis pour la Protection de la Propriété Intellectuelle (United International Bureau for the Protection of Intellectual Property or BIRPI). In 1893 BIRPI administered the Paris and Berne Conventions and two other treaties. Over time, as new treaties were added, the size of the organization had to increase. BIRPI maintained its headquarters in Berne until 1960, when it moved to Geneva to be closer to the United Nations. Seven years later, in 1967, BIRPI became WIPO. A new treaty, the Convention Establishing the World Intellectual Property Organization, became WIPO's organic document—its "constitution." Seven years after that, in 1974, WIPO became a specialized agency of the United Nations (WIPO 2001).

Nearly every country in the world is a member of WIPO; as of 2006, WIPO has 183 members. In addition, 247 organizations have observer status: 172 international nongovernmental organizations (NGOs), 10 national NGOs, and 65 intergovernmental organizations (WIPO 2006a). While many of these observers represent the content industry, some balance is provided by the presence of observers like the Electronic Frontier Foundation and Free Software Foundation Europe.

Today WIPO administers, in whole or in part, two dozen international intellectual property treaties. This task requires the work of nearly a thousand employees, mostly in Geneva and New York. In addition to administering these treaties, WIPO is also governed by three treaties: the Convention Establishing the World Intellectual Property Organization, the Agreement between the United Nations and WIPO, and the Agreement between WIPO and the WTO. The treaties administered by WIPO include the following:

1. The Berne Convention for the Protection of Literary and Artistic Works
2. The Brussels Convention Relating to the Distribution of Programme-Carrying Signals Transmitted by Satellite
3. The Budapest Treaty on the International Recognition of the Deposit of Microorganisms for the Purposes of Patent Procedure
4. The Convention for the Protection of Producers of Phonograms Against Unauthorized Duplication of Their Phonograms
5. The Hague Agreement Concerning the International Deposit of Industrial Designs
6. The International Convention for the Protection of New Varieties of Plants
7. The Lisbon Agreement for the Protection of Appellations of Origin and their International Registration
8. The Locarno Agreement Establishing an International Classification for Industrial Designs
9. The Madrid Agreement Concerning the International Registration of Marks
10. The Madrid Agreement for the Repression of False and Deceptive Indications of Source on Goods
11. The Nairobi Treaty on the Protection of the Olympic Symbol
12. The Nice Agreement Concerning the International Classification of Goods and Services for the Purposes of the Registration of Marks
13. The Paris Convention for the Protection of Industrial Property
14. The Patent Cooperation Treaty
15. The Patent Law Treaty
16. Protocol Relating to the Madrid Agreement Concerning the International Registration of Marks
17. The Rome Convention for the Protection of Performers, Producers of Phonograms and Broadcasting Organizations
18. The Strasbourg Agreement Concerning the International Patent Classification

19. The Trademark Law Treaty
20. The Treaty on the International Registration of Audiovisual Works
21. The Vienna Agreement Establishing an International Classification of the Figurative Elements of Marks
22. The Washington Treaty on Intellectual Property in Respect of Integrated Circuits
23. The WIPO Copyright Treaty
24. The WIPO Performances and Phonograms Treaty (WIPO 2005; WIPO 2001)

The Patent Cooperation Treaty is also a major source of revenue for WIPO. The fees inventors pay to use the Treaty's WIPO-administered international patent filing system enable WIPO to avoid dependence on contributions from member states.

Decisions within WIPO are made by voting; each member has one vote. This voting structure has been criticized as unrealistic and unjust, however, because the countries involved do not have equal populations or equal levels of participation in the global intellectual property marketplace. Large countries with high levels of market participation—the United States, China, India, Japan—are accorded no more voting weight than very small countries with low levels of market participation—such as Antigua and Barbuda, Comoros, and Monaco. On the whole, though, this imbalance seems more beneficial to consumer interests than otherwise. The developing countries that make up a majority of the membership tend to be net importers of intellectual property, which causes their interests to be those of consumers rather than producers. In the debate over licensing of pharmaceutical patents during the 1980s, this polarization became quite pronounced and was one of the factors leading the United States, in particular, to seek an additional international intellectual property treaty outside the WIPO regime.

The treaty that was ultimately adopted was the Agreement on Trade-Related Aspects of Intellectual Property Rights, Annex 1C to the Marrakesh Agreement Establishing the World Trade Organization. With such an unwieldy name, the treaty is almost always referred to by its acronym, TRIPs. Because TRIPs is part of the WTO Agreement, all countries that become parties to the WTO also become parties to TRIPs. One hundred forty-nine countries are now WTO members, the most recent to join being Saudi Arabia on 11 December 2005.

While previous treaties dealt with one or a few areas of intellectual property, TRIPs is comprehensive. It addresses not only copyright, trademark, and patent, but also geographical indications, industrial designs, integrated circuit layouts, and trade secrets. Like many subject-specific intellectual property treaties, TRIPs requires national treatment and most favored nation treatment (TRIPs, arts. 3 and 4). "National treatment" means that states that are parties to TRIPs must accord to all other parties the same level of protection that they accord to their own nationals. The term "most favored nation treatment" is confusing, and it is often misunderstood as meaning that a country is receiving preferential treatment. The actual meaning is the reverse: All WTO members are required to give to every other WTO member the same level of intellectual property protection that they give to the nation they most favor, so that no WTO member is favored or disfavored over any other (TRIPs makes a partial exception to avoid hardship to developing countries and allows those countries to phase in their obligations more slowly (TRIPs, arts. 65–67).) TRIPs also brings disputes arising under it within the scope of the WTO's dispute resolution mechanism. Specific provisions of TRIPs are examined in the relevant sections below.

# The World Wide Web

The terms "World Wide Web" and "Internet" are often confused. The Internet is the older and vaster of the two; it consists of the physical infrastructure and communications protocols that connect hundreds of millions of host systems and countless other computers and devices. The World Wide Web is a network of information contained on these host systems and accessible over the Internet; it consists of billions of hypertext pages, all of which can be accessed using a Web browser. While the Web is the best-known such network, it is not the only one. Other familiar uses of the Internet are e-mail and peer-to-peer networks.

While the Internet arose from a variety of sources and cannot be traced to a single inventor or event, the U.S. government was very heavily involved in its creation, a fact that continues to affect the law and politics of Internet administration. Histories of the Internet usually trace its inception to ARPANET, a U.S. Department of Defense project that, in 1969, linked four computers at locations in California and Utah (Kristula 2001). By 1972 e-mail was being sent over ARPANET, which by then connected more than two dozen computers. In 1983 ARPANET, now connecting hundreds of computers, switched to the TCP/IP networking protocols still in use today. In 1990 ARPANET ceased to exist, but the computers remained connected. New networks had grown up using those connections, including NSFNet, another government-sponsored project. These various networks were connected to each other, making it possible, in theory, for a computer connected to any one network to communicate with computers connected to one of the other networks. In the 1980s the Internet moved from universities and government research facilities to private homes, with the appearance of for-profit, proprietary networks like America Online, CompuServe, and Prodigy.

The World Wide Web, however, can be traced to a specific event. In the late 1980s Tim Berners-Lee and Robert Cailliau, working at the European Organization for Nuclear Research (CERN), created a hypertext to find documents on CERN's computers. The system differed from previous hypertext systems in using unidirectional, rather than bidirectional, links; this made it possible for a person creating a hypertext document to link to another document without having to alter that second document to include a reciprocal link. This made it possible to create a constantly expanding network of linked pages. Berners-Lee had created his first Web page and the first Web browser by 1991 (CERN no date).

The ease of creating additional pages was one factor in the success of the Web, but another was just as important: CERN chose to make the underlying technology freely available to all. Had CERN chosen to assert an intellectual property right in Berners-Lee's and Cailliau's inventions, the Web today would probably be as forgotten as many of the proprietary networks of the 1980s. This is a case in which intellectual property rights were more of a threat to innovation than an encouragement.

At this point using the Web still required a certain degree of technical sophistication. The third step in the development of the Web, and the one that ultimately resulted in connecting at least half the world in an ongoing, multisided exchange of information, was the development of easy-to-use Web browsers. This breakthrough came in 1993 with the release of the Mosaic browser by the National Center for Supercomputing Applications at the University of Illinois (CERN no date). This was followed by Netscape Navigator in 1994 and Microsoft Internet Explorer in

1995. The browser wars that followed are a saga in their own right; by the time they had run their course, the Web had grown into more or less its present form.

Governing the Internet and the Web has been difficult because they are not restrained by geographic boundaries. The involvement of the U.S. government and its citizens in setting up so much of the early Internet has led to a regime governing Web "real estate"—domain names—that many critics charge is unfairly skewed to reflect U.S. concerns. In the 1990s, as the Web expanded and the demand for domain names grew, the previously relatively informal allocation of domain names had to be made more systematic.

By the mid-1990s, the Internet Assigned Numbers Authority (IANA) was doing the actual work of assigning domain names and numbers. The IANA was essentially a one-man band, the one man being the late Dr. Jon Postel of the University of Southern California. In 1995 the function of registering domains within the .com, .net, and .org top-level domains was assigned to a private U.S. company, Network Solutions, Inc. (Gilwit 2003, 271).

Dr. Postel died in October 1998. A month later, the U.S. Department of Commerce, by agreement with representatives of IANA, created the Internet Corporation for Assigned Names and Numbers (ICANN), a nonprofit organization incorporated in California. ICANN has been embattled since its inception, but it still administers the top-level domain name system; it authorizes new top-level domains and authorizes private registrars to assign domain names within some of those top-level domains (ICANN 2005; ICANN 2006). It works with national governments to delegate administration of country-code top-level domains (".uk," ".jp," ".de," and so forth). And it resolves domain-name disputes, including cybersquatting and other trademark-related disputes. The controversy over ICANN, especially over its power over domain names and its connection to the U.S. government, is ongoing.

# The International Copyright Regime

By the nineteenth century it had become apparent that copyright protection was an international issue. A work copyrighted in one country might be freely and legally copied in another. And although some countries might allow foreign authors to register copyrights, no system existed for the global protection of foreign copyrights. Certain countries developed a reputation as havens for copyright pirates who engaged in widespread copying of works from other countries. Perhaps the most notorious of these countries was the United States. In opposing the idea of a global copyright convention, the United States argued that the ability to make copies without paying royalties aided developing countries (among which the United States, at the time, could be numbered) to achieve greater dissemination of knowledge and learning than would otherwise be possible (Tiefenbrun 1999, 5–6). Charles Dickens, one of the British authors whose work was heavily pirated in the United States, took a more cynical view in a conversation with fellow author (and fellow piracy victim) Anthony Trollope:

> [I]n this matter the American decision had been, according to [Dickens'] thinking, dishonest, therefore no other than dishonest decision was to be expected from Americans. Against that idea I [Trollope] protested, and now protest. American dishonesty is rampant; but it is rampant only among a few. It is the great misfortune of the community that those few have been able to dominate so large a portion of the population among which all men can vote, but so few can understand for what they are voting. (Trollope 1883, chapter 17)

In the case of international copyright, the "few" were American publishers, who made profits from the piracy of foreign works. American authors, however, suffered from piracy in England as well. *Uncle Tom's Cabin* sold over half a million copies in its first year of publication in England, for which Harriet Beecher Stowe received no compensation at all (Samuels 2000). Trollope himself traveled to the United States on behalf of the British government in an unsuccessful attempt to negotiate a bilateral copyright treaty. Despite the support of prominent American authors such as Louisa May Alcott, Mark Twain, Walt Whitman, and Oliver Wendell Holmes, the United States refused to grant protection to foreign works until 1891.

Five years earlier, in 1886, a group of European countries, responding to pressure from European copyright holders led by Victor Hugo, had adopted the Berne Convention protecting copyrights internationally. The Convention instantly became, and remains to this day, the primary instrument for such protection. The United States, however, was not to join the Convention for more than a hundred years.

In 1891, Congress enacted a statute giving limited copyright protection to some foreign authors. U.S. publishers were appeased with the Manufacturing Clause, an astonishing piece of protectionist legislation requiring all books sold in the United States to be printed in the United States. While this did not excuse U.S. publishers from paying royalties on protected foreign works, it insulated them from foreign competition in a way that must have been the envy of all other U.S. industries, even agriculture and defense. Although modified somewhat over the years, especially by the Universal Copyright Convention in 1955, this barrier to trade remained in place until 1986 (House Report No. 94-1476, sec. 601; Samuels 2000).

The early twentieth century saw an increase in copyright awareness and lawmaking around the world. The United States adopted a sweeping reform of copyright law in 1909; many more countries joined the Berne Convention; and many emerging industrial economies, notably in East Asia, adopted copyright codes based on European models. Japan joined the Berne Convention in 1899, but China and the two Koreas were to hold out even longer than the United States.

Copyright protection in the United States grew steadily more complex over the first nine decades of the twentieth century. Differing protection for works from different countries, revisions and renewals of copyright terms, parallel systems of state and federal copyright law, the need for U.S. authors to simultaneously publish works in one Berne Convention country (usually Canada) in order to be protected in all Berne Convention countries, and even the Manufacturing Clause combined to create a maze difficult for anyone but a professional copyright lawyer to navigate. Some simplification was achieved with two bilateral treaties, the Buenos Aires Convention of 1910 (ratified by the United States in 1911) and the Universal Copyright Convention, in force for the United States in 1955 and substantially revised in 1971. The Buenos Aires Convention provided that the United States and seventeen Latin American countries would honor each others' copyrights. Once a work was granted copyright protection in any member nation, that same protection would be extended by all without further formalities, other than the inclusion of the declaration "all rights reserved" or words to that effect.

(The Buenos Aires Convention is now a dead letter, having been superseded by later treaties, but the habit of including the words persists.)

The twentieth century brought new technologies and new challenges for copyright law. With the commercial development of movies and recorded music (both invented during the previous century), the role of the United States shifted from copyright pirate to major exporter of copyrighted works. With the 1909 Copyright Act making it impossible for the United States to join the Berne Convention, and Congress unwilling or unable to correct the situation, some alternative international structure was needed. This need was met by the Universal Copyright Convention, which allowed the United States to keep its shorter copyright term and its registration formalities while still enjoying copyright protection for its works in the territories of other member states. In turn, the United States was obligated to honor copyrights in works from member states, provided that the works included the copyright symbol "©," the year of first publication, and the name of the person claiming copyright (Universal Copyright Convention, art. III(1)). Nearly a hundred countries are now parties to the Universal Copyright Convention, yet the convention has become nearly as irrelevant as the Buenos Aires Convention: all but two of the parties to the Universal Copyright Convention (Cambodia and Laos) are also parties to the near-universal Berne Convention.

The complete revision of U.S. copyright law in the Copyright Act of 1976 replaced the fixed, renewable copyright term (dating back to the Statute of Anne) with a unitary term measured by the life of the author plus fifty years for individually or jointly authored works and by a set seventy-five-year term for most other works. This brought the duration of U.S. copyrights into compliance with Berne Convention norms. The 1976 Act did not, however, succeed in its goal of bringing the United States into compliance with the Berne Convention and thus making the United States eligible for membership. The 1976 Act still required registration formalities and the affixing of a copyright notice to the work—two things the Berne Convention rejected. Eliminating these provisions from U.S. copyright law required an additional twelve years. The Berne Convention Implementation Act of 1988 finally made it possible for the United States to join the Berne Convention, and the Convention came into force for the United States in 1989. Other major holdouts soon followed. China, where the printing revolution had begun, became a party in 1992, Russia in 1995, and the two Koreas in 1996 (South) and 2003 (North). Now, less than a thousand years after the invention of movable type, the world has achieved a relatively uniform and nearly universal system of copyright law.

Although copyrights are granted and enforced under national law, the nearly seamless coverage of the Berne/WIPO regime makes global copyright protection a relatively simple matter, at least by comparison with other forms of intellectual property protection. The Berne Convention, like TRIPs and the Universal Copyright Convention, requires national treatment. The parties must protect authors and works from other countries as they would their own:

> 1) The protection of this Convention shall apply to:
> (a) authors who are nationals of one of the countries of the Union, for their works, whether published or not;
> (b) authors who are not nationals of one of the countries of the Union, for their works first published in one of those countries, or simultaneously in a country outside the Union and in a country of the Union.
> (2) Authors who are not nationals of one of the countries of the Union but who have their habitual residence in one of them shall, for the purposes of this Convention, be assimilated to nationals of that country. (Berne Convention art. 3)

The definition of copyrightable subject matter is less succinct than and possibly not coextensive with the U.S. Copyright Act's "original works of authorship fixed in any tangible medium of expression" (17 U.S.C. § 102). The Berne Convention requires members to protect "every production in the literary and artistic domain whatever shall be the mode or form of its expression" (Berne Convention art. 2(1)). Enumerated types of subject matter include

> books, pamphlets and other writings; lectures, addresses, sermons and other works of the same nature; dramatic or dramatico-musical works; choreographic works and entertainments in dumb show; musical compositions with or without words; cinematographic works to which are assimilated works expressed by a

process analogous to cinematography; works of drawing, painting, architecture, sculpture, engraving and lithography; photographic works to which are assimilated works expressed by a process analogous to photography; works of applied art; illustrations, maps, plans, sketches and three-dimensional works relative to geography, topography, architecture or science. (Berne Convention art. 2(1))

Similarly, the Berne Convention's description of the exclusive rights of copyright holders differs somewhat from that in U.S. law, particularly in the area of the moral rights to integrity and attribution (Berne Convention art. 6*bis;* see also 17 U.S.C. § 106A). The Convention also allows for what has become known in the United States as fair use (Berne Convention arts. 9(2), 10, 10*bis*).

All parties to the Berne Convention must provide a minimum term of copyright protection of the lifetime of the author plus fifty years or, for anonymously or pseudonymously authored works, a minimum of fifty years; for cinematographic works, fifty years from the date the work is released to the public; and for photographic works or works of applied art, twenty-five years (Berne Convention art. 7; see also art. 5(3)).

Other important recent treaties under the WIPO umbrella include the WIPO Copyright Treaty (WCT) and the WIPO Performance and Phonograms Treaty (WPPT); the United States became a party to both in 2002. The WCT provides heightened protections for computer programs, original compilations of data, and sound recordings, but its most significant effect—and the most significant effect of the WPPT—was to require provisions for anticircumvention and digital rights management protection along the lines of those that were adopted in the United States in 1998 in the Digital Millennium Copyright Act (17 U.S.C. §§ 1201 through 1204; see also EU Directive 2001/29/EC). These are required under articles 11 and 12 of the WCT and articles 18 and 19 of the WPPT. Article 11 of the WCT requires the parties to "provide adequate legal protection and effective legal remedies against the circumvention of effective technological measures that are used" for copy protection. Article 18 of the WPPT is nearly identical. Article 12 of the WCT and Article 19 of the WPPT also require the parties to "provide adequate and effective legal remedies against any person knowingly" removing or altering "any electronic rights management information," or distributing, importing for distribution, broadcasting, or communicating to the public any works from which electronic rights management information has been removed, if in either case the person does not have the authority to do so and knows or has reason to know that doing so "will induce, enable, facilitate or conceal an infringement of any right covered by this Treaty or the Berne Convention" (Article 19 of the WPPT omits the words "or the Berne Convention").

The Berne Convention and the two WIPO treaties demonstrate some of the most dramatic effects that international law has had on U.S. intellectual property law—or on almost any area of U.S. law. The Berne Convention has brought about a lengthened duration of copyright, resulting in an as yet uncalculated transfer of property rights—probably measurable in billions of dollars—from the public domain to private copyright holders. The first, unsuccessful U.S. reaction—the Copyright Act of 1909—doubled the length of the copyright term; the second, successful reaction increased it yet further. U.S. law is now in compliance with—in fact, exceeds—the Berne Convention's duration requirement, although achieving this result took a century. The WIPO treaties, in contrast, took only a few years to complete—and led to one of the most deeply resented copyright statutes ever enacted in the United States. In one area, though, international law has not yet brought about a complete change. The WPPT was also intended in part to protect the moral rights of performers in live performances and phonograms (WPPT art. 5); U.S. law remains out of step with international norms on this issue.

The other major recent copyright treaty to which the United States is a party is TRIPs, which, as noted, requires national treatment and most favored nation treatment (TRIPs arts. 3–4). Through TRIPs, all members of the WTO agree to comply with the 1971 revision of the Berne Convention; TRIPs incorporates by references the major substantive provisions of the Berne Convention, with the exception of those dealing with moral rights (TRIPs arts. 1(3), 9; see also arts. 2(2), 3(1)). TRIPs also addresses, inconclusively, such still-debated issues as the protection of databases:

> Compilations of data or other material, whether in machine readable or other form, which by reason of the selection or arrangement of their contents constitute intellectual creations shall be protected as such. Such protection, which shall not extend to the data or material

itself, shall be without prejudice to any copyright subsisting in the data or material itself. (TRIPs art. 10(2))

TRIPs also requires WTO members to grant authors of computer programs and, in certain circumstances, of motion pictures
the right to prohibit the commercial rental of those works. The requirement only applies to movie rentals in countries where such
rentals have led to widespread piracy, and it only applies to software rentals where the software itself is not the object of the rental;
in other words, a rental of some piece of equipment, such as a car,
that contains software would not be covered (TRIPs art. 11).

Article 14 of TRIPs deals with live performances, sound
recordings, and broadcasting organizations. Performers "shall
have the possibility of preventing the fixation" (that is, recording)
or broadcast of their live audio performances. (The use of the
word "possibility" rather than "right" is interesting.) Producers
of phonograms (sound recordings) "shall enjoy the right to authorize or prohibit the direct or indirect reproduction of their
phonograms." Performers and producers are to be given the exclusive reproduction and rental rights to their recordings for a
minimum term of fifty years, although Article 14(4) provides a
grandfather clause: states that previously had "in force a system
of equitable remuneration of right holders in respect of the rental
of phonograms" may maintain their existing systems so long as
"the commercial rental of phonograms is not giving rise to the
material impairment of the exclusive rights of reproduction of
right holders"—that is, excessive unauthorized copying. Articles
14(3) and 14(5) set forth the right of broadcasting organizations to
prevent unauthorized recording, reproduction, or rebroadcast of
their broadcasts for a minimum term of twenty years. Here, as before the Sonny Bono Copyright Term Extension Act, there is an inconsistency between the duration of protection under U.S. and
European Union law, although this time it is the European Union
that offers the shorter term. Content-industry interests in the European Union are now lobbying to extend the European Union's
term, which complies with TRIPs' fifty-year minimum, to match
the ninety-five-year term provided by U.S. law (Withers 2006).

In the developing world and among information rights
activists in the United States, it was Article 13 of TRIPs that triggered the most discontent. A casual reading of Article 13 is unlikely to alarm anyone; the meaning only becomes apparent with
context. Article 13 provides that

> Members shall confine limitations or exceptions to ex-
> clusive rights to certain special cases which do not con-
> flict with a normal exploitation of the work and do not
> unreasonably prejudice the legitimate interests of the
> right holder.

Among developing countries, this was seen, in light of discussion leading up to the adoption of the article, as aimed at nations with poor records of copyright enforcement. In the United
States some saw it as a sneak attack on fair use, using the WTO
process to achieve what the content industry had been unable, despite its best efforts, to achieve in Congress.

The United States is also party to several other copyright-re-
lated treaties, including the Geneva Phonograms Convention, an
earlier treaty protecting sound recordings, and the Brussels Satellite Convention, which prohibits the hijacking of satellite transmission capability.

# The International Trademark Regime

While obtaining international copyright protection is automatic,
or nearly so, obtaining international trademark protection is
somewhat more difficult. The Paris Convention for the Protection
of Industrial Property requires its 169 members to accord nationals of other member states the same rights and protection in
trademark law that they would accord to their own nationals, and
to provide certain minimum levels of trademark protection. All
this does, though, is require countries to allow foreigners to obtain protection for marks in the same way and to the same extent
as local residents. To the extent that trademark registration is required for protection, the Paris Convention does nothing more to
simplify the international application process.

The Paris Union was followed a few years later by the 1891
Madrid Agreement Concerning the International Registration of
Marks. The United States never became a party to the Madrid
Agreement, but joined the Agreement's Madrid Union in 2003
when it became a party to the Madrid Protocol. The Madrid
Agreement (also known as the Madrid Arrangement) and its 1989
Madrid Protocol provide some simplification by making it possi-
ble for a mark holder to obtain protection in multiple countries
without having to register or otherwise apply for protection in

each individual country. The Protocol provides a single application process for the seventy-eight Madrid Union members. (Sixty-seven of these are parties to the Protocol; eleven are parties to the Agreement but not to the Protocol. The United States is a party to the Protocol but not to the Agreement.) While this is more convenient than filing seventy-eight separate applications, it leaves the majority of the world's countries uncovered. International trademark law is far less advanced in this respect than copyright or even patent.

Other important international trademark treaties to which the United States is a party include the Trademark Law Treaty (TLT) and the TRIPs. The TLT and the U.S. implementing legislation, the Trademark Law Treaty Act of 1998, help to simplify and reduce the cost of the trademark registration process. As of March 2006 it had thirty-three parties. The TLT applies to trademarks and service marks, making no distinction between the two, but it does not apply to "collective marks, certification marks and guarantee marks" (TLT art. 2(2)). All parties to the TLT must adopt uniform filing and renewal processes (TLT arts. 3, 13), with a renewable ten-year term of protection (TLT art. 13(7)). Through the TLT and the Trademark Law Treaty Act, the United States ostensibly abandoned its previously existing requirement that anyone seeking to register or renew a mark submit a declaration or proof that the mark was actually being used (TLT art. 13(6)), although in fact the United States retained the actual use requirement but made it independent of the registration and renewal process (McCarthy 2004, 614).

TRIPs brings trademark law within the WTO's enforcement and dispute-resolution framework and sets uniform standards for the eligible subject matter and other requirements for protection:

> Any sign, or any combination of signs, capable of distinguishing the goods or services of one undertaking from those of other undertakings, shall be capable of constituting a trademark. Such signs, in particular words including personal names, letters, numerals, figurative elements and combinations of colours as well as any combination of such signs, shall be eligible for registration as trademarks. Where signs are not inherently capable of distinguishing the relevant goods or services, Members may make registrability depend on

distinctiveness acquired through use. Members may require, as a condition of registration, that signs be visually perceptible. (TRIPs art. 15(1))

In contrast to the TLT, TRIPs permits WTO members to "make registrability depend on use" (TRIPs art. 15(3)). TRIPs also allows for prospective registration, though—registration in advance of an intended use: "[A]ctual use of a trademark shall not be a condition for filing an application for registration" (TRIPs art. 15(3)). While WTO members must grant the mark owner the right to prevent others from using the mark for similar goods and services (TRIPs art. 16), they may make exceptions for fair use (TRIPs art. 17). The term of trademark registration must be at least seven years (the United States, with its ten-year term, exceeds this), and must be renewable indefinitely (TRIPs art. 18; see also 15 U.S.C. §§ 1058–1059). Trademark registrations may be made dependent on use, as they are in the United States, but a trademark registration may be lost for nonuse "only after an uninterrupted period of at least three years of non-use," and even then it may not be lost if "valid reasons based on the existence of obstacles to such use are shown by the trademark owner" (TRIPs art. 19). Trademarks may be transferred and may not be made subject to compulsory licensing (TRIPs art. 21).

# The International Patent Regime

Toward the end of the nineteenth century, however, the increasing industrialization of many of the world's leading economies led to greater acceptance of patent laws, even among those who had previously opposed them as barriers to free trade. In 1883 eleven European and Latin American countries (including Switzerland, which did not yet have a patent law) signed the Paris Convention for the Protection of Industrial Property, setting up the Paris Union to govern international patent (and trademark) relations. The United States joined the Paris Union in 1887, around the time Switzerland finally adopted a domestic patent law. The Swiss statute, reflecting Swiss concerns about foreign copying of Swiss watches, covered mechanical inventions. At the time Switzerland's chemical industry was less advanced than Germany's; chemical process inventions were not covered by Swiss statute until 1907, giving the Swiss industry twenty years of protection from suits within Switzerland by German companies (Kaufer 1989, 9–10). Today 169 countries are parties to the Paris Convention and members of the Paris Union, the most recent being the island nation of Comoros, for which the Convention entered into force on 3 April 2005.

While the Paris Union remains an important tool in ensuring a degree of uniformity in international patent law, other agreements have been formed to address other problems. Particularly important are the patent provisions of TRIPs and the Patent Cooperation Treaty. TRIPs set a patent term "for any inventions, whether products or processes, in all fields of technology," with a few exceptions, for "a period of twenty years counted from the filing date" (TRIPs arts. 27, 33). Previously U.S. utility patents had been granted for a term of seventeen years from the date the patent was granted; the U.S. term was subsequently changed to conform to TRIPs (35 U.S.C. § 154(a)(2)). Another provision of TRIPs requiring member states to provide patent protection "for any inventions, whether products or processes" has been interpreted as requiring the granting of business methods patents. The Patent Cooperation Treaty provides a simplified multicountry application process.

A patent is a territorial grant. As with trademark, and in contrast to copyright, there is no automatic enforcement of patents among the member states of the various patent treaties. Instead, the patent holder must apply for a patent in each country in which he or she wishes to have patent protection. Unlike the Berne Convention, which provides copyright protection in multiple states for works copyrighted in any member state, the Paris Convention provides no easy road to global protection. An inventor who patents a device in the United States may exclude others from making that device in the United States and may prevent that device from being imported into the United States, but under the Paris Convention's regime may do nothing to prevent a person in, say, France from making that device in France and selling it in France. To be protected in France, the U.S. inventor would have to apply for and obtain a patent in France. To be protected around the world, the inventor would have to apply for and obtain patents in nearly 200 countries—a daunting task. The Patent Cooperation Treaty simplifies the task: An inventor who files an application in any state that is a party to the Patent Cooperation Treaty can simultaneously file patent applications in any or all of the other states. Including the United States, 128 states are now parties to the Patent Cooperation Treaty, the most recent being Libya and Saint Kitts-Nevis, for which the treaty came into force on 15 September 2005 and 27 October 2005, respectively.

The Patent Cooperation Treaty is not as seamless as the Berne Convention's effectively universal copyright process. While filing a single patent application will suffice for any or all member states, the inventor must still pay application fees—including translation fees, where necessary—for each state. And there is no guarantee that all of the states will grant the patent; a patent granted in one state may be denied in others. It is, however, more comprehensive in its coverage than the Madrid Union, as it has 128 member states to the Madrid Union's seventy-eight.

One of the major discrepancies remaining between U.S. patent law and the patent law of other countries is the "first-to-invent" rule applied in the United States, which, as discussed in Chapter 1, in certain cases can allow an inventor to substitute the conception date for the filing date. The Patent Law Treaty attempts to address this discrepancy, with so much circumlocution as to be nearly incomprehensible, by eliminating the first-to-invent rule (see Patent Law Treaty, arts. 5,6; see also *One Global Patent System* 2003). Inventors, and perhaps the people of the United States generally, are attached to the first-to-invent rule because it seems more fair, if less efficient. The United States signed the Patent Law Treaty in 2000 but has not ratified it. The treaty entered into force in 2005 for the handful of countries that have ratified it, but without the participation of the United States, it is meaningless (see also Takenaka 2003, 261).

The Patent Law Treaty's proponents see it as the first step to a single, harmonized system of international patent law. Such harmonization may still be a long way off; in the interim, the Patent Cooperation Treaty provides a unified filing system, and TRIPs provides a workable and enforceable means of addressing several remaining concerns. TRIPs incorporates by reference the basic protections of the Paris Convention (TRIPs art. 2) and provides for a uniform patent term of twenty years from the date of filing (TRIPs art. 33). As discussed earlier, it also requires the granting of business method patents (TRIPs art. 27; Conley 2003, 8). Under TRIPs, WTO members must grant patent holders the exclusive right to prevent others from "making, using, offering for sale, selling, or importing" a patented product, or products made by a patented process (TRIPs art. 28). As with other intellectual property rights, patents are made fully assignable, transferable, and licensable—which they already were in the United States (TRIPs art. 28(2)).

# Protection of Other Forms of Intellectual Property under U.S. and International Law

Copyrights, trademarks, and patents are the best-known categories of intellectual property, and they have the most fully evolved legal regimes to govern them. But there are other forms. Some, like semiconductor manufacturing mask works and vessel hull designs, are given the formal trappings of copyright, trademark, and patent law: They have a registration process, a fixed term of protection, and exclusive rights. The protection of others, like trade secrets and know-how, is somewhat more incomplete.

A semiconductor manufacturing mask work is necessary to the manufacture of computer chips. The design of the mask is a long and expensive process requiring the work of skilled and specialized engineers. Once the mask is designed, however, it can be copied somewhat more cheaply. Using the copied mask is not like playing a pirated DVD or a downloaded MP3—it requires a chip manufacturing factory, a supply of blank wafers, and, again, a skilled workforce. Even though the number of potential pirates is small, the U.S. Congress has created a form of intellectual property protection for the mask work: The Semiconductor Chip Protection Act of 1984 provides for the registration of mask work designs with the U.S. Copyright Office (17 U.S.C. § 908; 37 C.F.R. § 211.4). Notice of registration must be affixed to the finished chips or their receptacles (17 U.S.C. § 909; 37 C.F.R. § 211.6). The registrant will enjoy, for a ten-year term, the usual exclusive rights: the right to reproduce the mask work; the right to import or distribute a chip embodying it; and the sole right to authorize, induce, or knowingly cause any other person to reproduce the work or import or distribute the chips (17 U.S.C. §§ 904–905). It is also subject to a right of first sale (17 U.S.C. § 906(b)) and a reverse-engineering exception (17 U.S.C. § 906(a)); innocent infringers are also protected (17 U.S.C. § 907). Mask work registrations are also protected by articles 35–38 of TRIPs, which require WTO members to adopt protections similar to those in the U.S. statute, and potentially by the 1989 Treaty on Intellectual Property in Respect of Integrated Circuits (not yet in force).

This type of fully realized regime for a narrow category of intellectual property can also be found in the Vessel Hull Design Protection Act (17 U.S.C. §§ 1301–1332), which allows registration and protection of hull designs for vessels of 200 feet or less in length. A similar form of protection, not so narrowly defined, can be found in TRIPs, which protects industrial designs (TRIPs arts. 25–26; see also Hague Agreement Concerning the International Deposit of Industrial Designs; Locarno Agreement Establishing an International Classification for Industrial Designs). TRIPs also protects geographical indications (TRIPs arts. 22–24), as do the Madrid Agreement for the Repression of False or Deceptive Indications of Source on Goods and the Lisbon Agreement for the Protection of Appellations of Origin and their International Registration.

In addition to these formally registered and protected types of intellectual property, there are trade secrets and the wide variety of activities covered under state contract and unfair competition laws. The items in the latter category are too diverse to permit ready categorization here. Trade secrets are easier to categorize, but difficult indeed to protect, as their value depends on their not becoming widely known. For that reason they cannot be registered; even a "secret" registration would provide less security for the owner of the secret than nonregistration.

Trade secret law, in fact, is opposed to one of the policy interests that patent law seeks to further. Patent offers inventors a monopoly of limited duration as a reward for sharing their inventions and discoveries with the public (rather than keeping it as a trade secret). If the owners of the world's most celebrated trade secret—the secret formula for Coca-Cola—had patented the formula, it would have fallen into the public domain nearly a century ago. It is questionable how much of its success Coca-Cola owes to its formula rather than to aggressive marketing and trademark management, but the company evidently prefers to keep the secret a secret.

This—the vigilance of the secret's owner—is the main way in which trade secrets are protected. State and federal law can provide remedies to one whose trade secret is wrongfully taken, but can do nothing to recapture the secret once it has been widely disclosed (*Religious Technology Center*, 908 F. Supp. 1362). Nor are trade secrets, in contrast to patents, protected against independent discovery. Someone who innocently happens upon the secret by independent research is free to use or disclose it.

Trade secrets are protected at the state level by the Uniform Trade Secrets Act (UTSA), which has been adopted in various modified forms in forty-five states, the District of Columbia, and the U.S. Virgin Islands, and is currently under consideration in Massachusetts and New York. Under the UTSA, a trade secret is information that

> (i) derives independent economic value, actual or potential, from not being generally known to, and not being readily ascertainable by proper means by, other persons who can obtain economic value from its disclosure or use, and
> (ii) is the subject of efforts that are reasonable under the circumstances to maintain its secrecy. (UTSA § 1(4))

The UTSA prohibits misappropriation of trade secrets. "Misappropriation" means

> (i) acquisition of a trade secret of another by a person who knows or has reason to know that the trade secret was acquired by improper means; or
> (ii) disclosure or use of a trade secret of another without express or implied consent by a person who
> > (A) used improper means to acquire knowledge of the trade secret; or
> > (B) at the time of disclosure or use knew or had reason to know that his knowledge of the trade secret was
> > > (I) derived from or through a person who has utilized improper means to acquire it;
> > > (II) acquired under circumstances giving rise to a duty to maintain its secrecy or limit its use; or
> > > (III) derived from or through a person who owed a duty to the person seeking relief to maintain its secrecy or limit its use; or
> > (C) before a material change of his position, knew or had reason to know that it was a trade secret and that knowledge of it had been acquired by accident or mistake. (UTSA § 1(2))

What this rather complex definition boils down to is that anyone who comes into possession of someone else's trade secret by stealing it, by accident, by mistake, or under a duty to keep the secret cannot turn around and disclose the secret to someone else.

Trade secrets are protected not only at the state level but also at the national and international level. At the national level, the federal Economic Espionage Act of 1996 first defines trade secrets in terms substantially similar to those in the UTSA. The owner must have "taken reasonable measures to keep such information secret," and the information must derive "independent economic value, actual or potential, from not being generally known to, and not being readily ascertainable through proper means by, the public" (18 U.S.C. § 1839(3)). The activities prohibited by the federal statute are somewhat more limited. The statute prohibits anyone from taking the secret "intending or knowing that the offense will benefit any foreign government, foreign instrumentality, or foreign agent" (18 U.S.C. § 1831). Purely domestic economic espionage is not left unaddressed by federal law; the federal statute also prohibits taking a trade secret "with intent to convert" (that is, to deprive the owner of a property right) by any of a wide variety of listed means, provided that the taking is "to the economic benefit of anyone other than the owner" of the secret, that the taker intends or knows "that the offense will . . . injure any owner of that trade secret," and that the secret "is related to or included in a product that is produced for or placed in interstate or foreign commerce" (18 U.S.C. § 1832).

At the international level, trade secrets are protected by TRIPs. To be protected, a trade secret must meet a definition similar to those in the UTSA and the Economic Espionage Act. It must be lawfully under the owner's control; it must be "secret in the sense that it is not, as a body or in the precise configuration and assembly of its components, generally known among or readily accessible to persons within the circles that normally deal with the kind of information in question"; it must have "commercial value because it is secret"; and it must have "been subject to reasonable steps under the circumstances, by the person lawfully in control of the information, to keep it secret" (TRIPs art. 39(2)).

The prohibited conduct with regard to trade secrets is defined in more general terms, without the exhaustive list of prohibited acts found in the federal statute. Members of the WTO are to ensure, through appropriate legislation and enforcement, that trade secrets are not "disclosed to, acquired by, or used by others without their consent in a manner contrary to honest commercial practices" (TRIPs art. 39(2)).

# Summary

This chapter has examined the international legal regime governing intellectual property rights, as well as some of the challenges and controversies that have arisen regarding that regime. While most multilateral intellectual property agreements are administered under the auspices of WIPO, the WTO's comprehensive TRIPs treaty provides a parallel system, often in harmony but sometimes in conflict with the WIPO system. To a large extent the international regime has been successful in harmonizing national intellectual property laws, simplifying international rights protection for content owners, and reducing conflict. The copyright regime has been the most successful; after more than a century of independent development, the parallel U.S. and Berne Convention systems have finally been merged, and any copyrightable work is protected from the moment of its creation in most of the world.

The patent and trademark regimes have been less successful. Rather than a single patent or trademark process, they provide a process by which one may simultaneously apply for a patent or trademark in a large number of countries. The process remains costly, cumbersome, and, in the case of trademark, not particularly comprehensive.

International law has not hesitated to go beyond the traditional categories of copyright, trademark, and patent to provide protection for other categories of intellectual property, including industrial designs and trade secrets.

# Treaties

"Agreement Between the United Nations and the World Intellectual Property Organization." December 17, 1974. General Assembly Res. 3346, U.N. GAOR, 29th Sess., U.N. Doc. A/RES/3346 (XXIX).

"Agreement Between the World Intellectual Property Organization and the World Trade Organization." December 22, 1995. 35 I.L.M. 754.

"Agreement on Trade-Related Aspects of Intellectual Property Rights (TRIPs), Marrakesh Agreement Establishing the World Trade Organization, Annex 1C." April 15, 1994. 33 I.L.M. 81.

"Brussels Convention Relating to the Distribution of Programme-Carrying Signals Transmitted by Satellite." May 21, 1974. 13 I.L.M. 1444.

"Budapest Treaty on the International Recognition of the Deposit of Microorganisms for the Purposes of Patent Procedure." April 28, 1977, as amended on September 26, 1980. 32 U.S.T. 1241, 1861 U.N.T.S. 361.

"Buenos Aires Convention." August 20, 1910. 38 Stat. 1785, 155 L.N.T.S. 179.

"Convention Concerning the Creation of an International Union for the Protection of Literary and Artistic Works (Berne Convention)." September 9, 1886, as last revised at Paris, July 24, 1971 (amended 1979). 25 U.S.T. 1341, 828 U.N.T.S. 221.

"Convention Establishing the World Intellectual Property Organization." July 14, 1967, as amended on September 28, 1979 (WIPO Convention). 21 U.S.T. 1749, 828 U.N.T.S. 3.

"Convention for the Protection of Producers of Phonograms Against Unauthorized Duplication of Their Phonograms." October 29, 1971. 25 U.S.T. 309.

"Convention on the Grant of European Patents." October 5, 1973. 13 I.L.M. 276. Text as amended through December 10, 1998. http://www .european-patent-office.org/legal/epc/e/ma1.html.

"Hague Agreement Concerning the International Deposit of Industrial Design." November 6, 1925. 74 L.N.T.S. 343, revised at London, June 2, 1934, 205 L.N.T.S. 179, revised at The Hague, November 28, 1960. Supplemented by the Additional Act of Monaco, November 18, 1961, the Complementary Act of Stockholm, July 14, 1967, and the Protocol of Geneva, April 10, 1975, 26 U.S.T. 571; and as amended September 1979.

"Inter-American Convention for the Protection of Industrial Property." August 20, 1910. 39 Stat. 1675; TS 626; 1 Bevans 772. Replaced by "General Inter-American Convention for Trademark and Commercial Protection." February 20, 1929. 46 Stat. 2907, TS 833, 2 Bevans 751, 124 L.N.T.S. 357.

"Lisbon Agreement for the Protection of Appellations of Origin and their International Registration." October 31, 1958. As revised at Stockholm on July 14, 1967, and as amended on September 28, 1979. 923 U.N.T.S. 205.

"Locarno Agreement Establishing an International Classification for Industrial Designs." October 8, 1968. As amended September 28, 1979. 23 U.S.T. 1389.

"Madrid Agreement Concerning the International Registration of Marks." April 14, 1891. As revised at Brussels on December 14, 1900, at

Washington on June 2, 1911, at The Hague on November 6, 1925, at London on June 2, 1934, at Nice on June 15, 1957, and at Stockholm on July 14, 1967, and as amended on September 28, 1979. 828 U.N.T.S. 389.

"Madrid Agreement for the Repression of False or Deceptive Indications of Source on Goods." April 14, 1891. As revised at Washington on June 2, 1911, at The Hague on November 6, 1925, at London on June 2, 1934, and at Lisbon on October 31, 1958. Additional Act July 14, 1967. Stockholm. 828 U.N.T.S. 389.

"Nairobi Treaty on the Protection of the Olympic Symbol." September 26, 1981. 1863 U.N.T.S. 367.

"Nice Agreement Concerning the International Classification of Goods and Services for the Purposes of the Registration of Marks." June 15, 1957. As revised at Stockholm on July 14, 1967, and at Geneva on May 13, 1977, and amended on September 28, 1979. 23 U.S.T. 1336, 550 U.N.T.S. 45.

"Paris Convention for the Protection of Industrial Property." March 20, 1883. As revised at Brussels on December 14, 1900, at Washington on June 2, 1911, at The Hague on November 6, 1925, at London on June 2, 1934, at Lisbon on October 31, 1958, and at Stockholm on July 14, 1967, and as amended on September 28, 1979. 21 U.S.T. 1583, 828 U.N.T.S. 305.

"Patent Cooperation Treaty." Washington. June 19, 1970. As amended on September 28, 1979, and as modified on February 3, 1984, and October 3, 2001. 28 U.S.T. 7645, 9 I.L.M. 978.

"Patent Law Treaty." June 1, 2000. 39 I.L.M. 1047.

"Protocol Relating to the Madrid Agreement Concerning the International Registration of Marks." June 27, 1989. http://www.wipo .int/madrid/en/legal_texts/.

"Rome Convention for the Protection of Performers, Producers of Phonograms and Broadcasting Organizations." October 26, 1961. 496 U.N.T.S. 43.

"Statute of the International Court of Justice." Art. 38(1), 59 Stat. 1055, 1060 (1945), T.S. No. 993, 3 Bevans 1153, 1976 Y.B.U.N. 1052.

"Strasbourg Agreement Concerning the International Patent Classification." March 24, 1971. As amended on September 28 1979. 26 U.S.T. 1793.

"Trademark Law Treaty." October 27, 1994. http://www.wipo .int/clea/docs/en/wo/wo027en.htm.

"Treaty on Intellectual Property in Respect of Integrated Circuits." Washington. May 26, 1989. 28 I.L.M. 1477 (not in force).

"Treaty on the International Registration of Audiovisual Works." April 20, 1989. http://www.wipo.int/treaties/en/ip/frt/trtdocs_wo004.html.

"Universal Copyright Convention." September 6, 1952. 6 U.S.T. 2731. Revised at Paris. July 24, 1971. 25 U.S.T. 1341.

"Vienna Agreement Establishing an International Classification of the Figurative Elements of Marks." June 12, 1973. As amended October 1, 1985. http://www.wipo.int/clea/docs/en/wo/wo031en.htm.

"WIPO Copyright Treaty." December 20, 1996. 36 I.L.M. 65 (1997).

"WIPO Performance and Phonograms Treaty." December 20, 1996. 36 I.L.M. 76 (1997).

# European Union, ICANN, WIPO, and WTO Documents

"Articles of Incorporation of Internet Corporation for Assigned Names and Numbers." Revised November 21, 1998. http://www.icann .org/general/articles.htm.

"Bylaws for Internet Corporation for Assigned Names and Numbers, a California Nonprofit Public-Benefit Corporation." Amended effective April 19, 2004. http://www.icann.org/general/archive-bylaws/bylaws-13oct03.htm.

"Council Directive 93/98/EEC of 29 October 1993 Harmonizing the Term of Protection of Copyright and Certain Related Rights," 1993 O.J. (L 290) 9.

"EU Directive 2001/29/EC on the Harmonisation of Certain Aspects of Copyright and Related Rights in the Information Society," 2001 O.J. (L 167) 10.

ICANN. 2006. "ICANN-Accredited Registrars." March 10. http://www .icann.org/registrars/accredited-list.html.

ICANN. 2005. "ICANN Information." December 21. http://www.icann .org/general/.

ICANN. 1999. "Internet Domain Name System Structure and Delegation (ccTLD Administration and Delegation)." May. http://www.icann .org/icp/icp-1.htm.

ICANN. 1998. "Memorandum of Understanding between the U.S. Department of Commerce and the Internet Corporation for Assigned Names and Numbers." http://www.icann.org/general/icann-mou-25nov98.htm.

World Intellectual Property Organization. 2006a. *Direct Filing of PCT Applications with the International Bureau as PCT Receiving Office.* http://www.wipo.int/pct/en/filing/filing.htm#P20_2204.

World Intellectual Property Organization. 2006b. *Treaties and Contracting Parties.* Geneva, Switzerland: WIPO.

World Intellectual Property Organization. 2005. *New Parties to WIPO-Administered Treaties in 2004.* WIPO Update 235/2005. Geneva, Switzerland: WIPO, January 14.

World Intellectual Property Organization. 2002. *Basic Facts about the Patent Cooperation Treaty.* (Leaflet.) Geneva, Switzerland: WIPO, April.

World Intellectual Property Organization. 2001. *About WIPO.* WIPO Publication No. 400(E). June. http://www.wipo.int/about-wipo/en/gib .htm#P9_1980.

World Intellectual Property Organization. No date. *Organisations Intergouvernmentales Admises en Qualite d'Observateurs aux Reunions des Assemblees des États Membres,* BIG/158/17. Geneva, Switzerland: WIPO.

World Trade Organization. *Members and Observers.* http://www.wto .org/English/thewto_e/whatis_e/tif_e/org6_e.htm.

Uniform Domain Name Dispute Resolution Policy. 1999. August 26. http://www.icann.org/udrp/udrp-policy-24oct99.htm.

# Statutes and Legislative Materials

Copyright Act of 1976, 17 U.S.C. §§ 101–1331.

Digital Millennium Copyright Act, 17 U.S.C. §§ 512, 1201–1204.

Economic Espionage Act of 1996, 18 U.S.C. § 1831 et seq.

House Report on the Copyright Act of 1976, H.R. Rep. No. 94-1476, sec. 601.

Lanham Trademark Act, 15 U.S.C. §§ 1058–1059.

National Conference of Commissioners on Uniform State Laws, Uniform Trade Secrets Act, as amended 1985. http://nsi.org/Library/Espionage /utsa.htm.

Patent Code, 35 U.S.C. §§ 1–376.

Patent Code, Right of Priority, 35 U.S.C. § 119.

Semiconductor Chip Protection Act, 17 U.S.C. §§ 901–914.

Trademark Law Treaty Act of 1998, 15 U.S.C. § 1051.

Vessel Hull Design Protection Act, 17 U.S.C. §§ 1301–1332.

Visual Artists' Rights Act, 17 U.S.C. § 106A.

# Cases

*Feist Publications v. Rural Telephone Service Co.*, 499 U.S. 340 (1991).

*Religious Technology Center v. Lerma*, 908 F. Supp. 1362 (E.D. Va. 1995).

*State Street Bank & Trust Co. v. Signature Financial Group*, 149 F.3d 1368 (Fed. Cir. 1998); *cert. denied*, 525 U.S. 1093.

# Sources and Further Reading

Biegel, Stuart. 2001. *Beyond Our Control? Confronting the Limits of Our Legal System in the Age of Cyberspace.* Cambridge, MA: MIT Press.

Buergenthal, Thomas, and Sean D. Murphy. 2002. *Public International Law in a Nutshell.* 3rd ed. St. Paul, MN: West.

CERN. "The World Wide Web." http://public.web.cern.ch/Public/Content/Chapters/AboutCERN/Achievements/WorldWideWeb/WWW-en.html.

Conley, John M. 2003. "The International Law of Business Method Patents." *U.S. Patent and Trademark Office Economic Review.* October. http://ideas.repec.org/a/fip/fedaer/y2003p15-33nv.88no.4.html.

D'Amato, Anthony, and Doris Estelle Long, eds. *1996. International Intellectual Property Anthology.* Cincinnati, OH: Anderson Publishing.

Dinwoodie, Graeme B., William O. Hennessey, and Shira Perlmutter. 2002. *International and Comparative Patent Law.* Newark, NJ: LexisNexis Matthew Bender.

Froomkin, A. Michael. 2000. "Wrong Turn in Cyberspace: Using ICANN to Route Around the APA and the Constitution." *Duke Law Journal* 50: 17.

Gilwit, Dara B. 2003. "The Latest Cybersquatting Trend: Typosquatters, their Changing Tactics, and How to Prevent Public Deception and Trademark Infringement." *Washington University Journal of Law and Policy* 11: 267.

Goldstein, Paul. 2000. *International Copyright: Principles, Law, and Practice.* Oxford: Oxford University Press.

Kaufer, Erich. 1989. *The Economics of the Patent System.* Chur, Switzerland: Harwood Academic Publishers.

Kristula, Dave. 2001. "The History of the Internet." August. http://www.davesite.com/webstation/net-history.shtml.

Leaffer, Marshall. 1990. "International Copyright from an American Perspective." *Arkansas Law Review* 43: 373.

McCarthy, J. Thomas, Roger Schechter, and David J. Franklyn. 2004. *Mc-Carthy's Desk Encyclopedia of Intellectual Property.* 3rd ed. Washington, DC: Bureau of National Affairs.

*One Global Patent System? WIPO's Substantive Patent Law Treaty.* 2003. GRAIN. October. http://www.grain.org/briefings_files/wipo-splt-2003-en.pdf.

Pires de Carvalho, Nuno. 2002. *The TRIPs Regime of Patent Rights.* The Hague: Kluwer Law International.

Samuels, Edward. 2000. *The Illustrated History of Copyright.* New York: St. Martin's Press. http://www.edwardsamuels.com/illustratedstory/isc10.htm.

Samuelson, Pamela. 1997. "The U.S. Digital Agenda at WIPO." *Virginia Journal of International Law* 37: 369.

Takenaka, Toshiko. 2003. "The Best Patent Practice or Mere Compromise? A Review of the Current Draft of the Substantive Patent Law Treaty and a Proposal for a First-to-Invent Exception for Domestic Applicants." *Texas Intellectual Property Law Journal* 11: 259.

Tiefenbrun, Susan. 1999. "A Hermeneutic Methodology and How Pirates Misread the Berne Convention." *Wisconsin International Law Journal* 17: 1.

Trimble, Phillip R. 2002. *International Law: United States Foreign Relations Law.* New York: Foundation.

Trollope, Anthony. 1883. *Autobiography of Anthony Trollope.* Project Gutenberg ed., 2004. Available at http://www.gutenberg.org/dirs/etext04/8auto10.txt

Withers, Kay. 2006. "Copyright Sings to a Different Tune." BBC.com. February 17. http://news.bbc.co.uk/2/hi/technology/4724664.stm.

*World v Web: America Does Not Want the United Nations to Run the Internet.* 2004. *The Economist,* November 20, 65.

# 4

# Chronology

**560–561**   Columba, later to become Saint Columba, copies a
psalter without permission. The dispute over the
ownership of the copy leads to a battle in which thousands are killed.

**563**   Columba leaves Ireland for exile on Iona.

**578**   The Kongo family emigrates from Korea to Japan and
founds the construction company Kongo Gumi.
Today the company, led by Toshitaka Kongo, is still in
the construction business under the same name, making it the owner of possibly the world's oldest trademark.

**717**   The Hoshi Ryokan hotel begins operating in Awazu,
Japan.

**868**   Wang Jie publishes what is now the world's oldest
surviving block-printed work, a Chinese translation
of the *Diamond Sutra*. The work bears the notice "Reverently made for universal free distribution by Wang
Jie on behalf of his two parents on the 13th day of the
4th moon of the 9th year of Xiantong." With a bit of
wishful thinking, this might be seen as the first open-
source license.

1040  Benedictine monks in Weihenstephan (in what is now Germany) open the Weihenstephan Brewery. Other claimants for the title of the European business name in longest continuous use include the Château de Goulaine Vineyard in France and the Fonderia Pontificia Marinelli, a bell foundry in Agnone, Italy; both also date from the eleventh century.

1041  Bi Sheng, also in China, builds a printing machine that uses movable type—probably the first in the world to do so.

c. 1234 Yi Gyu-bo publishes the *New Code of Etiquette* in Korea; today it is the world's oldest surviving work printed with movable type.

1266  The Bakers Marking Law requires English bakers to place identifying marks on their loaves of bread.

1421  The government of the city of Florence grants a three-year patent of monopoly to Filippo Brunelleschi for the manufacture of a new type of ship for transporting marble. The ship is built and later sinks in the Arno River.

c. 1430– Johannes Gutenberg and perhaps Laurens Coster
1450  build printing presses in Europe; the extent to which they are influenced by awareness of Chinese and Korean printing technology is uncertain, although they were quite possibly aware of it.

1446  The Korean government adopts a phonetic script, making typesetting much cheaper; an explosion in the printing industry follows. The Korean government responds to complaints about copying by granting printing monopolies over certain works to certain printers.

1449  In England, King Henry VI grants John of Utynam a patent of monopoly for the manufacture of stained glass.

1455        Johannes Gutenberg prints his first Bible.

1455–1468 After several lawsuits, Johannes Gutenberg loses control of his printing business.

1474        William Caxton prints *The Recuyell of the Historyes of Troye*, the first book to be printed in English using movable type.

            The city of Venice adopts the world's first patent statute in the modern sense, granting a ten-year patent of monopoly to any inventor of a "new and ingenious device," and requiring disclosure of the way in which the device might be duplicated.

1476        William Caxton prints Geoffrey Chaucer's *Canterbury Tales*.

1537        King Francis I of France requires all printers to deposit a copy of each work they publish and offer for sale in the National Library. This requirement of *dépôt légale* will influence U.S. copyright law and will persist in the United States long after it is abandoned in France.

1557        The Stationer's Company receives a monopoly on printing from the English government.

1618        The British case of *Southern v. How*, the first published trademark infringement case in the Anglo-American common law tradition, is decided.

1623        In England, Parliament enacts the Statute of Monopolies, granting a fourteen-year patent of monopoly to "the true and first inventor" of any invention. This "first to invent" rule later becomes the standard for U.S. patent law, where it persists, even though it has been abandoned by the rest of the world.

1641        In North America, the British colony of Massachusetts adopts its first patent law.

**1661–1663** The first book is printed in English North America.

**1695** The Stationer's Company's printing monopoly ends.

**1695–1710** England sees a printing free-for-all as multiple printing companies vie for market share.

**1707** The Act of Union unites Scotland and England.

**1710** The newly united British Parliament enacts the Statute of Anne, the first modern copyright law. The Statute sets a copyright term of fourteen years for new works, renewable once.

**1774** In Britain, the House of Lords decides *Donaldson v. Beckett*, establishing that copyright terms are of finite duration.

**1777** The government of France sets the term of copyrights granted to publishers at the lifetime of the author, and copyrights are granted to authors in perpetuity. While the perpetual copyright will eventually be abandoned, the difference between the lifetime-based copyright in French law and the set term of years approach taken at the time in English law, and later in U.S. law, will persist for another two centuries.

**1789** Article I, Section 8, Clause 8 of the U.S. Constitution declares that Congress shall have the power "To promote the Progress of Science and useful Arts, by securing for limited Times to Authors and Inventors the exclusive Right to their respective Writings and Discoveries." This gives Congress the power to grant copyrights and patents, but not, it later turns out, trademarks.

**1790** The first U.S. Copyright Act, modeled on the Statute of Anne, provides for a fourteen-year copyright term, renewable once. The first U.S. Patent Act also takes its lead from English law (the 1623 Statute of Monopolies), setting the patent term at fourteen years. The Patent Act requires an official examination before a patent can be granted. Samuel Hopkins of Pittsford, Vermont, obtained the first U.S. patent on July 31.

1793    In the United States, Congress eliminates the 1790 Patent Act's requirement of an examination.

1809    Mary Kies of Killingly, Connecticut, becomes the first woman to obtain a U.S. patent.

1836    In the United States, Congress restores the requirement of an official examination before a patent can be granted.

Nearly all of the existing models and records in the U.S. Patent Office are destroyed in a fire.

1838    In France, the Société des Gens de Lettres, a writers' group, is founded.

1843    In the United States, Annie Ellsworth, daughter of Patent Commissioner Henry Ellsworth, becomes an employee of the U.S. Patent Office.

1847    French composer Ernest Bourget is appalled to find a Paris café playing his music for the entertainment of patrons, including himself. He refuses to pay for his drinks and later sues the café, successfully.

1849    The Cour d'Appel de Paris orders the *Café Concert les Ambassadeurs* to pay royalties to Bourget for performing his music.

1850    Bourget and others form the *Agence Centrale pour la Perception Droits Auteurs et Compositeurs de Musique* to license and enforce music performance rights.

1854    Clara Barton, who would later found the American Red Cross, becomes a clerk in the U.S. Patent Office.

1865    Photographs, a relatively new type of printed matter, are made copyrightable under U.S. law.

**1867–1895** Moving pictures invented.

**1870** The U.S. Congress enacts the first federal Trademark Act, later declared unconstitutional by the Supreme Court, and the Patent Act of 1870, which revises and simplifies existing U.S. patent law.

**1873** The International Law Association is founded in Brussels.

**1877** In the United States, Thomas Edison invents the phonograph, and Eadweard Muybridge takes "The Horse in Motion," a series of photographs that represent an important step toward the development of motion-picture technology; these two innovations will open new worlds of copyrightable material and potential infringement.

**1878** Victor Hugo and other copyright holders establish the Association Littéraire et Artistique Internationale, an organization whose goal is to push for an international copyright protection system.

The International Trademark Association is founded.

**1879** The Supreme Court strikes down the Trademark Act of 1870, pointing out that the Patent and Copyright Clause does not give Congress the authority to grant trademarks.

**1881** In the United States, Congress enacts a trademark act allowing national registration of marks used in commerce with foreign nations and Indian tribes, but not in interstate commerce.

**1883** Several countries, not including the United States, adopt the Paris Convention for the Protection of Industrial Property. The Convention creates the Paris Union to govern international patent and trademark law.

**1886** Several countries, not including the United States, adopt the Berne Convention, beginning the process of creating the international copyright regime in effect today.

1887      The United States joins the Paris Union.

Switzerland adopts a domestic patent law, after several unsuccessful attempts.

1890      In the United States, the court in *Merriam v. Holloway Publishing Co.* holds that trademark cannot be used to protect the entire content of a text on which copyright had expired; to do so would be to grant an effectually perpetual copyright.

1891      The United States grants copyright protection to some foreign works.

Several countries, not including the United States, adopt the Madrid Agreement Concerning the International Registration of Marks and the Madrid Agreement for the Repression of False or Deceptive Indications of Source on Goods.

1893      The Paris and Berne convention treaty organizations unite to form the Bureaux Internationaux Réunis pour la Protection de la Propriété Intellectuelle, precursor to the World Intellectual Property Organization.

1894      In the United States, the American Bar Association forms its Section of Intellectual Property Law, which will eventually grow to become the world's largest intellectual property law organization.

1895      In the United States, the Music Publishers Association is founded.

1897      In the United States, the American Intellectual Property Law Association is founded.

In Europe, the International Association for the Protection of Industrial Property is founded.

1899    In the United States, the Supreme Court decides
        *Singer Manufacturing Co. v. June Manufacturing Co.*,
        holding that just as trademark law cannot be used to
        prevent others from duplicating a copyrighted work
        after the copyright has expired, it cannot be used to
        prevent others from duplicating a patented invention
        after the patent has expired.

1905    In the United States, Congress enacts a trademark act
        allowing national registration of fanciful and arbitrary
        (but not descriptive) marks used in interstate com-
        merce.

1906    The International Federation of Intellectual Property
        Attorneys is founded.

1909    The U.S. Congress enacts the Copyright Act of 1909,
        which doubles the length of the copyright term but
        fails in almost all of its goals, most notably in bringing
        U.S. law into compliance with Berne Convention stan-
        dards. The Act's deficiencies also give rise to an awk-
        ward parallel system of state copyright law.

1910    The United States and several Latin American coun-
        tries adopt the Inter-American Convention for the
        Protection of Industrial Property and the Buenos Aires
        Convention on Literary and Artistic Copyrights.

1911    The United States ratifies the Buenos Aires Conven-
        tion on Literary and Artistic Copyrights.

1914    In the United States, the American Society of Com-
        posers, Authors and Publishers (ASCAP), a music
        copyright clearinghouse, is formed.

1920    In the United States, Congress enacts a new Trade-
        mark Act to carry out the obligations of the United
        States under the 1910 convention.

        In the United Kingdom, the Trade Marks, Patents and
        Designs Federation is founded.

1925    The International Association for the Protection of Industrial Property finds a permanent home in Switzerland.

1930    In the United States, Congress enacts the Plant Patent Act.

1934    In the United Kingdom, the Institute of Trade Mark Attorneys is founded.

1938    In Japan, the Japan Intellectual Property Association is founded.

1940    In the United States, Broadcast Music, Incorporated (BMI), a music copyright clearinghouse, is formed.

1946    In the United States, Congress enacts the Lanham Trademark Act of 1946, the foundation of modern federal trademark law.

1955    The United States becomes a party to the Universal Copyright Convention, an alternative to the Berne Convention.

1962    In Gabon, twelve French-speaking African countries form the Organisation Africaine de la Propriété Intellectuelle, a regional intellectual property organization.

1963    In France, the Centre for International Industrial Property Studies is founded.

1966    In the United States, the Association of Corporate Patent Counsel is founded.

1967    The Bureaux Internationaux Réunis pour la Protection de la Propriété Intellectuelle becomes the World Intellectual Property Organization.

1969    ARPANET links four computers, three in California and one in Utah.

1970    Patent Cooperation Treaty concluded.

1971    Project Gutenberg begins distributing e-books online for free.

1972    The U.S. Supreme Court decides *Gottschalk v. Benson,* which holds that a mathematical algorithm used in a computer program is not patentable.

The U.S. Patent Office suspends all pending computer program patent applications.

European countries adopt the Convention on the Grant of European Patents. Among other things, the Convention excludes computer programs from its definition of patentable subject matter.

E-mail begins to be sent over ARPANET.

1974    The World Intellectual Property Organization becomes an agency of the United Nations.

1975    The U.S. Patent Office becomes the U.S. Patent and Trademark Office.

1976    The U.S. Congress enacts the Copyright Act of 1976, the most radical revision of copyright law in U.S. history. The Act eliminates the parallel state copyright system and replaces the renewable term with a unitary term in compliance with the Berne Convention. It does not, however, eliminate the notice requirement.

In Zambia, a group of English-speaking African countries adopts the Agreement on the Creation of the Industrial Property Organization for English-speaking Africa, forming the English-Speaking Africa Regional Intellectual Property Organization, later to become the African Regional Intellectual Property Organization.

1977    The International Association of Entertainment Lawyers is founded.

In the Central African Republic (shortly before it became the ill-fated and short-lived Central African

Empire), the parties to the Organisation Africaine de la Propriété Intellectuelle revise their 1962 agreement to cover a broader range of intellectual property rights and admit new members.

1978      Patent Cooperation Treaty enters into force for the United States.

1981      The U.S. Supreme Court holds in *Diamond v. Diehr* that some computer programs are patentable; U.S. Patent and Trademark Office begins to accept applications for software patents.

1982      In the United States, the Federal Circuit Court of Appeals is created to hear, among other things, patent appeals.

1983      ARPANET switches to TCP/IP protocol.

1984      In the United States, Congress enacts the Computer Fraud and Abuse Act, an antihacking law, and the Semiconductor Chip Protection Act, protecting semiconductor manufacturing mask works.

     The U.S. Supreme Court decides *Sony Corporation of America v. Universal City Studios,* holding that the fact that a VCR can be used for copyright infringement does not make the device unlawful, nor does it make Sony liable for infringement by purchasers of VCRs; the VCR is capable of substantial noninfringing uses and is thus a "staple article of commerce."

     The Federal Circuit decides *Atari, Inc. v. JS & A Group, Inc.,* preventing the sale of a device allowing users to make copies of game cartridges and marketed for that purpose.

1985      Microsoft agrees "that the visual displays in Windows 1.0 are derivative works of the visual displays generated by Apple's Lisa and Macintosh graphical user interface programs."

| | |
|---|---|
| 1985 *(cont.)* | In Africa, the member states of the English-Speaking Africa Regional Intellectual Property Organization agree to open membership to most African countries; the organization is renamed the African Regional Intellectual Property Organization. |
| 1988 | In the United States, Congress enacts the Berne Convention Implementation Act, eliminating the notice requirement and making it possible for the United States to join the Berne Convention. |
| | Congress also enacts the Trademark Law Revision Act. |
| | Microsoft releases Windows 2.03 and Hewlett-Packard releases NewWave; Apple sues for copyright infringement. |
| 1989 | The United States joins the Berne Convention. |
| | Many of the parties to the Madrid Agreement Concerning the International Registration of Marks adopt the Madrid Protocol. |
| 1990 | In the United States, Congress enacts the Visual Artists Rights Act, granting very limited recognition to moral rights in federal copyright law. |
| | The Electronic Frontier Foundation is founded. |
| 1991 | Tim Berners-Lee's first Web page, created the previous year, becomes available online. By the end of the year the first U.S. Web page (at the Stanford Linear Accelerator Center) is also online, as are many others. |
| | In deciding *Feist Publications v. Rural Telephone Service Co.*, the U.S. Supreme Court rejects the "sweat of the brow" theory—the idea that copyright can be a reward for hard work even in the absence of originality. |
| 1992 | The Internet Underground Music Archive enables |

users with technical sophistication and lots of free time to download copyrighted music files.

The U.S. Congress enacts the Audio Home Recording Act and the Copyright Renewal Act.

The Ninth Circuit holds, in *New Kids on the Block v. News America Publishing, Inc.,* that the newspaper *USA Today* had the right to use the name *New Kids on the Block* in a contest asking readers to vote for their favorite member of the band of that name.

**1993**     The National Center for Supercomputing Applications at the University of Illinois releases Mosaic, the first Web browser easily usable by the technically unsophisticated.

In the United States, the Ninth Circuit Court of Appeals decides *MAI Systems v. Peak Computer,* holding that the creation of copies of computer programs during maintenance can infringe on a copyright. The effect of the decision is to grant computer makers and software vendors exclusive rights to maintain their own equipment, preventing independent operators from doing so; five years later Congress passes the Computer Maintenance Competition Assurance Act to restore competition in this industry.

**1994**     Netscape releases Netscape Navigator.

The Uruguay Round of the General Agreement on Tariffs and Trade leads to the creation of the World Trade Organization (WTO). Annex 1C of the WTO agreement, adopted by all the parties, is the Agreement on Trade-Related Aspects of Intellectual Property Rights, better known as TRIPs.

In the United States, the Federal Circuit holds, in *In re Alappat,* that a wide range of computer programs are patentable. The government fails to convict accused warez trader David LaMacchia.

1994
(cont.)

The Ninth Circuit holds that Microsoft's Windows operating system does not infringe on Apple's copyright in the Mac and Lisa operating systems. The decision limits possible future actions for "look and feel" infringement.

The Trademark Law Treaty is opened for signature.

1995

On 1 January, TRIPs enters into force.

The U.S. Patent and Trademark Office somewhat belatedly publishes guidelines for software patent applications.

The First Circuit, in *Lotus Development v. Borland*, holds that the menu command hierarchy of a computer program is not copyrightable. The U.S. Supreme Court declines to review the Ninth Circuit's decision in *Apple Computer, Inc. v. Microsoft Corp.*

Microsoft releases Internet Explorer.

1996

The U.S. Supreme Court decides *State Street Bank & Trust v. Signature Financial Group*, holding that methods of doing business are patentable subject matter.

Congress enacts the Economic Espionage Act, providing some protection for trade secrets.

Also in the United States, the National Association of Patent Practitioners is founded.

The European Union adopts its Database Directive, protecting compilations of data even without the originality required in U.S. law under *Feist*, although for a far shorter term (fifteen years) than traditional copyright protection.

The World Intellectual Property Organization (WIPO) concludes and opens for signature the WIPO Copyright Treaty and the WIPO Performance and Phonograms Treaty.

1997        MP3.com is founded in San Diego, California.

            The U.S. Congress enacts the No Electronic Theft Act.

1998        The Internet Corporation for Assigned Names and Numbers is founded.

            Diamond Multimedia markets a portable MP3 player and is promptly sued by the Recording Industry Association of America (RIAA).

            The U.S. Congress enacts the Federal Trademark Dilution Act, the Trademark Law Treaty Act, and the Anticounterfeiting Consumer Protection Act.

            The U.S. Congress also enacts a suite of laws designed to address the developing crisis in copyright law, including the Sonny Bono Copyright Term Extension Act and the five sections of the Digital Millennium Copyright Act.

            The Ninth Circuit, in *Playboy Enterprises, Inc. v. Welles,* holds that Welles has a right to refer to herself as "Playmate of the Year 1981" on her website and to use the terms "playmate" and "playboy" in metatags on the site.

1999        In Norway, fifteen-year-old Jon Lech Johansen posts DeCSS on the Internet. Johansen is arrested and prosecuted in Norway. In the United States, many people distribute DeCSS or provide links to sites from which it can be downloaded; they are sued by motion picture content companies.

            In the United States, Napster begins operations and is sued by the RIAA and others.

            The U.S. Congress enacts the Anticybersquatting Consumer Protection Act and the First Inventor Defense Act.

1999
(*cont.*)

Diamond Multimedia prevails in the lawsuit brought against it by the RIAA.

Amazon.com obtains a U.S. patent for its one-click ordering system and obtains an injunction prohibiting Barnes & Noble from using a similar system.

**2000**

In the Netherlands, Consumer Empowerment begins distributing KaZaA Media Desktop and is sued by Dutch content industry group Buma/Stemra.

In the United States, a federal trial court in *Universal City Studios, Inc. v. Reimerdes* rejects the constitutional arguments of the defendants who distributed or linked to the decryption program DeCSS.

Also in the United States, MP3.com loses a lawsuit brought by Universal Music Group and others and is ordered to pay $250 million in damages.

The Trademark Law Treaty enters into force for the United States. The Patent Law Treaty is concluded; the United States signs the treaty but does not ratify it.

Vivendi, a French company, purchases MP3.com.

Bertelsmann Music Group, a German company, invests in Napster.

**2001**

In the United States, Napster is found potentially liable as a third-party copyright infringer.

The Federal Circuit decides, in *Amazon.com, Inc. v. Barnesandnoble.com, Inc.*, that the 1999 injunction against Barnes & Noble should not have been issued, because Barnes & Noble has "raised substantial questions as to the validity" of Amazon's patent on one-click ordering.

The Second Circuit, in *Universal City Studios, Inc. v. Corley*, affirms the 2000 decision of the trial court in *Universal City Studios, Inc. v. Reimerdes*.

Also in the United States, Dmitri Sklyarov, the author of a program that can break the copy protection on Adobe e-books, is arrested while visiting the country for a conference.

2002    The WIPO Copyright Treaty and the WIPO Performance and Phonograms Treaty come into force; the United States is a party to both.

In the United States, the Supreme Court upholds the constitutionality of the Sonny Bono Copyright Term Extension Act.

In the United States, Aimster is found liable for indirect copyright infringement. In the Netherlands, the Amsterdam Court of Appeals holds that KaZaA is not liable for indirect copyright infringement in the suit brought by Buma/Stemra.

In Europe, European Digital Rights, a users' rights group, is founded.

The Open Society Institute adopts the Budapest Open Access Initiative, an attempt to create greater access to academic work.

2003    Apple launches iTunes.

In the United States, Verizon Internet Services wins a court battle against the RIAA, which had attempted to compel Verizon to disclose a subscriber's name.

The United States becomes a party to the Madrid Protocol, an international trademark agreement.

The RIAA begins suing individual users for file sharing.

In Norway, Jon Lech Johansen is acquitted of charges arising from the distribution of DeCSS; the acquittal is upheld on appeal.

2005   The U.S. Supreme Court finds that Grokster may be liable as an indirect copyright infringer and remands the case for further proceedings.

The European Parliament rejects a bill authorizing software patents.

The Patent Law Treaty enters into force for those countries that have ratified it, but not for the United States.

2006   The U.S. Congress enacts the Trademark Dilution Revision Act.

In Japan, Kongo Gumi Construction is taken over by relative upstart Takamatsu Corporation, a construction company slightly less than 400 years old. The new owners keep the Kongo Gumi name, however.

# 5

# Biographies

## Clara Barton (1821–1912)

Clara Barton is internationally famous as the founder of the American Red Cross. In her earlier career, however, she played a role in the development of American intellectual property administration: Before the Civil War, she worked in the U.S. Patent Office as a patent clerk, rising to a position of considerable responsibility. At the beginning of the war, when Colonel Ephraim Elmer Ellsworth (a former patent solicitor) was killed by Virginia innkeeper James Jackson, becoming the first Union officer to die in the war, Barton attended his funeral. Afterward she wrote "I . . . wondered if he had not sold himself at his highest price for his Country's good—if the inspiration of 'Ellsworth dead' were not worth more to our cause than the life of *any* man could be" (Barton 1922, 117).

The U.S. Patent Office was disrupted by the war. In 1861 the First Rhode Island Infantry Regiment was quartered in the model rooms, where they broke hundreds of glass cases and stole many of the models (Letter from Our Washington House 1861, 374). During the war the U.S. Patent Office became a hospital; the poet Walt Whitman, who worked as a volunteer in the hospital, wrote:

> The vast area of the second story of that noblest of Washington buildings, the Patent Office, is crowded close with rows of sick, badly wounded and dying soldiers. . . . Two of the immense apartments are filled with high and ponderous glass cabinets, crowded with models in miniature

**149**

of every kind of utensil, machine or invention it ever entered into the mind of man to conceive and with curiosities and foreign gifts. Between these cabinets are lateral openings, perhaps eight feet wide and quite deep, and in these openings are placed many of the sick. Many of them are very bad cases, wounds and amputations. There is also a great long double row of them up and down through the middle of the hall. Then there is a gallery running above the hall in which there are beds also. It is, indeed, a curious scene, especially at night when lit up. The glass cabinets, the beds, the forms lying there, the gallery above, and the marble pavement under foot—the suffering, and the fortitude to bear it in various degrees—occasionally, from some, the groan that cannot be repressed—sometimes a poor fellow dying, with emaciated face and glassy eye, the nurse by his side, the doctor also there, but no friend, no relative—such are the sights in the Patent Office. (Whitman 1963)

After the war the U.S. Patent Office returned to its traditional function, but Barton went on to work with the International Red Cross, eventually returning to the United States to found the American Red Cross. The Red Cross symbol itself, along with the Red Crescent, is protected from misuse both during the conduct of war and in commercial and other nonmilitary activities. The latter protection amounts to a form of intellectual property protection similar to that accorded to service marks (see, for example, 18 U.S.C. § 706; Paris Convention, art. 6*ter*; Geneva Convention I, art. 44; Geneva Convention II, arts. 44–45; Protocol Additional to the Geneva Convention, art. 85(3)(f)).

### Sources and Further Reading

18 U.S.C. § 706.

Barton, William E. 1922. *The Life of Clara Barton*. Reprinted. New York: AMS, 1969.

Geneva Convention I. Convention for the Amelioration of the Condition of the Wounded and Sick in Armed Forces in the Field, August 12, 1949, 6 U.S.T. 3114, 75 U.N.T.S. 31.

Geneva Convention II. Convention for the Amelioration of the Condition of the Wounded, Sick and Shipwrecked Members of the Armed Forces at Sea, August 12, 1949, 6 U.S.T. 3217, 75 U.N.T.S. 85.

"Letter from Our Washington House." 1861. *Scientific American.* June 15, 374. http://cdl.library.cornell.edu/cgi-bin/moa/pageviewer?frames =1&coll=moa&view=50&root=%2Fmoa%2Fscia%2Fscia1004%2F&tif =00378.TIF&cite=http%3A%2F%2Fcdl.library.cornell.edu%2Fcgi-bin%2 Fmoa%2Fmoa-cgi%3Fnotisid%3DABF2204-1004-26.

Paris Convention for the Protection of Industrial Property, March 20, 1883, as revised at Brussels on December 14, 1900, at Washington on June 2, 1911, at The Hague on November 6, 1925, at London on June 2, 1934, at Lisbon on October 31, 1958, and at Stockholm on July 14, 1967, and as amended on September 28, 1979, 21 U.S.T. 1583, 828 U.N.T.S. 305.

Protocol Additional to the Geneva Conventions of 12 August 1949, and Relating to the Protection of Victims of International Armed Conflicts, June 8, 1977, 1125 U.N.T.S. 3.

Whitman, Walt. 1963. *Prose Works, Volume I.* Ed. Floyd Stovall. New York: New York University Press.

# Ernest Bourget (fl. 1847–1850)

Ernest Bourget was a French composer of popular music and light works in the 1840s. It was as a litigant, however, and not as a musician, that Bourget was to have the greatest impact on future generations of musicians. In 1847 Bourget and two other composers, Victor Parizot and Paul Henrion, visited the Café Concert les Ambassadeurs, a popular café in Paris, where they drank sugared ice-water. (This seems an odd choice today, but it was very much in fashion in Paris at the time.) The Ambassadeurs provided live musical entertainment, and Bourget was incensed to hear the musicians playing songs that he had written. He demanded that the manager of the Ambassadeurs pay him royalties for the songs. When the manager refused, Bourget and his companions refused to pay for their drinks.

The matter wound up in court, and in 1849 the Cour d'Appel de Paris ordered the Ambassadeurs to pay royalties to Bourget. This had two dramatic effects on the music world. First, it recognized that the author of a musical work had the right to control not only the copying of the work but also the public performance of it. A musician or café owner who had purchased authorized copies of sheet music had already paid a royalty by doing so, but that royalty covered only the right to reproduce the sheet music. The right to perform the work before an audience was separate, and it required a separate royalty payment. (This right had been set out in a 1793 statute but widely ignored until the 1849 decision.)

The second effect was indirect. While the decision of the Cour d'Appel recognized the performance right, it left the enforcement of that right in the hands of the composer. To collect all of the royalties due to him, Bourget would have had to visit all the musical venues not only in Paris but also in all of France, leaving him no time to compose future works. (International copyright protection still lay in the future.) Some more efficient administrative mechanism was needed. Ideally, the performance right royalties could be collected by a single entity and distributed to the right holders.

In the following year, 1850, Bourget and others formed the Agence Centrale pour la Perception Droits Auteurs et Compositeurs de Musique, the first such music copyright clearinghouse. In 1851 the licensing functions of the Agence Central, as well as some licensing functions of the Société des Gens de Lettres (founded in 1838 by French authors, including Victor Hugo and Honoré de Balzac—see Chapter 7), were taken over by a new organization, the Société des Auteurs, Compositeurs et Éditeurs de Musique (SACEM). Music copyright clearinghouses modeled on SACEM soon appeared in other European countries and, with the founding of the American Society of Composers, Authors and Publishers in 1914 and Broadcast Music, Inc. in 1940, in the United States (BMI 1990; Caslon Analytics 2002; SACEM no date).

Ironically, considering the enormous benefit he conferred on musicians who came after him, Bourget's music is forgotten. Today he is remembered as a figure in copyright law rather than in music; musically he is remembered mostly for his association with Jacques Offenbach, creator of *The Tales of Hoffman*.

### Sources and Further Reading

Broadcast Music, Inc. 1990. *BMI 50th Anniversary History Book.* http://www.bmi.com/library/brochures/historybook/index.asp.

Caslon Analytics. 2002. "Copyright Collecting Societies." http://www.caslon.com.au/colsocietiesprofile.htm.

SACEM. *La Sacem: Une Histoire d'amour Entre la Musique et le Droit d'auteur.* http://www.sacem.fr/portailSacem/jsp/ep/channelView.do?channelId=-536881293&channelPage=ACTION%3BBVCONTENT%3B0%3B%2Fep%2FprogramView.do&pageTypeId=8586 (in French).

# Filippo Brunelleschi (1377–1446)

The Italian Renaissance sculptor, mathematician, and architect Filippo Brunelleschi is best known for building the Duomo—the Basilica di Santa Maria del Fiore—in Florence. He devoted the greatest part of his professional life to the project, and during the course of the construction earned another historical distinction, becoming the first person to be awarded a patent, in the modern sense, for an invention (see Chapter 1). The construction of the Duomo required a great deal of marble, which had to be transported up the Arno River from Pisa to Florence. To transport this marble Brunelleschi designed and built a barge, *Il Badalone (The Monster)*, which was quite different from earlier riverboats used for the same purpose. *Il Badalone* used special hoisting gear to lift the heavy blocks of marble on and off the boat. In the preamble to his patent, Brunelleschi argued that he should be granted "some prerogative concerning" his invention. This would actually increase the eventual availability of the invention: If granted this prerogative, "he would open up what he is hiding and would disclose it to all." If not, he would "[refuse] to make such machine available to the public, in order that the fruit of his genius and skill [might] not be reaped by another without his will and consent" (King 2005).

Brunelleschi's plans for *Il Badalone* brought derision from university lecturer and architectural rival Giovanni da Prato, who wrote:

> O you deep fountain, pit of ignorance,
> You Miserable beast and imbecile,
> Who thinks uncertain things can be made visible:
> There is no substance to your alchemy.
> The fickle mob, eternally deceived
> In all its hope, may still believe in you,
> But never will you, worthless nobody,
> Make that come true which is impossible.
> So if the Badalon, your water bird,
> Were ever finished—which can never be—
> I would no longer read on Dante at school
> But finish my existence with my hand.
> For surely you are mad. You hardly know
> Your own profession. Leave us, please, alone.

Brunelleschi responded with another sonnet, equally insulting:

When hope is given us by Heaven,
O you ridiculous-looking beast,
We rise above corruptible matter
And gain the strength of clearest sight.
A fool will lose what hope he has,
For all experience disappoints him.
For wise men nothing that exists
Remains unseen; they do not share
The idle dreams of would-be scholars.
Only the artist, not the fool
Discovers that which nature hides.
Therefore untangle the web of your verses,
Lest they strike sour notes in the dance
When your "impossible" comes to pass.
(Translations reproduced in Walker 2002, 136–137)

Da Prato later lost his job teaching Dante because of budget cuts, but he did not take his life when *Il Badalone* was completed (Walker 2002, 137).

In 1421 Brunelleschi received his groundbreaking patent, which gave him a monopoly on the manufacture of vessels to his design for three years—and the right to burn any infringing vessel. Brunelleschi's arguments and the city's response were entirely modern. To this day patent law is viewed as serving two functions: encouraging inventors to invent by granting them a monopoly, and ensuring that the public will eventually gain access to the invention by placing a time limit on the monopoly.

Possession of what may have been the world's first utility patent brought Brunelleschi no wealth, however. *Il Badalone's* loading mechanism may have been ingenious, but its seaworthiness (or riverworthiness) was less impressive. *Il Badalone* sank on its first voyage, perhaps taking a hundred Florentine tons (about 37 avoirdupois tons) of Carrara marble to the bottom of the Arno River near Empoli. History, unfortunately, has not preserved Giovanni da Prato's reaction to this news, although he must have been delighted (King 2005; but see Walker 2002, 164–165: *Il Badalone* may not have sunk, and thus "perhaps it was not a total failure; yet it could hardly be called a success").

Despite the loss of *Il Badalone*, Brunelleschi managed to see the Duomo through nearly to completion by the time of his death and to leave his architectural stamp on Florence in the form of the Ospedale degli Innocenti, the Basilica di San Lorenzo di Firenze, and the Chiesa di Santa Maria del Santo Spirito. He is interred in his masterpiece, the Basilica di Santa Maria del Fiore.

### Sources and Further Reading

King, Jamie. 2005. "The Dissolving Fortress." *European Journal of Higher Arts Education*. February. http://www.ejhae.elia-artschools.org/Issue2/2d-king.htm.

Misa, Thomas J. 2004. *Leonardo to the Internet: Technology & Culture from the Renaissance to the Present*. Baltimore, MD: Johns Hopkins University Press.

O'Connor, J. J., and E. F. Robertson. 2002. *Filippo Brunelleschi*. School of Mathematics and Statistics, University of St. Andrews, Scotland. February. http://www-history.mcs.st-andrews.ac.uk/Biographies/Brunelleschi.html.

Walker, Paul Robert. 2002. *The Feud that Sparked the Renaissance: How Brunelleschi and Ghiberti Changed the Art World*. New York: HarperCollins (William Morrow).

# Laurens Coster (ca. 1370–1440)

Laurens Janszoon Coster may have been an early printer—or may not have been. The generally accepted view is that Johannes Gutenberg was the first European to print with movable type. Coster, who died more than a decade before Gutenberg printed his first Bible, was a prominent citizen of Haarlem, in the Netherlands, where among other offices he served as a church sexton and as city treasurer. Coster is rumored to have printed several books in Haarlem. In one version of the story, Coster's assistant, Johann Fust, stole Coster's printing presses, perhaps after Coster's death, and took them to Gutenberg.

The debate over whether Coster or Gutenberg was "first" can grow quite heated, yet the answer is less interesting than the Eurocentric view of history that the question reveals. Movable-type printing had been in use in China, Korea, and elsewhere in East Asia for centuries before either Coster or Gutenberg was born.

Coster, Gutenberg, and other pioneering European printers of the fifteenth century were products of history rather than shapers of it. Printing came about more because of the availability of cheaper paper and other materials than because of any brilliant technological breakthrough. The Costerites, for example, suggest that the idea for his printing press came to Coster when he was cutting letters from the bark of a tree for the amusement of his grandchildren: "The letters fell into the sand, and from the impression that they left the idea came to him that letters such as these might also be impressed upon paper in order to print books" (Psymon Web Bindery).

This is nonsense. Coster may or may not have printed books before Gutenberg, and he may or may not have cut letters from tree bark. But even if he was unaware of Chinese and Korean innovations in printing, he would have been familiar with block printing. Block printing, in which an entire page is carved from a single block, was already widely in use in Europe for pictures and text. It would have required no moment of inspiration for Coster, or for that matter Gutenberg or anyone else, to realize that individual letters could also be used for printing. What was required instead was a great deal of work to iron out the inevitable problems. Coster may have done some of this work, and Gutenberg undoubtedly did. But development of printing did not stop after Gutenberg, and today, ironically, it has come full circle: Typesetting is nearly a vanished art, and pages today are "set" by computer as a single piece, rather than as collections of bits of removable (and reusable) type. Nonetheless, a statue of Coster still stands in Haarlem's central marketplace.

### Sources and Further Reading

Hadrianus Junius. *Batavia* (Antwerp, 1588; in Latin), page referring to Coster available at http://www.psymon.com/koster/batavia.html.

Psymon Web Bindery. *The Legend of Koster.* http://www.psymon.com/koster/.

# Annie Ellsworth (1826–1900)

The Patent Act of 1836 (see Chapter 1) radically revamped and modernized U.S. patent law. The Act created the modern U.S. Patent Office (now the U.S. Patent and Trademark Office) to evaluate patent applications and grant patents. A year earlier Henry Ellsworth had been appointed patent commissioner; in 1836 the U.S. Patent Office suffered a disastrous fire, destroying almost all of the existing patent models and records. By 1843 Henry had employed his seventeen-year-old daughter, Annie, as a patent copyist. (In those days before the invention and patenting of copying machines, copies of original patents had to be made by hand.)

Henry's nepotism might raise eyebrows today, but a truly meritocratic civil service did not yet exist. Henry himself was the son of Oliver Ellsworth, third chief justice of the U.S. Supreme Court; Henry's twin brother William became governor of Connecticut shortly after Henry became patent commissioner.

Nepotism notwithstanding, the two Ellsworths, father and daughter, proved to be good hires, and they played a crucial role in creating a modern patent review process in the United States. From copying patents at the age of seventeen, Annie progressed to more difficult assignments, paving the way for future female U.S. Patent Office employees (such as Clara Barton) to rise yet higher in the system. In 1844 Annie Ellsworth also initiated the first link in the global electronic information network, sending the world's first telegraph message: "What hath God wrought?" (Brown 1994, 177; the words are from Numbers 23:23). According to family tradition, Annie was at the time infatuated with fifty-two-year-old Samuel Morse, the inventor of the telegraph. If this is true, there is an interesting postscript: A century and a half later, Annie's descendant Jennie Jackson married Samuel's descendant Brian Morse. The two were unaware of their historical connection until after announcing their engagement (Dobyns 1994, 205–206).

## Sources and Further Reading

Brown, Travis. 1994. *Historical First Patents: The First United States Patents for Many Everyday Things*. Metuchen, NJ: The Scarecrow Press.

Dinwoodie, Graeme B., William O. Hennessey, and Shira Perlmutter. 2002. *International and Comparative Patent Law*. Newark, NJ: LexisNexis Matthew Bender.

Dobyns, Kenneth W. 1994. *The Patent Office Pony: A History of the Early Patent Office*. Spotsylvania, VA: Sergeant Kirklands Museum.

Kaufer, Erich. 1989. *The Economics of the Patent System*. Chur, Switzerland: Harwood Academic Publishers.

# Johannes Gutenberg (ca. 1395–1468)

Johannes Gutenberg has become indelibly associated in the popular imagination with one of history's greatest revolutions in information technology—the spread throughout Europe and the Americas of commercial printing using movable type. Gutenberg may or may not have been the first European to use movable type (see the Laurens Coster entry in this chapter). However, even if others in Europe had already experimented with movable type, Gutenberg and his colleagues made dramatic innovations, bringing European printing up to the technological level of East Asian printing.

In the early to mid-fifteenth century, Gutenberg moved from his hometown of Mainz to Strasbourg, where he became a partner in a printing shop. The shop used the cumbersome block-printing techniques of the day. The tremendous amount of labor required to cut out each page-printing block meant that printing was expensive, which in turn meant that most block-printed works were short, often no more than a single page. The cost of printing entire books by this method was prohibitive.

While in Strasbourg, Gutenberg experimented with movable type. Three technological problems had to be solved to make movable type practical. First, Gutenberg had to find a metal alloy with a sufficiently low melting point; the higher the melting point, the greater the cost (in fuel and time, and thus in money) of making the type. Second, he had to develop an ink that would adhere to the metal, but would not be so viscous as to gum up the printing press. Third, the press itself had to be made. The equipment used for block printing was unsuitable, so a wine press was used instead.

In 1448 Gutenberg, having made considerable progress on solving these problems, returned to his hometown of Mainz and opened his own printing shop, with the financial backing of Johann Fust. (An alternate theory is that Fust, not Gutenberg, provided the necessary technological know-how, perhaps having stolen it from Laurens Coster.) Seven years later, in 1455, Gutenberg exhibited his Bible at the Frankfurt Trade Fair. This first Bible, made with more than 300 pieces of type, was still expensive and was probably aimed at institutional buyers. Within a few years, however, Gutenberg and others had refined and simplified the printing process, bringing printed books within the reach of most literate persons—and many illiterate ones, increasing the incentive to become literate.

Far more is known about the Gutenberg Bible, many copies of which are still in existence, than about Gutenberg's life—it is not even certain that he actually printed the Bible. One thing that is known, however, is that in 1455, the year in which the Bible was exhibited at Frankfurt, Fust sued Gutenberg. Fust had advanced a great deal of money to Gutenberg, possibly for the preparation of the Bible. Gutenberg lost the suit and Fust apparently gained control of part or all of the printing operation, which he then operated with his son-in-law Peter Schoffer (Misa 2004, 21; Harry Ransom Center 2002; Gray 1999). Gutenberg died thirteen years later, but not, apparently, in poverty: He was granted a pension by the archbishop of Mainz, and he may have started a new printing business.

### Sources and Further Reading

Gies, Frances, and Joseph Gies. 1994. *Cathedral, Forge and Waterwheel: Technology and Invention in the Middle Ages.* New York: HarperCollins.

Gray, Paul. 1999. "Most Important People of the Millennium—Johann Gutenberg (c. 1395–1468): The Obscure Printer's Innovation Kindled Reformations and a Yet Unfinished Information Revolution." *Time,* December 31.

Harry Ransom Center (University of Texas at Austin). 2002. "The Gutenberg Bible at the Ransom Center." http://www.hrc.utexas.edu/exhibitions/permanent/gutenberg/.

Misa, Thomas J. 2004. *Leonardo to the Internet: Technology and Culture from the Renaissance to the Present.* Baltimore, MD: Johns Hopkins University Press.

# Victor Hugo (1802–1885)

France's most celebrated author and poet of the nineteenth century, the author of *Les Misérables* and *The Hunchback of Notre Dame,* did perhaps more than any other individual to bring about the current international copyright regime. In 1838 (seven years after the publication of *The Hunchback of Notre Dame*) he cofounded the Société des Gens de Lettres with other famous writers including

Honoré de Balzac, Alexandre Dumas, and George Sand. The Société is still in existence and continues to advise writers on intellectual property issues. Forty years later, in 1878 (sixteen years after the first publication of *Les Misérables*), the Société served as a vehicle for Hugo to found the Association Littéraire et Artistique Internationale (ALAI), an organization that had as its purpose the pursuit of an international copyright convention (see Chapter 7). Like the Société des Gens de Lettres, the ALAI is still in existence. Across the top of its home page are the words "Fondée à Paris par Victor Hugo en 1878" ("Founded in Paris by Victor Hugo in 1878").

The ALAI's moment of triumph came in 1886, with the creation of the Berne Convention—but Hugo did not live to see it. He died in May 1885, more than a year before the signing of the Berne Convention in September 1886.

### Sources and Further Reading

Association Littéraire et Artistique Internationale. Home page. http://www.alai.org/index-f.php?sm=0 (in French); English translation at http://www.alai.org/index-a.php?sm=0.

Convention Concerning the Creation of an International Union for the Protection of Literary and Artistic Works (Berne Convention), Sept. 9, 1886, as last revised at Paris, July 24, 1971 (amended 1979), 25 U.S.T. 1341, 828 U.N.T.S. 221.

Société des Gens de Lettres. *Découvrez la SGDL: Historique.* http://www.sgdl.org (in French).

# Jon Lech Johansen (1983–)

Movies sold on DVD are encrypted to make them harder to copy. The encryption method used, Content Scramble System (CSS) is owned by the DVD Copy Control Association (DVD CCA). The DVD CCA licenses decryption keys to the makers of DVD players; without these keys, the players would be unable to play encrypted DVDs. The distribution of the decryption keys is carefully controlled, because any technically sophisticated person who gained access to a decryption key would be able to decrypt (and make or enable the making of unauthorized copies of) the encrypted work. Even stringent security precautions, however, cannot prevent the decryption keys from being reverse engineered.

In 1999, a program called DeCSS, which was capable of decrypting CSS-encrypted DVDs, appeared. It was first posted on 6 October 1999, by a fifteen-year-old Norwegian, Jon Lech Johansen. The DVD CCA, the Motion Picture Association of America, and other content-industry groups were outraged; lawyers in Norway for these groups demanded that the Norwegian government do something, and on 23 January 2000, Johansen was arrested at his home by three police officers. Two years later, on 9 January 2002, he was indicted for violating Norwegian copyright law.

Breaking the copy protection encryption on copyrighted DVDs was forbidden under Norwegian law at the time, as it is under U.S. law. However, the attempt to prosecute "DVD Jon" backfired on those in the content industry who had encouraged it. Johansen became an instant celebrity, a poster child for consumer rights advocates. Many consumers had bitterly resented the restrictions placed on copyrighted DVD content that they had purchased, and Johansen's trial provided a focus for that anger. Information rights advocacy groups, including the Electronic Frontier Foundation (see Chapter 7), assisted in Johansen's defense.

At the time, no decryption keys were licensed for playing CSS-encrypted DVDs on Linux systems. A consumer who had a Linux system, but no Macintosh or Windows system and no licensed DVD player, could not play an encrypted DVD. Johansen did not copy DVDs; he ostensibly intended DeCSS to be used to play CSS-encrypted DVDs on Linux systems. On 7 January 2003, a year after his indictment and three years after his arrest, Johansen was acquitted by the trial court. In Norway, however, as in many countries (but not the United States), the prosecution can appeal an acquittal, and Økokrim, the Norwegian government's economic crimes division, chose to do so.

The appeal was heard by the Borgarting Appellate Court, which upheld the trial court's decision on 22 December 2003. Johansen had committed no crime, the appellate court decided (without using his name, because he was a minor). In January 2004, Økokrim announced that it would not pursue the case further.

While the decision of the Borgarting Appellate Court was a victory for consumer and information rights advocates, as well as for Johansen personally, it was a limited one. DeCSS had taken on a life of its own outside Norway, and information rights activists in other countries, notably the United States, had deliberately challenged laws forbidding its distribution. In the United States, especially, these challenges were less successful than in Norway (see *Universal City Studios, Inc. v. Corley*, 273 F.3d 429; *DVD Copy Control Association, Inc. v. Bunner*, 4 Cal.Rptr.3d 69).

Like DeCSS, Johansen (who now lives in the United States) has not vanished from the public eye. Shortly before his appeal was heard by the Borgarting Appellate Court, someone—apparently Johansen—posted a program capable of decrypting the .aap files used by Apple's iTunes. Throughout 2004, 2005, and 2006 Johansen's website (http://nanocrew.net/) has continued to provide downloadable software.

### Sources and Further Reading

Chu, Jeff. 2002. "Enemy At The Gates? Jon Johansen's Trial for Hacking May Be a Key Battle in the Struggle between Industry and Innovation." *Time*, July 8, 46.

*DVD Copy Control Association, Inc. v. Bunner*, 4 Cal.Rptr.3d 69 (2003).

Johansen, Jon Lech. So Sue Me: Jon Lech Johansen's Blog. http://nanocrew.net/.

Lessig, Lawrence. 2004. *Free Culture: How Big Media Uses Technology and the Law to Lock Down Culture and Control Creativity.* New York: Penguin.

"Norwegian Hacker Cracks iTunes Code." 2003. November 27. http://www.cnn.com/2003/TECH/internet/11/27/itunes.code.ap/index.html.

*Sunde (for Norway) v. Johansen*, Oslo First Instance Trial Court, January 7, 2003, No. 02-507 M/94, English translation by Professor Jon Bing available at http://www.eff.org/IP/Video/Johansen_DeCSS_case/20030109_johansen_decision.html; on appeal, Borgarting Appellate Court, Dec. 22, 2003, No. LB-2003-00731, English translation by Professor Jon Bing available at http://www.efn.no/DVD-dom-20031222-en.html.

*Universal City Studios, Inc. v. Corley*, 273 F.3d 429 (2nd Cir. 2001).

# Mary Kies (1752–1837)

In 1809, Mary Kies, of Killingly, Connecticut, became the first woman to obtain a U.S. patent. Kies invented an improved method of weaving straw with silk or thread for making hats. She was not the first U.S. woman to create an innovation in hatmaking. In 1798 Betsy Metcalf had invented, but not patented, a method of braiding straw that was in widespread use at the time of Kies' invention. Kies, however, applied for a patent. The patent was signed by then-President James Madison; Dolley Madison, the president's wife, wrote a note to Kies congratulating her.

Her achievement earned her a small place in history, but unfortunately no money. Her son Daniel and others invested considerable money in a hatmaking enterprise using her invention, but they failed to profit, perhaps because of changes in fashion and the resumption of trade with Europe after the end of the Napoleonic wars. After her husband died in 1813, Kies moved in with Daniel and lived with him until her death. She died in poverty and was buried in a pauper's grave, although a belated recognition of her significance to U.S. history led to a monument in 1965.

No copy of the Kies patent survives; a fire in the U.S. Patent Office in 1836 destroyed thousands of patent records, including hers. However, two samples of her patented straw fabric, woven by Kies herself, can be seen at the Bugbee Memorial Library in Killingly.

### Sources and Further Reading

Killingly Historical Society. 2005. "Mary (Dixon) Kies, America's First Female Patent Holder." http://www.killinglyhistory.org/jol7/page5.htm.

Massachusetts Institute of Technology. 2004. Inventor of the Week Archive. "Mary Kies: Process for Weaving Straw." January. http://web.mit.edu/invent/iow/kies.html.

# Antonio Meucci (1808–1889)

Landmark accomplishments often invite controversy; just as Johannes Gutenberg had his Laurens Coster, Alexander Graham Bell, inventor of the telephone, had his Antonio Meucci.

Meucci was an immigrant from Italy. Between 1859 and 1883 he received fourteen U.S. patents, none for a telephone or any form of electric communications device. According to his supporters, though, he exhibited a telephone in New York in 1860. It is known that in 1871 he filed a patent caveat for a telephonic communications device. This caveat was a notice of an impending patent, preserving the inventor's rights for a renewable one-year period. The caveat expired in 1874 when the impoverished Meucci was unable to pay the ten-dollar renewal fee; had Meucci been able to maintain the caveat, Bell's 1876 patent could not have been granted (H.Res. 269, 2002).

Meucci had invented his communications device, which may or may not have been a telephone, to communicate with his paralyzed wife from various parts of his house. Later, when Meucci was severely injured in a steamship explosion, his wife sold his working models to pay for his medical care; she received six dollars. In a striking similarity to the Coster-Fust-Gutenberg theory, Meucci's advocates believe the models may have eventually found their way into Bell's hands.

Meucci sued Bell; eventually the U.S. government joined in, filing suit against Bell for fraud. Meucci was not the only person to feel wronged by Bell; other claimants for inventor of the telephone include Charles Bourseul, Sylvanus Cushman, Amos Dolbear, Daniel Drawbaugh, Edward Farrar, Elisha Gray (who filed a caveat on the same day Bell filed his patent application, although Bell's application was received earlier in the day), Innocenzo Manzetti, James McDonough, and Johann Philipp Reis (Bellis no date). Meucci died in poverty in 1889, and in 1893 Bell's patent expired. The underlying issue in Meucci's lawsuit—the question of who invented the telephone—was never resolved (H.Res. 269, 2002). In 2002 his accomplishments were belatedly recognized by the U.S. House of Representatives.

### Sources and Further Reading

Bellis, Mary. "Antonio Meucci and the Invention of the Telephone." http://inventors.about.com/library/inventors/bl_Antonio_Meucci.htm.

H.Res. 269, 107th Cong., June 11, 2002.

Levy, Daniel S. 2000. "Man-Made Marvels; and Other Bumps on the Road of Progress . . ." *Time*, December 4, 91.

# Eadweard Muybridge (1830–1904)

A technology as complex as that required for making and displaying motion pictures cannot be said to have a single inventor; many innovators played a part in bringing still pictures to life on the screen. One of the more notable—and controversial—pioneers in the motion picture industry was Eadweard Muybridge, inventor of the zoopraxiscope.

Muybridge (born Edward Muggeridge) emigrated from England to the United States in 1850, at the age of twenty, and in the early days of photography became known for his photographs of California's coast and Yosemite region. In 1877 he took "The Horse in Motion," the series of photographs that guaranteed his place in the history of photography and is regarded as an important milestone in the development of motion picture technology.

In 1872, former California governor Leland Stanford commissioned Muybridge to take the photographs to determine whether, when a horse is galloping, there is ever a point at which all four of the horse's hooves are off the ground simultaneously. (Debate rages between Stanford's biographer and Muybridge's as to whether Stanford wanted to answer the question to settle a bet or from simple curiosity.) Muybridge's first attempts were inconclusive, but in 1877 he set up 12 cameras along a Palo Alto racetrack, triggered by threads at the height of the horse's chest; his photos showed that there is indeed a moment at which all four of the horse's hooves are tucked underneath its body.

Muybridge's breakthrough inspired a wave of innovation in stop-motion camera technology, and Muybridge himself became perhaps the best-known taker of such pictures. His second innovation was the zoopraxiscope, which displayed pictures in rapid succession, creating the illusion of motion. With the zoopraxiscope, the horse begins to gallop again, and it is no longer possible for the unaided eye to tell whether all of its feet are off the ground simultaneously.

Muybridge was a pioneer not only of Hollywood's technology but also of its mystique. He became a celebrity. His many "films" of moving male and female nudes raised eyebrows, and his "Woman Walking Downstairs" inspired Marcel Duchamp's "Nude Descending a Staircase, No. 2," although Muybridge was not alive to enjoy the controversy Duchamp's painting generated.

The lesser scandals of Muybridge's life were eclipsed by his pioneering of what has become another entertainment-industry tradition, however: the celebrity trial (and inexplicable acquittal). In 1870, or perhaps earlier, Muybridge met Flora Stone, the wife of San Francisco saddler Lucius Stone. In December 1870, Flora and Lucius Stone divorced. At the time Muybridge was forty-one, and Flora Stone was nineteen. Two years later the two were married, and shortly after that Flora (now Flora Muybridge) began an affair with Harry Larkyns. In 1874 Flora bore a son, Floredo Helios Muybridge; she and Harry Larkyns continued their affair. At one point Muybridge threatened to kill Harry if the affair continued. Late in

1874 Muybridge discovered a photograph of Floredo with the name "Little Harry" written on the back, suggesting that Flora and Harry considered Floredo to be their son. He then spent most of the day traveling by boat and stagecoach to Calistoga, eighty miles away. Along the way he fired a test round from his pistol. In Calistoga he knocked on the door of the mine superintendent and asked for Harry Larkyns. Larkyns, who had been playing cribbage, came to the door. Muybridge said "Good evening, Major. My name is Muybridge. Here is the answer to the message you sent my wife." He then shot Harry in the chest, killing him.

It seems incredible that Muybridge was not convicted. He was undeniably guilty, beyond any reasonable doubt, of premeditated murder. There were multiple witnesses to the shooting. The length of the journey to Calistoga, the lack of any reason for going there other than to kill Harry Larkyns, the test shot, and the previous death threat all amounted to overwhelming evidence of premeditation. Nonetheless, Muybridge was acquitted. His attorneys used an "honor killing" defense: "Muybridge was not only avenging the wrongs done him when he shot the man dead, but was protecting Mrs. Muybridge against him in the future" (Prodger 2003, 261).

After his acquittal, Muybridge left for Central America. Flora, who had filed for divorce, died, and Floredo was placed in an orphanage. As an adult, Floredo greatly resembled Muybridge. Muybridge returned to the United States to create "The Horse in Motion" and the many works that followed from it. Eventually this too would lead to what has become an entertainment-industry tradition: the intellectual property dispute. Stanford commissioned a book based on "The Horse in Motion," crediting Muybridge not as the creator of the work but as a technician and using lithographic reproductions rather than the higher-quality (and more expensive to print) original photographs. Muybridge sued Stanford, but lost. The rights he sought to protect were the moral rights of integrity and paternity—the right to protect one's work against alteration and to be identified as the author of a work—and, with very limited exceptions, these rights have never been acknowledged in U.S. copyright law (see Chapter 1).

### Sources and Further Reading

Prodger, Phillip. 2003. *Time Stands Still: Muybridge and the Instantaneous Photography Movement*. New York: Oxford University Press.

Sandler, Martin W. 2002. *Photography: An Illustrated History.* New York: Oxford University Press.

# Dmitri Sklyarov (1974– )

Like Jon Lech Johansen, Dmitri Sklyarov wrote a decryption program; also like Johansen, Sklyarov probably did not expect to become a symbol of the information rights movement by doing so. Sklyarov, a Russian citizen living in Russia and working for a Russian company, ElcomSoft, wrote a program called Advanced E-Book Processor. E-books, like DVDs, are often encrypted to protect their content from unauthorized copying. Advanced E-Book Processor made it possible to decrypt e-books protected by encryption used by Adobe Systems, Inc. for its Adobe e-Book Reader. Like Johansen's distribution of DeCSS, this might be characterized as resistance to expanded controls on copyrighted content. Unlike Johansen, however, Sklyarov and ElcomSoft had a financial motive: They sold the Advanced E-Book Processor, presumably with the knowledge that it would be used to circumvent copyright protection. However, this was apparently not illegal in Russia at the time.

In July 2001, Sklyarov came to the United States to deliver a presentation, "eBook Security—Theory and Practice," at DefCon, a hacker convention in Las Vegas. Acting on a complaint from Adobe, the FBI arrested Sklyarov (see, for example, Newman 2001).

Sklyarov's arrest was a public relations disaster for Adobe and a diplomatic embarrassment for the United States. Sklyarov had indeed written Advanced E-Book Processor, and Advanced E-Book Processor was illegal in the United States. However, Sklyarov had not written the program in the United States, nor had he sold or distributed it while he was in the United States. In Russia, at the time only recently emerged from communism, the press seized on the Sklyarov case to ridicule perceived U.S. hypocrisy on issues of free speech. In the United States and around the world, the information rights community instantly went into action. Within hours of the arrest the Free Dmitri Sklyarov campaign was distributing information, suggesting a boycott of Adobe, and arranging Sklyarov's defense.

Adobe backed down almost immediately. On July 23, a week after the arrest, Adobe issued a press release saying that Sklyarov should be released ("Adobe, in a Reversal" 2001). The U.S. government, however, was less flexible. Sklyarov remained in jail, first in Las Vegas, then in Oklahoma City, and finally in San Jose, until 6 August, when he was released on $50,000 bail. He was not allowed to return to Russia until 13 December, and then only on condition that he return the following year to testify in the case against his employer, ElcomSoft. Unlike Johansen, Sklyarov has not remained in the public eye. He announced his intention to seek "a quiet life from here on," and at last report was living in Russia with his family (Silicon.com 2003).

### Sources and Further Reading

"Adobe, in a Reversal, Says U.S. Should Free Russian Programmer." 2001. *Wall Street Journal,* July 24, B11.

"Charges Dropped Against Russian Programmer." 2001. *Wall Street Journal,* December 14, A12.

Chu, Jeff. 2002. "Enemy At The Gates? Jon Johansen's Trial for Hacking May Be a Key Battle in the Struggle between Industry and Innovation." *Time,* July 8, 46.

Newman, Matthew. 2001. "The Rules—So Many Countries, So Many Laws: The Internet May Not Have Borders; but the Legal System Certainly Does." *Wall Street Journal,* April 28, R8.

"Programmer Claims Microsoft's Technology For E-Book Is Defeatable." 2001. *Wall Street Journal,* August 30, B7.

"Russian Programmer In Copyright Case Is Released on Bail." 2001. *Wall Street Journal,* August 7, B11.

Samuelson, Pamela, and Suzanne Scotchmer. 2002. "The Law and Economics of Reverse Engineering," *Yale Law Journal* 111: 1575.

Silicon.com. 2003. *Top 50 Agenda Setters 2003.* http://www.siliconagendasetters .com/list29.html.

*United States v. Elcom Ltd.,* 203 F. Supp.2d 1111 (N.D. Cal. 2002).

"U.S. Agents Arrest Russian Programmer Over Allegations of Copyright Violation." 2001. *Wall Street Journal,* July 18, B4.

Vaidhyanathan, Siva. 2004. *The Anarchist in the Library: How the Clash Between Freedom and Control is Hacking the Real World and Crashing the System.* New York: Basic Books.

# Jack Valenti (1921– )

While modern intellectual property disputes have made celebrities of perceived rebels like Jon Lech Johansen and Dmitri Sklyarov, the content industry is not without colorful, mediagenic personalities of its own. One of the most colorful and most durable is Jack Valenti, the octogenarian former president of the Motion Picture Association of America (MPAA).

A child prodigy, Valenti graduated from high school at fifteen. In World War II, he served with the U.S. Army Air Corps as a bomber pilot and flew 51 combat missions over Italy. After the war he received an M.B.A. from Harvard and became a political consultant. He can be seen in the famous picture of Lyndon B. Johnson being sworn in as president on Air Force One after the assassination of John F. Kennedy. Immediately afterward, he was appointed a special assistant to the president; he worked with the Johnson White House until 1966, when he resigned to become the president of the MPAA. During the next thirty-eight years Valenti redefined the MPAA and its role in copyright enforcement and the film industry. His first target was the MPAA's censorship of the movie industry: At the time, the MPAA's Motion Picture Production Code (also known as the Hays Code, after the MPAA's first president) explicitly forbade or restricted a wide variety of depictions, from interracial dating and marriage to the portrayal of a minister as a comic character or villain. Valenti created the now-familiar MPAA rating system, which classifies movies according to the age of the audience for which they are deemed appropriate.

The 1970s brought the Sony Betamax VCR into American households, and Valenti became notorious for his colorfully worded attacks on the technology. He told a Congressional panel that "the VCR is to the American film producer and the American public as the Boston strangler is to the woman home alone" (Greenhouse 2004). Later he declared that twin-drive VCRs were "the latest piece of evil magic doing the devil's work . . . It's like being able to market an ignition key that would start any car in America" ("Hollywood Nightmares" 1985). The VCR, Valenti claimed, provided a test of whether "copyright is real or whether it is mush . . . the future of creative entertainment of the American family is what's at stake here" (Stengel 1984). Another problem, Valenti pointed out, was the threat to TV networks' advertising revenue: With a VCR, viewers could "assassinate" commercials (Stengel 1984).

The movie industry's first battle against the VCR, however, ended in defeat. In 1984 the U.S. Supreme Court held that recording television programs for time-shifting purposes was a protected fair use (see Chapter 1). Improvements in copying technology led to more court battles, but Valenti was more directly involved with lobbying and was instrumental in bringing about some of the major revisions of U.S. copyright law in the 1990s. The Digital Millennium Copyright Act of 1998, with its anticircumvention and digital rights managements provisions and its requirement that anti–copying enabling technology be included in VCRs sold in the United States, went a long way toward solving the VCR problem and even the problem of more sophisticated copying technologies. The Sonny Bono Copyright Term Extension Act of the same year extended copyright terms by twenty years, providing movie studios with a continued income stream for its older properties, perhaps measured in the billions of dollars. In arguing for the latter statute, Representative Mary Bono proposed that at some point Congress might want to consider "Jack Valenti's proposal for [the copyright] term to last forever less one day" (Statement of Representative Mary Bono 1998).

Online file sharing threatened (and continues to threaten) the movie industry, although perhaps to a lesser degree than it threatened the music industry. Anxious to avoid making enemies of its customers, as the music industry had, Valenti handled file sharing cautiously, saying "The movie studios are trying to prevent themselves from becoming the next music industry" (Greenhouse 2004). In confronting online rebroadcaster iCrave TV, however, he was characteristically blunt, calling iCrave's service "one of the largest and most brazen thefts of intellectual property ever committed in the U.S." (Borland 2000).

Valenti retired as MPAA president in 2004, at the age of eighty-two. Since then he has continued to be an active voice in the ongoing debate over mass media and copyright.

### Sources and Further Reading

Bansal, Monisha. 2006. "Parents in 'Complete Control' of TV, Says Jack Valenti." CNS News, May 11. http://www.cnsnews.com/ViewCulture.asp?Page=/Culture/archive/200605/CUL20060511a.html.

Borland, John. iCraveTV.com exec discusses his start-up's short life. C/Net News.com, Feb. 29, 2000, http://news.com.com/2100-1033-237450.html.

Digital Millennium Copyright Act, 17 U.S.C. §§ 1201–1205.

Greenhouse, Linda. 2004. "Justices Agree To Hear Case On File Sharing." *NY Times*, December 11, 5.

Hamilton, Anita. 2004. "Failed Merger: TV On The Net." *NY Times*, December 11, 1.

"Hollywood Nightmares." 1985. *Time*, February 11, 73.

Landro, Laura. 1984. "The Scene-Stealer: Hollywood's Lobbyist, Jack Valenti, Upstages Industry's Opponents." *Wall Street Journal*, October 2.

*Sony Corp. of America v. Universal City Studios, Inc.*, 464 U.S. 417 (1984).

Statement of Representative Mary Bono Regarding the Sonny Bono Copyright Term Extension Act. 1998. October 7. 144 Cong. Rec. H9946-01, H9952.

Stengel, Richard. 1984. "Tape It to the Max; The Supreme Court Says a VCR Switch in Time Is Not a Crime." *Time*, January 30, 67.

Valenti, Jack. 1982. "Protecting the Artist." *Time*, January 4, 6.

Valenti, Jack. 1981. "Renew America." *Time*, March 16, 6.

# Terri Welles (1956– )

While in recent years copyright battles have captured the head-lines (when intellectual property disputes make the news at all, that is), the Internet has brought about a somewhat quieter crisis in trademark law. Questions that have been addressed in traditional media often have to be addressed anew online, and the Internet also raises new questions.

In May and December 1980, United Airlines flight attendant Terri Welles posed for *Playboy* magazine. In 1981 the magazine proclaimed her its "Playmate of the Year," a term that has commercial value and is claimed as a trademark by Playboy Enterprises, Inc. Sixteen years later, in 1997, Welles set up a commercial website, terriwelles.com, offering pictures of herself and other content to subscribers. On the site she used Playboy's trademarks in three ways: She used the term "Playmate of the Year" in banner advertisements and in the headline of the Web page, she used the repeated term "PMOY 1981" as a wallpaper design, and she used the terms "playboy" and "playmate" in metatags. The first two uses were similar to uses that might have occurred in the pre-Internet era and might still occur in print media. The third use was specific to the Internet: The metatags were invisible to persons viewing the site, but were visible to search engines. Welles used them, as many Web designers did, to direct search-engine traffic to her site. Thus, persons searching for "playboy" or "playmate" would be directed to her site (as well as to others using those terms, including Playboy Enterprises' own site).

The Court of Appeals for the Ninth Circuit held that the use of the terms in metatags and the use of "Playmate of the Year" in banner ads and the headline were permissible (see Chapter 2). The "PMOY 1981" wallpaper design was not, however, and Welles subsequently removed it from her site. Her blog entry for 11 February 2002 celebrates the Ninth Circuit's decision and points out that Playboy Enterprises would have fared better had it paid her not to use the name rather than suing her:

> It's finally OVER!
> *** Playboy could have saved millions on lawyers, (giving me a mere pittance of what they actually spent to LOSE the . . . case), saved face and looked as if they won. The other Playmates would have had nowhere to go but to the Playboy site to sell their goods. Now, the Playmates can actually STATE they are PLAYMATES!!!!! And on their own web sites!!!! (Welles 2002)

In other words, Welles's victory affirmed the right of other people—models, contest winners, professional athletes, actors—to use the trademark of the event or enterprise for which they are known in order to identify themselves. Welles's blog and the Ninth Circuit's opinion both refer to former Chicago Bulls player Michael Jordan, pointing out that there is no practical way for him to describe his team affiliation without using the (trade-marked) name of the team.

Welles's blog was last updated in late 2003; the last entries are concerned with the unusual California gubernatorial election of that year, in which 135 candidates for governor appeared on the ballot. Welles expresses support for the Republican Party, Arnold Schwarzenegger, U.S. troops, and the University of Southern California Trojans, among others.

### Sources and Further Reading

*Playboy Enterprises, Inc. v. Welles*, 279 F.3d 796 (9th Cir. 2002).

Welles, Terri. *My Autobiography—and a Few Other Facts . . .* http://www.terriwelles.com/free/faq.html.

Welles, Terri. *TerriTalk* (blog). http://www.terriwelles.com/free/talk.html.

# Samuel Winslow (fl. 1641) and Joseph Jenks (1602–1683)

The first patent granted to an inventor in the British North American colonies was granted in 1641 by the Massachusetts Bay Colony to Samuel Winslow. Little is known about Winslow other than the information contained in his patent, granted in accordance with Massachusetts' first patent law, which provided that "there shall be no monopolies granted or allowed among us, but of such new inventions as are profitable to the country, and that for a short time" (Brown 1994, 88). Winslow's patent was for the manufacture of salt "by a means and way which hitherto hath not been discovered[.]" The patent granted "to him and his associates, for the space of ten years," the exclusive right to use the salt-making process, although the monopoly did not extend to other means of making salt (Brown 1994, 88; spelling modernized).

Five years later, in 1646, Massachusetts granted Joseph Jenks a patent "for the making of engines for mills, to go with water, for the more speedy dispatch of work than formerly, and mills for the making of scythes and other edged tools, with a new invented sawmill" (Brown 1994, 88; spelling modernized). By the end of the seventeenth century the British colonies in Virginia and South

Carolina had also granted patents to inventors. New York's first patent was granted somewhat later, in 1712.

Jenks was a prominent figure in early Massachusetts history. He had come to Massachusetts from England in 1643 to set up British colonies' first ironworks. In 1652 he created the dies used to make the first money minted in the British colonies, and in 1654 he built the colonies' first fire engine. While these innovations resulted in no patents, in 1655 he obtained a second patent, this time for a new type of scythe blade (Brown 1994, 89).

### Sources and Further Reading

Brown, Travis. 1994. *Historical First Patents: The First United States Patents for Many Everyday Things.* Metuchen, NJ: The Scarecrow Press.

Dahn, Frank W. 1921. "Colonial Patents in the United States of America." *Journal of the Patent Office Society* 3: 342.

Dinwoodie, Graeme B., William O. Hennessey, and Shira Perlmutter. 2002. *International and Comparative Patent Law.* Newark, NJ: LexisNexis Matthew Bender.

# 6

# Data and Documents

This chapter presents a selection of documents on U.S. and international intellectual property law. Space does not permit the inclusion of all of the relevant documents, or even all of the important ones—such a collection of documents would be considerably longer than this book. Instead, this chapter presents selected documents from the three traditional areas of intellectual property (omitted sections are indicated by three asterisks [***]). For each, crucial U.S. statutes are included, along with relevant sections from one treaty (the World Trade Organization's [WTO] Agreement on Trade-Related Aspects of Intellectual Property Rights [TRIPs]). Each of the three sections—copyright, trademark, and patent—also includes one reported court opinion.

All of these documents and other statutes, cases, regulations, treaties, international organization documents, and other materials produced by governmental and intergovernmental organizations can be found online. Chapter 8 provides an expanded list of source materials, and Chapter 7 includes a list of organizations from which many of these documents are available. Most of these materials can also be located using Google or another search engine. Materials created by governments and international organizations are almost always available for free. Academic articles, reports from nongovernmental organizations, and some books are also available online for free. Some materials may be available online only from fee-based proprietary databases, such as those listed at the end of Chapter 8; however, these may also be available in hard copy in libraries.

# Copyright

*The Copyright Act of 1976, as amended, is the current U.S. copyright law; it is contained in Title 17 of the United States Code. Section 102 of the law sets the scope of copyright protection by defining the things that can and cannot be copyrighted. A careful examination will show that Section 102 also sets forth (as much by omission as by specification) the process (or lack thereof) by which copyright protection may be obtained: No formalities are required. The act of fixing an original work of authorship in a tangible medium of expression is sufficient.*

## Copyright Act of 1976, 17 U.S.C. § 102. Subject matter of copyright: In general

(a) Copyright protection subsists, in accordance with this title, in original works of authorship fixed in any tangible medium of expression, now known or later developed, from which they can be perceived, reproduced, or otherwise communicated, either directly or with the aid of a machine or device. Works of authorship include the following categories:

(1) literary works;
(2) musical works, including any accompanying words;
(3) dramatic works, including any accompanying music;
(4) pantomimes and choreographic works;
(5) pictorial, graphic, and sculptural works;
(6) motion pictures and other audiovisual works;
(7) sound recordings; and
(8) architectural works.

(b) In no case does copyright protection for an original work of authorship extend to any idea, procedure, process, system, method of operation, concept, principle, or discovery, regardless of the form in which it is described, explained, illustrated, or embodied in such work.

## Copyright Act of 1976, 17 U.S.C. § 106. Exclusive rights in copyrighted works

*While Section 102 describes what may be protected by copyright, it does not explain the extent or nature of that protection. Section 106 fills this gap by according six rights to the copyright holder. (Moral rights, which are not widely recognized in U.S. law, are the subject of a separate statute, Section 106A).*

Subject to sections 107 through 122, the owner of copyright under this title has the exclusive rights to do and to authorize any of the following:

(1) to reproduce the copyrighted work in copies or phonorecords;
(2) to prepare derivative works based upon the copyrighted work;
(3) to distribute copies or phonorecords of the copyrighted work to the public by sale or other transfer of ownership, or by rental, lease, or lending;
(4) in the case of literary, musical, dramatic, and choreographic works, pantomimes, and motion pictures and other audiovisual works, to perform the copyrighted work publicly;
(5) in the case of literary, musical, dramatic, and choreographic works, pantomimes, and pictorial, graphic, or sculptural works, including the individual images of a motion picture or other audiovisual work, to display the copyrighted work publicly; and
(6) in the case of sound recordings, to perform the copyrighted work publicly by means of a digital audio transmission.

# Copyright Act of 1976, 17 U.S.C. § 107. Limitations on exclusive rights: Fair use

*The rights granted to the copyright holder by Section 106 are not absolute; they are subject to several exceptions. Perhaps the most important and most controversial of these exceptions is the right of fair use.*

Notwithstanding the provisions of sections 106 and 106A, the fair use of a copyrighted work, including such use by reproduction in copies or phonorecords or by any other means specified by that section, for purposes such as criticism, comment, news reporting, teaching (including multiple copies for classroom use), scholarship, or research, is not an infringement of copyright. In determining whether the use made of a work in any particular case is a fair use the factors to be considered shall include—

(1) the purpose and character of the use, including whether such use is of a commercial nature or is for nonprofit educational purposes;
(2) the nature of the copyrighted work;
(3) the amount and substantiality of the portion used in relation to the copyrighted work as a whole; and
(4) the effect of the use upon the potential market for or value of the copyrighted work.

The fact that a work is unpublished shall not itself bar a finding of fair use if such finding is made upon consideration of all the above factors.

# Digital Millennium Copyright Act, 17 U.S.C. § 1201. Circumvention of copyright protection systems

*The advent of digital recording, and in particular the advent of digitally recorded movies, posed a threat to the content industry: Any number of copies, and copies of copies, of a work could be made, with no diminution in quality. To prevent such copying, content owners encrypted their content, then licensed decryption keys to equipment makers. The problem with such an approach was that eventually someone would figure out how to break the encryption. The content industry succeeded in convincing the U.S. Congress to back up technological measures such as encryption with a law prohibiting anyone from breaking the encryption. However, this anticircumvention provision proved enormously unpopular with consumers; it may have done more than anything else to galvanize organized opposition to the content industry's attempts to expand the scope of intellectual property protection.*

*Take a look at Section 1201(k). What all of this verbiage is aiming at is requiring the use of Macrovision's copy-protection system for analog video recorders (see Chapter 2). Could you think of a less verbose way to have drafted the law?*

(a) Violations regarding circumvention of technological measures.—
   (1)
      (A) No person shall circumvent a technological measure that effectively controls access to a work protected under this title. The prohibition contained in the preceding sentence shall take effect at the end of the 2-year period beginning on the date of the enactment of this chapter.
      (B) The prohibition contained in subparagraph (A) shall not apply to persons who are users of a copyrighted work which is in a particular class of works, if such persons are, or are likely to be in the succeeding 3-year period, adversely affected by virtue of such prohibition in their ability to make noninfringing uses of that particular class of works under this title, as determined under subparagraph (C).
      (C) During the 2-year period described in subparagraph (A), and during each succeeding 3-year period, the Librarian of

Congress, upon the recommendation of the Register of Copyrights, who shall consult with the Assistant Secretary for Communications and Information of the Department of Commerce and report and comment on his or her views in making such recommendation, shall make the determination in a rulemaking proceeding for purposes of subparagraph (B) of whether persons who are users of a copyrighted work are, or are likely to be in the succeeding 3-year period, adversely affected by the prohibition under subparagraph (A) in their ability to make noninfringing uses under this title of a particular class of copyrighted works. In conducting such rulemaking, the Librarian shall examine—

> (i) the availability for use of copyrighted works;
> (ii) the availability for use of works for nonprofit archival, preservation, and educational purposes;
> (iii) the impact that the prohibition on the circumvention of technological measures applied to copyrighted works has on criticism, comment, news reporting, teaching, scholarship, or research;
> (iv) the effect of circumvention of technological measures on the market for or value of copyrighted works; and
> (v) such other factors as the Librarian considers appropriate.

(D) The Librarian shall publish any class of copyrighted works for which the Librarian has determined, pursuant to the rulemaking conducted under subparagraph (C), that noninfringing uses by persons who are users of a copyrighted work are, or are likely to be, adversely affected, and the prohibition contained in subparagraph (A) shall not apply to such users with respect to such class of works for the ensuing 3-year period.

(E) Neither the exception under subparagraph (B) from the applicability of the prohibition contained in subparagraph (A), nor any determination made in a rulemaking conducted under subparagraph (C), may be used as a defense in any action to enforce any provision of this title other than this paragraph.

(2) No person shall manufacture, import, offer to the public, provide, or otherwise traffic in any technology, product, service, device, component, or part thereof, that—

(A) is primarily designed or produced for the purpose of circumventing a technological measure that effectively controls access to a work protected under this title;

(B) has only limited commercially significant purpose or use other than to circumvent a technological measure that effectively controls access to a work protected under this title; or

(C) is marketed by that person or another acting in concert with that person with that person's knowledge for use in circumventing a technological measure that effectively controls access to a work protected under this title.

(3) As used in this subsection—

(A) to "circumvent a technological measure" means to descramble a scrambled work, to decrypt an encrypted work, or otherwise to avoid, bypass, remove, deactivate, or impair a technological measure, without the authority of the copyright owner; and

(B) a technological measure "effectively controls access to a work" if the measure, in the ordinary course of its operation, requires the application of information, or a process or a treatment, with the authority of the copyright owner, to gain access to the work.

(b) Additional violations. —

(1) No person shall manufacture, import, offer to the public, provide, or otherwise traffic in any technology, product, service, device, component, or part thereof, that—

(A) is primarily designed or produced for the purpose of circumventing protection afforded by a technological measure that effectively protects a right of a copyright owner under this title in a work or a portion thereof;

(B) has only limited commercially significant purpose or use other than to circumvent protection afforded by a technological measure that effectively protects a right of a copyright owner under this title in a work or a portion thereof; or

(C) is marketed by that person or another acting in concert with that person with that person's knowledge for use in circumventing protection afforded by a technological measure that effectively protects a right of a copyright owner under this title in a work or a portion thereof.

(2) As used in this subsection—

(A) to "circumvent protection afforded by a technological measure" means avoiding, bypassing, removing, deactivating, or otherwise impairing a technological measure; and

(B) a technological measure "effectively protects a right of a copyright owner under this title" if the measure, in the ordinary course of its operation, prevents, restricts, or otherwise limits the exercise of a right of a copyright owner under this title.

(c) Other rights, etc., not affected. —
(1) Nothing in this section shall affect rights, remedies, limitations, or defenses to copyright infringement, including fair use, under this title.
(2) Nothing in this section shall enlarge or diminish vicarious or contributory liability for copyright infringement in connection with any technology, product, service, device, component, or part thereof.
(3) Nothing in this section shall require that the design of, or design and selection of parts and components for, a consumer electronics, telecommunications, or computing product provide for a response to any particular technological measure, so long as such part or component, or the product in which such part or component is integrated, does not otherwise fall within the prohibitions of subsection (a)(2) or (b)(1).
(4) Nothing in this section shall enlarge or diminish any rights of free speech or the press for activities using consumer electronics, telecommunications, or computing products.

(d) Exemption for nonprofit libraries, archives, and educational institutions. [omitted]
***

(e) Law enforcement, intelligence, and other government activities. [omitted]
***

(f) Reverse engineering. [omitted]
***

(g) Encryption research. [omitted]
***

(h) Exceptions regarding minors. [omitted]
***

(i) Protection of personally identifying information. [omitted]
***

(j) Security testing. [omitted]
***

(k) Certain analog devices and certain technological measures. —
(1) Certain analog devices. —

(A) Effective 18 months after the date of the enactment of this chapter, no person shall manufacture, import, offer to the public, provide or otherwise traffic in any—
    (i) VHS format analog video cassette recorder unless such recorder conforms to the automatic gain control copy control technology;
    (ii) 8mm format analog video cassette camcorder unless such camcorder conforms to the automatic gain control technology;
    (iii) Beta format analog video cassette recorder, unless such recorder conforms to the automatic gain control copy control technology, except that this requirement shall not apply until there are 1,000 Beta format analog video cassette recorders sold in the United States in any one calendar year after the date of the enactment of this chapter;
    (iv) 8mm format analog video cassette recorder that is not an analog video cassette camcorder, unless such recorder conforms to the automatic gain control copy control technology, except that this requirement shall not apply until there are 20,000 such recorders sold in the United States in any one calendar year after the date of the enactment of this chapter; or
    (v) analog video cassette recorder that records using an NTSC format video input and that is not otherwise covered under clauses (i) through (iv), unless such device conforms to the automatic gain control copy control technology.

(B) Effective on the date of the enactment of this chapter, no person shall manufacture, import, offer to the public, provide or otherwise traffic in—
    (i) any VHS format analog video cassette recorder or any 8mm format analog video cassette recorder if the design of the model of such recorder has been modified after such date of enactment so that a model of recorder that previously conformed to the automatic gain control copy control technology no longer conforms to such technology; or
    (ii) any VHS format analog video cassette recorder, or any 8mm format analog video cassette recorder that is not an 8mm analog video cassette camcorder, if the design of the model of such recorder has been modified after such date of enactment so that a model of recorder that previously

conformed to the four-line colorstripe copy control technology no longer conforms to such technology. Manufacturers that have not previously manufactured or sold a VHS format analog video cassette recorder, or an 8mm format analog cassette recorder, shall be required to conform to the four-line colorstripe copy control technology in the initial model of any such recorder manufactured after the date of the enactment of this chapter, and thereafter to continue conforming to the four-line colorstripe copy control technology. For purposes of this subparagraph, an analog video cassette recorder "conforms to" the four-line colorstripe copy control technology if it records a signal that, when played back by the playback function of that recorder in the normal viewing mode, exhibits, on a reference display device, a display containing distracting visible lines through portions of the viewable picture.

(2) Certain encoding restrictions.—No person shall apply the automatic gain control copy control technology or colorstripe copy control technology to prevent or limit consumer copying except such copying—

(A) of a single transmission, or specified group of transmissions, of live events or of audiovisual works for which a member of the public has exercised choice in selecting the transmissions, including the content of the transmissions or the time of receipt of such transmissions, or both, and as to which such member is charged a separate fee for each such transmission or specified group of transmissions;

(B) from a copy of a transmission of a live event or an audiovisual work if such transmission is provided by a channel or service where payment is made by a member of the public for such channel or service in the form of a subscription fee that entitles the member of the public to receive all of the programming contained in such channel or service;

(C) from a physical medium containing one or more prerecorded audiovisual works; or

(D) from a copy of a transmission described in subparagraph (A) or from a copy made from a physical medium described in subparagraph (C).

In the event that a transmission meets both the conditions set forth in subparagraph (A) and those set forth in subparagraph (B), the transmission shall be treated as a transmission described in subparagraph (A).

(3) Inapplicability. —This subsection shall not—
(A) require any analog video cassette camcorder to conform to the automatic gain control copy control technology with respect to any video signal received through a camera lens;
(B) apply to the manufacture, importation, offer for sale, provision of, or other trafficking in, any professional analog video cassette recorder; or
(C) apply to the offer for sale or provision of, or other trafficking in, any previously owned analog video cassette recorder, if such recorder was legally manufactured and sold when new and not subsequently modified in violation of paragraph (1)(B).

(4) Definitions. —For purposes of this subsection:
(A) An "analog video cassette recorder" means a device that records, or a device that includes a function that records, on electromagnetic tape in an analog format the electronic impulses produced by the video and audio portions of a television program, motion picture, or other form of audiovisual work.
(B) An "analog video cassette camcorder" means an analog video cassette recorder that contains a recording function that operates through a camera lens and through a video input that may be connected with a television or other video playback device.
(C) An analog video cassette recorder "conforms" to the automatic gain control copy control technology if it—
(i) detects one or more of the elements of such technology and does not record the motion picture or transmission protected by such technology; or
(ii) records a signal that, when played back, exhibits a meaningfully distorted or degraded display.
(D) The term "professional analog video cassette recorder" means an analog video cassette recorder that is designed, manufactured, marketed, and intended for use by a person who regularly employs such a device for a lawful business or industrial use, including making, performing, displaying, distributing, or transmitting copies of motion pictures on a commercial scale.
(E) The terms "VHS format", "8mm format", "Beta format", "automatic gain control copy control technology", "colorstripe copy control technology", "four-line version of the colorstripe copy control technology", and "NTSC" have the meanings that are commonly understood in the consumer electronics and motion picture industries as of the date of the enactment of this chapter.

(5) Violations. —Any violation of paragraph (1) of this subsection shall be treated as a violation of subsection (b)(1) of this section. Any violation of paragraph (2) of this subsection shall be deemed an "act of circumvention" for the purposes of section 1203(c)(3)(A) of this chapter.

# TRIPs: Agreement on Trade-Related Aspects of Intellectual Property Rights

*TRIPs is the WTO's intellectual property agreement. Section 1 of TRIPs addresses copyright. It is not the only copyright treaty, nor is it even the most important one (that would be the Berne Convention). It is, however, the only major multilateral treaty to address every aspect of intellectual property law. Also, because it is part of the WTO agreement, it is more enforceable than some other treaties: Disputes arising under TRIPs can be brought before the WTO's dispute resolution body.*

# Part II: Standards Concerning the Availability, Scope and Use of Intellectual Property Rights

## Section 1: Copyright and Related Rights

### Article 9: Relation to the Berne Convention

1. Members shall comply with Articles 1 through 21 of the Berne Convention (1971) and the Appendix thereto. However, Members shall not have rights or obligations under this Agreement in respect of the rights conferred under Article 6*bis* of that Convention or of the rights derived therefrom.
2. Copyright protection shall extend to expressions and not to ideas, procedures, methods of operation or mathematical concepts as such.

### Article 10: Computer Programs and Compilations of Data

1. Computer programs, whether in source or object code, shall be protected as literary works under the Berne Convention (1971).
2. Compilations of data or other material, whether in machine readable or other form, which by reason of the selection or arrangement of their contents constitute intellectual creations shall be protected as such. Such protection, which shall not extend to the data or material itself, shall be without prejudice to any copyright subsisting in the data or material itself.

## Article 11: Rental Rights

In respect of at least computer programs and cinematographic works, a Member shall provide authors and their successors in title the right to authorize or to prohibit the commercial rental to the public of originals or copies of their copyright works. A Member shall be excepted from this obligation in respect of cinematographic works unless such rental has led to widespread copying of such works which is materially impairing the exclusive right of reproduction conferred in that Member on authors and their successors in title. In respect of computer programs, this obligation does not apply to rentals where the program itself is not the essential object of the rental.

## Article 12: Term of Protection

Whenever the term of protection of a work, other than a photographic work or a work of applied art, is calculated on a basis other than the life of a natural person, such term shall be no less than 50 years from the end of the calendar year of authorized publication, or, failing such authorized publication within 50 years from the making of the work, 50 years from the end of the calendar year of making.

## Article 13: Limitations and Exceptions

Members shall confine limitations or exceptions to exclusive rights to certain special cases which do not conflict with a normal exploitation of the work and do not unreasonably prejudice the legitimate interests of the right holder.

## Article 14: Protection of Performers, Producers of Phonograms (Sound Recordings) and Broadcasting Organizations [omitted]
\*\*\*

# *Metro-Goldwyn-Mayer Studios, Inc. v. Grokster, Ltd.,* 125 S.Ct. 2764 (2005)

*The recent case of* MGM v. Grokster *spelled the end of a winning streak for P2P (peer-to-peer) file-sharing networks and an expansion of the reach of third-party liability for copyright infringement. The defendants in* Grokster *were P2P networks, some of whose users had committed copyright infringement by sharing copyrighted files over the networks. Two courts—first a trial court and then the federal Ninth Circuit Court of Appeals—had found the defendants not liable for the infringements by their users. The U.S. Supreme Court reversed the Ninth Circuit's decision, setting a precedent that is binding on all federal trial and appellate courts in the United States. Exactly what the precedent means, however, is a bit confusing. While all of the justices seemed to agree that the defendants in this particular case were liable, they were less able to agree on why. Three justices wrote opinions, each representing themselves and two colleagues; none of the opinions represented a majority of the Court. The text of Justice Souter's opinion below has been slightly edited, removing long citations and other material that interferes with readability; some footnotes have been retained. The other opinions have been omitted.*

Justice Souter delivered the opinion of the Court.

The question is under what circumstances the distributor of a product capable of both lawful and unlawful use is liable for acts of copyright infringement by third parties using the product. We hold that one who distributes a device with the object of promoting its use to infringe copyright, as shown by clear expression or other affirmative steps taken to foster infringement, is liable for the resulting acts of infringement by third parties.

# I
## A

Respondents, Grokster, Ltd., and StreamCast Networks, Inc., defendants in the trial court, distribute free software products that allow computer users to share electronic files through peer-to-peer networks, so called because users' computers communicate directly with each other, not through central servers. The advantage of peer-to-peer networks over information networks of other types shows up in their substantial and growing popularity. Because they need no central computer server to mediate the exchange of information or files among users, the high-bandwidth communications capacity for a server may be dispensed with, and the need for costly server storage space is eliminated. Since copies of a file (particularly a popular one) are available on many users' computers, file requests and retrievals may be faster than on other types of networks, and since file exchanges do not travel through a server, communications can take place between any computers that remain connected to the network without risk that a glitch in the server will disable the network in its entirety. Given these benefits in security, cost, and efficiency, peer-to-peer networks are employed to store and distribute electronic files by universities, government agencies, corporations, and libraries, among others.[1]

Other users of peer-to-peer networks include individual recipients of Grokster's and StreamCast's software, and although the networks that they enjoy through using the software can be used to share any type of digital file, they have prominently employed those networks in sharing copyrighted music and video files without authorization. A group of copyright holders (MGM for short, but including motion picture studios, recording companies, songwriters, and music publishers) sued Grokster and StreamCast for their users' copyright infringements, alleging that they knowingly and intentionally distributed their software to enable users to reproduce and distribute the copyrighted works in violation of the Copyright Act, 17 U.S.C. § 101 *et seq.* (2000 ed. and Supp. II).[2] MGM sought damages and an injunction.

Discovery during the litigation revealed the way the software worked, the business aims of each defendant company, and the predilections of the users. Grokster's eponymous software employs what is known as FastTrack technology, a protocol developed by others and licensed to Grokster. StreamCast distributes a very similar product except that its software, called Morpheus, relies on what is known as Gnutella technology.[3] A user who downloads and installs either software possesses the protocol to send requests for files directly to the computers of others using software compatible with FastTrack or Gnutella. On the FastTrack network opened by the Grokster software, the user's request goes to a computer given an indexing capacity by the software and designated a supernode, or to some other computer with comparable power and capacity to collect temporary indexes of the files available on the computers of users connected to it. The supernode (or indexing computer) searches its own index and may communicate the search request to other supernodes. If the file is found, the supernode discloses its location to the computer requesting it, and the requesting user can download the file directly from the computer located. The copied file is placed in a designated sharing folder on the requesting user's computer, where it is available for other users to download in turn, along with any other file in that folder.

In the Gnutella network made available by Morpheus, the process is mostly the same, except that in some versions of the Gnutella protocol there are no supernodes. In these versions, peer computers using the protocol communicate directly with each other. When a user enters a search request into the Morpheus software, it sends the request to computers connected with it, which in turn pass the request along to other connected peers. The search results are communicated to the requesting computer, and the user can download desired files directly from peers' computers. As this description indicates, Grokster and StreamCast use no servers to intercept the content of the search requests or to mediate the file transfers conducted by users of the software, there being no central point through which the substance of the communications passes in either direction.[4]

Although Grokster and StreamCast do not therefore know when particular files are copied, a few searches using their software would show what is available on the networks the software reaches. MGM commissioned a statistician to conduct a systematic search, and his study showed that nearly 90% of the files available for download on the FastTrack system were copyrighted works.[5] Grokster and StreamCast dispute this figure, raising methodological problems and arguing that free copying even of copyrighted works may be authorized by the rightholders. They also argue that potential noninfringing uses of their software are significant in kind, even if infrequent in practice. Some musical performers, for example, have gained new audiences by distributing their copyrighted works for free across peer-to-peer networks, and some distributors of unprotected content have used peer-to-peer networks to disseminate files, Shakespeare being an example. Indeed, StreamCast has given Morpheus users the opportunity to download the briefs in this very case, though their popularity has not been quantified.

As for quantification, the parties' anecdotal and statistical evidence entered thus far to show the content available on the FastTrack and Gnutella networks does not say much about which files are actually downloaded by users, and no one can say how often the software is used to obtain copies of unprotected material. But MGM's evidence gives reason to think that the vast majority of users' downloads are acts of infringement, and because well over 100 million copies of the software in question are known to have been downloaded, and billions of files are shared across the FastTrack and Gnutella networks each month, the probable scope of copyright infringement is staggering.

Grokster and StreamCast concede the infringement in most downloads, ***, and it is uncontested that they are aware that users employ their software primarily to download copyrighted files, even if the decentralized FastTrack and Gnutella networks fail to reveal which files are being copied, and when. From time to time, moreover, the companies have learned about their users' infringement directly, as from users who have sent e-mail to each company with questions about playing copyrighted movies they had downloaded, to whom the companies have responded with guidance.[6] ***And MGM notified the companies of 8 million copyrighted files that could be obtained using their software.

Grokster and StreamCast are not, however, merely passive recipients of information about infringing use. The record is replete with evidence that from the moment Grokster and StreamCast began to distribute their free software, each one clearly voiced the objective that recipients use it to download copyrighted works, and each took active steps to encourage infringement.

After the notorious file-sharing service, Napster, was sued by copyright holders for facilitation of copyright infringement . . ., StreamCast gave away a software program of a kind known as OpenNap, designed as compatible with the Napster program and open to Napster users for downloading files from other Napster and OpenNap users' computers. Evidence indicates that "[i]t was always [StreamCast's] intent to use [its OpenNap network] to be able to capture email addresses of [its] initial target market so that [it] could promote [its] StreamCast Morpheus interface to them," . . .; indeed, the OpenNap program was engineered "'to leverage Napster's 50 million user base . . .'"

StreamCast monitored both the number of users downloading its OpenNap program and the number of music files they downloaded . . . It also used the resulting OpenNap network to distribute copies of the Morpheus software and to encourage users to adopt it . . . Internal company documents indicate that StreamCast hoped to attract large numbers of former Napster users if that company was shut down by court order or otherwise, and that StreamCast planned to be the next Napster . . . A kit developed by StreamCast to be delivered to advertisers, for example, contained press articles about StreamCast's potential to capture former Napster users . . ., and it introduced itself to some potential advertisers as a company "which is similar to what Napster was. . . ." It broadcast banner advertisements to users of other Napster-compatible software, urging them to adopt its OpenNap. . . . An internal e-mail from a company executive stated: "'We have put this network in place so that when Napster pulls the plug on their free service . . . or if the Court orders them shut down prior to that . . . we will be positioned to capture the flood of their 32 million users that will be actively looking for an alternative. . . .'"

Thus, StreamCast developed promotional materials to market its service as the best Napster alternative. One proposed advertisement read: "Napster Inc. has announced that it will soon begin charging you a fee. That's if the courts don't order it shut down first. What will you do to get around it?" Another proposed ad touted StreamCast's software as the "# 1 alternative to Napster" and asked "[w]hen the lights went off at Napster . . . where did the users go?" . . . (ellipsis in original).[7] StreamCast even planned to flaunt the illegal uses of its software; when it launched the OpenNap network, the chief technology officer of the company averred that "[t]he goal is to get in trouble with the law and get sued. It's the best way to get in the new[s]."

The evidence that Grokster sought to capture the market of former Napster users is sparser but revealing, for Grokster launched its own OpenNap system called Swaptor and inserted digital codes into its website so that computer users using Web search engines to look for "Napster" or "[f]ree filesharing" would be directed to the Grokster website, where they could download the Grokster software. And Grokster's name is an apparent derivative of Napster.

StreamCast's executives monitored the number of songs by certain commercial artists available on their networks, and an internal communication indicates they aimed to have a larger number of copyrighted songs available on their networks than other file-sharing networks . . . The point, of course, would be to attract users of a mind to infringe, just as it would be with their promotional materials developed showing copyrighted songs as examples of the kinds of files available through Morpheus . . . Morpheus in fact allowed users to search specifically for "Top 40" songs . . ., which were inevitably copyrighted. Similarly, Grokster sent users a newsletter promoting its ability to provide particular, popular copyrighted materials . . .

In addition to this evidence of express promotion, marketing, and intent to promote further, the business models employed by Grokster and StreamCast confirm that their principal object was use of their software to download copyrighted works. Grokster and StreamCast receive no revenue from users, who obtain the software itself for nothing. Instead, both companies generate income by selling advertising space, and they stream the advertising to Grokster and Morpheus users while they are employing the programs. As the number of users of each program increases, advertising opportunities become worth more. . . . While there is doubtless some demand for free Shakespeare, the evidence shows that substantive volume is a function of free access to copyrighted work. Users seeking Top 40 songs, for example, or the latest release by Modest Mouse, are certain to be far more numerous than those seeking a free Decameron, and Grokster and StreamCast translated that demand into dollars.

Finally, there is no evidence that either company made an effort to filter copyrighted material from users' downloads or otherwise impede the sharing of copyrighted files. Although Grokster appears to have sent e-mails warning users about infringing content when it received threatening notice from the copyright holders, it never blocked anyone from continuing to use its software to share copyrighted files. . . . StreamCast not only rejected another company's offer of help to monitor infringement . . ., but blocked the Internet Protocol addresses of entities it believed were trying to engage in such monitoring on its networks. . . .

## B

After discovery, the parties on each side of the case cross-moved for summary judgment. The District Court limited its consideration to the asserted liability of Grokster and StreamCast for distributing the current versions of their software, leaving aside whether either was liable "for damages arising from past versions of their software, or from other past activities." 259 F.Supp.2d 1029, 1033 (C.D.Cal.2003). The District Court held that those who used the Grokster and Morpheus software to download copyrighted media files directly infringed MGM's copyrights, a conclusion not contested on appeal, but the court nonetheless granted summary judgment in favor of Grokster and StreamCast as to any liability arising from distribution of the then current versions of their software.

Distributing that software gave rise to no liability in the court's view, because its use did not provide the distributors with actual knowledge of specific acts of infringement.

\*\*\*

The Court of Appeals affirmed. 380 F.3d 1154 (C.A.9 2004). In the court's analysis, a defendant was liable as a contributory infringer when it had knowledge of direct infringement and materially contributed to the infringement. But the court read *Sony Corp. of America v. Universal City Studios, Inc.*, 464 U.S. 417, 104 S.Ct. 774, 78 L.Ed.2d 574 (1984), as holding that distribution of a commercial product capable of substantial noninfringing uses could not give rise to contributory liability for infringement unless the distributor had actual knowledge of specific instances of infringement and failed to act on that knowledge. The fact that the software was capable of substantial noninfringing uses in the Ninth Circuit's view meant that Grokster and StreamCast were not liable, because they had no such actual knowledge, owing to the decentralized architecture of their software. The court also held that Grokster and StreamCast did not materially contribute to their users' infringement because it was the users themselves who searched for, retrieved, and stored the infringing files, with no involvement by the defendants beyond providing the software in the first place.

The Ninth Circuit also considered whether Grokster and StreamCast could be liable under a theory of vicarious infringement. The court held against liability because the defendants did not monitor or control the use of the software, had no agreed-upon right or current ability to supervise its use, and had no independent duty to police infringement. \*\*\*

## II

## A

MGM and many of the *amici* fault the Court of Appeals's holding for upsetting a sound balance between the respective values of supporting creative pursuits through copyright protection and promoting innovation in new communication technologies by limiting the incidence of liability for copyright infringement. The more artistic protection is favored, the more technological innovation may be discouraged; the administration of copyright law is an exercise in managing the trade-off. \*\*\*

The tension between the two values is the subject of this case, with its claim that digital distribution of copyrighted material threatens copyright holders as never before, because every copy is identical to the original, copying is easy, and many people (especially the young) use file-sharing software to download copyrighted works. This very breadth of the software's use may well draw the public directly into the debate over copyright policy, Peters, Brace Memorial Lecture: Copyright Enters the Public Domain, 51 J. Copyright Soc. 701, 705-717 (2004) (address by Register of Copyrights), and the indications are that the ease of copying songs or movies using software like Grokster's and Napster's is fostering disdain for copyright protection, Wu, When Code Isn't Law, 89 Va. L.Rev. 679, 724-726 (2003). As the case has been presented to us, these fears are said to be offset by the different concern that imposing liability, not only on infringers but on distributors of software based on its potential for unlawful use, could limit further development of beneficial technologies.\*\*\*[8]

The argument for imposing indirect liability in this case is, however, a powerful one, given the number of infringing downloads that occur every day using StreamCast's and Grokster's software. When a widely shared service or product is used to commit infringement, it may be impossible to enforce rights in the protected work effectively against all direct infringers, the only practical alternative being to go against the distributor of the copying device for secondary liability on a theory of contributory or vicarious infringement. . . .

One infringes contributorily by intentionally inducing or encouraging direct infringement . . ., and infringes vicariously by profiting from direct infringement while declining to exercise a right to stop or limit it. . . .[9] Although "[t]he Copyright Act does not expressly render anyone liable for infringement committed by another," *Sony Corp. v. Universal City Studios,* 464 U.S., at 434, 104 S.Ct. 774, these doctrines of secondary liability emerged from common law principles and are well established in the law. . . .

### B

Despite the currency of these principles of secondary liability, this Court has dealt with secondary copyright infringement in only one recent case, and because MGM has tailored its principal claim to our opinion there, a look at our earlier holding is in order. In *Sony Corp. v. Universal City Studios, supra,* this Court addressed a claim that secondary liability for infringement can arise from the very distribution of a commercial product. There, the product, novel at the time, was what we know today as the videocassette recorder or VCR. Copyright holders sued Sony as the manufacturer, claiming it was contributorily liable for infringement that occurred when VCR owners taped copyrighted programs because it supplied the means used to infringe, and it had constructive knowledge that infringement would occur. At the trial on the merits, the evidence showed that the principal use of the VCR was for "time-shifting," or taping a program for later viewing at a more convenient time, which the Court found to be a fair, not an infringing, use. *Id.*, at 423-424, 104 S.Ct. 774. There was no evidence that Sony had expressed an object of bringing about taping in violation of copyright or had taken active steps to increase its profits from unlawful taping. *Id.*, at 438, 104 S.Ct. 774. Although Sony's advertisements urged consumers to buy the VCR to "record favorite shows" or "build a library" of recorded programs . . ., neither of these uses was necessarily infringing. . . .

On those facts, with no evidence of stated or indicated intent to promote infringing uses, the only conceivable basis for imposing liability was on a theory of contributory infringement arising from its sale of VCRs to consumers with knowledge that some would use them to infringe. *Id.*, at 439, 104 S.Ct. 774. But because the VCR was "capable of commercially significant noninfringing uses," we held the manufacturer could not be faulted solely on the basis of its distribution. *Id.*, at 442, 104 S.Ct. 774.

This analysis reflected patent law's traditional staple article of commerce doctrine, now codified, that distribution of a component of a patented device will not violate the patent if it is suitable for use in other ways[.] The doctrine was devised to identify instances in which it may be presumed from distribution of an article in commerce that the distributor intended the article to be used to infringe another's patent, and so may justly be held liable for that infringement. "One who makes and sells articles which are only adapted to be used in a patented combination will be presumed to intend the natural consequences of his acts; he will be presumed to intend that they shall be used in the combination of the patent." *New York Scaffolding Co. v. Whitney*, 224 F. 452, 459 (C.A.8 1915); ***.

In sum, where an article is "good for nothing else" but infringement . . ., there is no legitimate public interest in its unlicensed availability, and there is no injustice in presuming or imputing an intent to infringe[.] Conversely, the doctrine absolves the equivocal conduct of selling an item with substantial lawful as well as unlawful uses, and limits liability to instances of more acute fault than the mere understanding that some of one's products will be misused. It leaves breathing room for innovation and a vigorous commerce . . .

The parties and many of the *amici* in this case think the key to resolving it is the *Sony* rule and, in particular, what it means for a product to be "capable of commercially significant noninfringing uses." *Sony Corp. v. Universal City Studios, supra,* at 442, 104 S.Ct. 774. MGM advances the argument that granting summary judgment to Grokster and StreamCast as to their current activities gave too much weight to the value of innovative technology, and too little to the copyrights infringed by users of their software, given that 90% of works available on one of the networks was shown to be copyrighted. Assuming the remaining 10% to be its noninfringing use, MGM says this should not qualify as "substantial," and the Court should quantify Sony to the extent of holding that a product used "principally" for infringement does not qualify. . . . As mentioned before, Grokster and StreamCast reply by citing evidence that their software can be used to reproduce public domain works, and they point to copyright holders who actually encourage copying. Even if infringement is the principal practice with their software today, they argue, the noninfringing uses are significant and will grow.

We agree with MGM that the Court of Appeals misapplied Sony, which it read as limiting secondary liability quite beyond the circumstances to which the case applied. Sony barred secondary liability based on presuming or imputing intent to cause infringement solely from the design or distribution of a product capable of substantial lawful use, which the distributor knows is in fact used for infringement. The Ninth Circuit has read Sony's limitation to mean that whenever a product is capable of substantial lawful use, the producer can never be held contributorily liable for third parties' infringing use of it; it read the rule as being this broad, even when an actual purpose to cause infringing use is shown by evidence independent of design and distribution of the product, unless the distributors had "specific knowledge of infringement at a time at which they contributed to the infringement, and failed to act upon that information." 380 F.3d, at 1162 [internal quotation marks and alterations omitted]. Because the Circuit found the StreamCast and Grokster software capable of substantial lawful use, it concluded on the basis of its reading of Sony that neither company could be held liable, since there was no showing that their software, being without any central server, afforded them knowledge of specific unlawful uses.

This view of Sony, however, was error, converting the case from one about liability resting on imputed intent to one about liability on any theory. Because Sony did not displace other theories of secondary liability, and because we find below that it was error to grant summary judgment to the companies on MGM's inducement claim, we do not revisit Sony further, as MGM requests, to add a more quantified description of the point of balance between protection and commerce when liability rests solely on distribution with knowledge that unlawful use will occur. It is enough to note that the Ninth Circuit's judgment rested on an erroneous understanding of Sony and to leave further consideration of the Sony rule for a day when that may be required.

## C

Sony's rule limits imputing culpable intent as a matter of law from the characteristics or uses of a distributed product. But nothing in Sony requires courts to ignore evidence of intent if there is such evidence, and the case was never meant to foreclose rules of fault-based liability derived from the common law.[10] *Sony Corp. v. Universal City Studios,* 464 U.S., at 439, 104 S.Ct. 774 ("If vicarious liability is to be imposed on Sony in this case, it must rest on the fact that it has sold equipment with constructive knowledge" of the potential for infringement). Thus, where evidence goes beyond a product's characteristics or the knowledge that it may be put to infringing uses, and shows statements or actions directed to promoting infringement, Sony's staple-article rule will not preclude liability.

The classic case of direct evidence of unlawful purpose occurs when one induces commission of infringement by another, or "entic[es] or persuad[es] another" to infringe, Black's Law Dictionary 790 (8th ed. 2004), as by advertising. Thus at common law a copyright or patent defendant who "not only expected but invoked [infringing use] by advertisement" was liable for infringement "on principles recognized in every part of the law." *Kalem Co. v. Harper Brothers,* 222 U.S., at 62-63, 32 S.Ct. 20 (copyright infringement). ***

The rule on inducement of infringement as developed in the early cases is no different today.[11] Evidence of "active steps . . . taken to encourage direct infringement," *Oak Industries, Inc. v. Zenith Electronics Corp.,* 697 F.Supp. 988, 992 (N.D.Ill.1988), such as advertising an infringing use or instructing how to engage in an infringing use, show an affirmative intent that the product be used to infringe, and a showing that infringement was encouraged overcomes the law's reluctance to find liability when a defendant merely sells a commercial product suitable for some lawful use, ***

For the same reasons that Sony took the staple-article doctrine of patent law as a model for its copyright safe-harbor rule, the inducement rule, too, is a sensible one for copyright. We adopt it here, holding that one who distributes a device with the object of promoting its use to infringe copyright, as shown by clear expression or other affirmative steps taken to foster infringement, is liable for the resulting acts of infringement by third parties. We are, of course, mindful of the need to keep from trenching on regular commerce or discouraging the development of technologies with lawful and unlawful potential. Accordingly, just as Sony did not find intentional inducement despite the knowledge of the VCR manufacturer that its device could be used to infringe . . ., mere knowledge of infringing potential or of actual infringing uses would not be enough here to subject a distributor to liability. Nor would ordinary acts incident to product distribution, such as offering customers technical support or product updates, support liability in themselves. The inducement rule, instead, premises liability on purposeful, culpable expression and conduct, and thus does nothing to compromise legitimate commerce or discourage innovation having a lawful promise.

## III
### A [omitted]
\***

### B

In addition to intent to bring about infringement and distribution of a device suitable for infringing use, the inducement theory of course requires evidence of actual infringement by recipients of the device, the software in this case. As the account of the facts indicates, there is evidence of infringement on a gigantic scale, and there is no serious issue of the adequacy of MGM's showing on this point in order to survive the companies' summary judgment requests. Although an exact calculation of infringing use, as a basis for a claim of damages, is subject to dispute, there is no question that the summary judgment evidence is at least adequate to entitle MGM to go forward with claims for damages and equitable relief.
\***

In sum, this case is significantly different from Sony and reliance on that case to rule in favor of StreamCast and Grokster was error. Sony dealt with a claim of liability based solely on distributing a product with alternative lawful and unlawful uses, with knowledge that some users would follow the unlawful course. The case struck a balance between the interests of protection and innovation by holding that the product's capability of substantial lawful employment should bar the imputation of fault and consequent secondary liability for the unlawful acts of others.

MGM's evidence in this case most obviously addresses a different basis of liability for distributing a product open to alternative uses. Here, evidence of the distributors' words and deeds going beyond distribution as such shows a purpose to cause and profit from third-party acts of copyright infringement. If liability for inducing infringement is ultimately found, it will not be on the basis of presuming or imputing fault, but from inferring a patently illegal objective from statements and actions showing what that objective was.

There is substantial evidence in MGM's favor on all elements of inducement, and summary judgment in favor of Grokster and

StreamCast was error. On remand, reconsideration of MGM's motion for summary judgment will be in order.

The judgment of the Court of Appeals is vacated, and the case is remanded for further proceedings consistent with this opinion.

*It is so ordered.*

Justice Ginsburg, with whom the Chief Justice and Justice Kennedy join, concurring [omitted]

\*\*\*

Justice Breyer, with whom Justice Stevens and Justice O'Connor join, concurring [omitted]

\*\*\*

# Trademark

*Trademark, unlike copyright and patent, is governed by state and federal law. Section 1125 sets out the federal rules for infringement, dilution, and cybersquatting, discussed in Chapter 2.*

## 15 U.S.C. § 1125. False designations of origin, false descriptions, and dilution forbidden

(a) Civil action

(1) Any person who, on or in connection with any goods or services, or any container for goods, uses in commerce any word, term, name, symbol, or device, or any combination thereof, or any false designation of origin, false or misleading description of fact, or false or misleading representation of fact, which—

(A) is likely to cause confusion, or to cause mistake, or to deceive as to the affiliation, connection, or association of such person with another person, or as to the origin, sponsorship, or approval of his or her goods, services, or commercial activities by another person, or

(B) in commercial advertising or promotion, misrepresents the nature, characteristics, qualities, or geographic origin of his or her or another person's goods, services, or commercial activities,

shall be liable in a civil action by any person who believes that he or she is or is likely to be damaged by such act.

(2) As used in this subsection, the term "any person" includes any State, instrumentality of a State or employee of a State or instrumentality of a State acting in his or her official capacity. Any

State, and any such instrumentality, officer, or employee, shall be subject to the provisions of this chapter in the same manner and to the same extent as any nongovernmental entity.

(3) In a civil action for trade dress infringement under this chapter for trade dress not registered on the principal register, the person who asserts trade dress protection has the burden of proving that the matter sought to be protected is not functional.

(b) Importation

Any goods marked or labeled in contravention of the provisions of this section shall not be imported into the United States or admitted to entry at any customhouse of the United States. The owner, importer, or consignee of goods refused entry at any customhouse under this section may have any recourse by protest or appeal that is given under the customs revenue laws or may have the remedy given by this chapter in cases involving goods refused entry or seized.

(c) Remedies for dilution of famous marks

(1) The owner of a famous mark shall be entitled, subject to the principles of equity and upon such terms as the court deems reasonable, to an injunction against another person's commercial use in commerce of a mark or trade name, if such use begins after the mark has become famous and causes dilution of the distinctive quality of the mark, and to obtain such other relief as is provided in this subsection. In determining whether a mark is distinctive and famous, a court may consider factors such as, but not limited to—

(A) the degree of inherent or acquired distinctiveness of the mark;

(B) the duration and extent of use of the mark in connection with the goods or services with which the mark is used;

(C) the duration and extent of advertising and publicity of the mark;

(D) the geographical extent of the trading area in which the mark is used;

(E) the channels of trade for the goods or services with which the mark is used;

(F) the degree of recognition of the mark in the trading areas and channels of trade used by the mark's owner and the person against whom the injunction is sought;

(G) the nature and extent of use of the same or similar marks by third parties; and

(H) whether the mark was registered under the Act of March 3, 1881, or the Act of February 20, 1905, or on the principal register.

(2) In an action brought under this subsection, the owner of the famous mark shall be entitled only to injunctive relief as set forth in section 1116 of this title unless the person against whom the injunction is sought willfully intended to trade on the owner's reputation or to cause dilution of the famous mark. If such willful intent is proven, the owner of the famous mark shall also be entitled to the remedies set forth in sections 1117 (a) and 1118 of this title, subject to the discretion of the court and the principles of equity.

(3) The ownership by a person of a valid registration under the Act of March 3, 1881, or the Act of February 20, 1905, or on the principal register shall be a complete bar to an action against that person, with respect to that mark, that is brought by another person under the common law or a statute of a State and that seeks to prevent dilution of the distinctiveness of a mark, label, or form of advertisement.

(4) The following shall not be actionable under this section:

(A) Fair use of a famous mark by another person in comparative commercial advertising or promotion to identify the competing goods or services of the owner of the famous mark.

(B) Noncommercial use of a mark.

(C) All forms of news reporting and news commentary.

(d) Cyberpiracy prevention

(1)

(A) A person shall be liable in a civil action by the owner of a mark, including a personal name which is protected as a mark under this section, if, without regard to the goods or services of the parties, that person—

(i) has a bad faith intent to profit from that mark, including a personal name which is protected as a mark under this section; and

(ii) registers, traffics in, or uses a domain name that—

(I) in the case of a mark that is distinctive at the time of registration of the domain name, is identical or confusingly similar to that mark;

(II) in the case of a famous mark that is famous at the time of registration of the domain name, is identical or confusingly similar to or dilutive of that mark; or

(III) is a trademark, word, or name protected by reason of section 706 of title 18 or section 220506 of title 36.

(B)

    (i) In determining whether a person has a bad faith intent described under subparagraph (A), a court may consider factors such as, but not limited to—

        (I) the trademark or other intellectual property rights of the person, if any, in the domain name;

        (II) the extent to which the domain name consists of the legal name of the person or a name that is otherwise commonly used to identify that person;

        (III) the person's prior use, if any, of the domain name in connection with the bona fide offering of any goods or services;

        (IV) the person's bona fide noncommercial or fair use of the mark in a site accessible under the domain name;

        (V) the person's intent to divert consumers from the mark owner's online location to a site accessible under the domain name that could harm the goodwill represented by the mark, either for commercial gain or with the intent to tarnish or disparage the mark, by creating a likelihood of confusion as to the source, sponsorship, affiliation, or endorsement of the site;

        (VI) the person's offer to transfer, sell, or otherwise assign the domain name to the mark owner or any third party for financial gain without having used, or having an intent to use, the domain name in the bona fide offering of any goods or services, or the person's prior conduct indicating a pattern of such conduct;

        (VII) the person's provision of material and misleading false contact information when applying for the registration of the domain name, the person's intentional failure to maintain accurate contact information, or the person's prior conduct indicating a pattern of such conduct;

        (VIII) the person's registration or acquisition of multiple domain names which the person knows are identical or confusingly similar to marks of others that are distinctive at the time of registration of such domain names, or dilutive of famous marks of others that are famous at the time of registration of such domain names, without regard to the goods or services of the parties; and

(IX) the extent to which the mark incorporated in the person's domain name registration is or is not distinctive and famous within the meaning of subsection (c)(1) of this section.

(ii) Bad faith intent described under subparagraph (A) shall not be found in any case in which the court determines that the person believed and had reasonable grounds to believe that the use of the domain name was a fair use or otherwise lawful.

(C) In any civil action involving the registration, trafficking, or use of a domain name under this paragraph, a court may order the forfeiture or cancellation of the domain name or the transfer of the domain name to the owner of the mark.

(D) A person shall be liable for using a domain name under subparagraph (A) only if that person is the domain name registrant or that registrant's authorized licensee.

(E) As used in this paragraph, the term "traffics in" refers to transactions that include, but are not limited to, sales, purchases, loans, pledges, licenses, exchanges of currency, and any other transfer for consideration or receipt in exchange for consideration.

(2)

(A) The owner of a mark may file an in rem civil action against a domain name in the judicial district in which the domain name registrar, domain name registry, or other domain name authority that registered or assigned the domain name is located if—

(i) the domain name violates any right of the owner of a mark registered in the Patent and Trademark Office, or protected under subsection (a) or (c) of this section; and

(ii) the court finds that the owner—

(I) is not able to obtain in personam jurisdiction over a person who would have been a defendant in a civil action under paragraph (1); or

(II) through due diligence was not able to find a person who would have been a defendant in a civil action under paragraph (1) by—

(aa) sending a notice of the alleged violation and intent to proceed under this paragraph to the registrant of the domain name at the postal and e-mail address provided by the registrant to the registrar; and

(bb) publishing notice of the action as the court may direct promptly after filing the action.

(B) The actions under subparagraph (A)(ii) shall constitute service of process.

(C) In an in rem action under this paragraph, a domain name shall be deemed to have its situs in the judicial district in which—

(i) the domain name registrar, registry, or other domain name authority that registered or assigned the domain name is located; or

(ii) documents sufficient to establish control and authority regarding the disposition of the registration and use of the domain name are deposited with the court.

(D)

(i) The remedies in an in rem action under this paragraph shall be limited to a court order for the forfeiture or cancellation of the domain name or the transfer of the domain name to the owner of the mark. Upon receipt of written notification of a filed, stamped copy of a complaint filed by the owner of a mark in a United States district court under this paragraph, the domain name registrar, domain name registry, or other domain name authority shall—

(I) expeditiously deposit with the court documents sufficient to establish the court's control and authority regarding the disposition of the registration and use of the domain name to the court; and

(II) not transfer, suspend, or otherwise modify the domain name during the pendency of the action, except upon order of the court.

(ii) The domain name registrar or registry or other domain name authority shall not be liable for injunctive or monetary relief under this paragraph except in the case of bad faith or reckless disregard, which includes a willful failure to comply with any such court order.

(3) The civil action established under paragraph (1) and the in rem action established under paragraph (2), and any remedy available under either such action, shall be in addition to any other civil action or remedy otherwise applicable.

(4) The in rem jurisdiction established under paragraph (2) shall be in addition to any other jurisdiction that otherwise exists, whether in rem or in personam.

# Trademark Dilution Revision Act of 2006

*The law of trademark dilution was revisited and dramatically revised by Congress in 2006. The Trademark Dilution Revision Act of 2006 appears below in the form in which it was approved by Congress and sent to the president for signature; President Bush signed the act into law on 6 October 2006.*

# Trademark Dilution Revision Act of 2006 (Enrolled as Agreed to or Passed by Both House and Senate), H.R.683, One Hundred Ninth Congress of the United States of America

### SECTION 1. SHORT TITLE.

(a) Short Title- This Act may be cited as the 'Trademark Dilution Revision Act of 2006'.

(b) References- Any reference in this Act to the Trademark Act of 1946 shall be a reference to the Act entitled 'An Act to provide for the registration and protection of trademarks used in commerce, to carry out the provisions of certain international conventions, and for other purposes', approved July 5, 1946 (15 U.S.C. 1051 et seq.).

### SECTION 2. DILUTION BY BLURRING; DILUTION BY TARNISHMENT.

Section 43 of the Trademark Act of 1946 (15 U.S.C. 1125) is amended—

(1) by striking subsection (c) and inserting the following:

(c) Dilution by Blurring; Dilution by Tarnishment-

(1) INJUNCTIVE RELIEF- Subject to the principles of equity, the owner of a famous mark that is distinctive, inherently or through acquired distinctiveness, shall be entitled to an injunction against another person who, at any time after the owner's mark has become famous, commences use of a mark or trade name in commerce that is likely to cause dilution by blurring or dilution by tarnishment of the famous mark, regardless of the presence or absence of actual or likely confusion, of competition, or of actual economic injury.

(2) DEFINITIONS-

(A) For purposes of paragraph (1), a mark is famous if it is widely recognized by the general consuming public of the United States as a designation of source of the goods or services of the mark's owner. In determining whether a mark possesses the requisite degree of recognition, the court may consider all relevant factors, including the following:

(i) The duration, extent, and geographic reach of advertising and publicity of the mark, whether advertised or publicized by the owner or third parties.

(ii) The amount, volume, and geographic extent of sales of goods or services offered under the mark.

(iii) The extent of actual recognition of the mark.

(iv) Whether the mark was registered under the Act of March 3, 1881, or the Act of February 20, 1905, or on the principal register.

(B) For purposes of paragraph (1), 'dilution by blurring' is association arising from the similarity between a mark or trade name and a famous mark that impairs the distinctiveness of the famous mark. In determining whether a mark or trade name is likely to cause dilution by blurring, the court may consider all relevant factors, including the following:

(i) The degree of similarity between the mark or trade name and the famous mark.

(ii) The degree of inherent or acquired distinctiveness of the famous mark.

(iii) The extent to which the owner of the famous mark is engaging in substantially exclusive use of the mark.

(iv) The degree of recognition of the famous mark.

(v) Whether the user of the mark or trade name intended to create an association with the famous mark.

(vi) Any actual association between the mark or trade name and the famous mark.

(C) For purposes of paragraph (1), 'dilution by tarnishment' is association arising from the similarity between a mark or trade name and a famous mark that harms the reputation of the famous mark.

(3) EXCLUSIONS- The following shall not be actionable as dilution by blurring or dilution by tarnishment under this subsection:

(A) Any fair use, including a nominative or descriptive fair use, or facilitation of such fair use, of a famous mark by another person other than as a designation of source for the person's own goods or services, including use in connection with—

(i) advertising or promotion that permits consumers to compare goods or services; or

(ii) identifying and parodying, criticizing, or commenting upon the famous mark owner or the goods or services of the famous mark owner.

(B) All forms of news reporting and news commentary.

(C) Any noncommercial use of a mark.

(4) BURDEN OF PROOF- In a civil action for trade dress dilution under this Act for trade dress not registered on the principal register, the person who asserts trade dress protection has the burden of proving that—

(A) the claimed trade dress, taken as a whole, is not functional and is famous; and

(B) if the claimed trade dress includes any mark or marks registered on the principal register, the unregistered matter, taken as a whole, is famous separate and apart from any fame of such registered marks.

(5) ADDITIONAL REMEDIES- In an action brought under this subsection, the owner of the famous mark shall be entitled to injunctive relief as set forth in section 34. The owner of the famous mark shall also be entitled to the remedies set forth in sections 35(a) and 36, subject to the discretion of the court and the principles of equity if—

(A) the mark or trade name that is likely to cause dilution by blurring or dilution by tarnishment was first used in commerce by the person against whom the injunction is sought after the date of enactment of the Trademark Dilution Revision Act of 2006; and

(B) in a claim arising under this subsection—

(i) by reason of dilution by blurring, the person against whom the injunction is sought willfully intended to trade on the recognition of the famous mark; or

(ii) by reason of dilution by tarnishment, the person against whom the injunction is sought willfully intended to harm the reputation of the famous mark.

(6) OWNERSHIP OF VALID REGISTRATION A COMPLETE BAR TO ACTION- The ownership by a person of a valid registration under the Act of March 3, 1881, or the Act of February 20, 1905, or on the principal register under this Act shall be a complete bar to an action against that person, with respect to that mark, that—

(A)

(i) is brought by another person under the common law or a statute of a State; and

(ii) seeks to prevent dilution by blurring or dilution by tarnishment; or

(B) asserts any claim of actual or likely damage or harm to the distinctiveness or reputation of a mark, label, or form of advertisement.

(7) SAVINGS CLAUSE- Nothing in this subsection shall be construed to impair, modify, or supersede the applicability of the patent laws of the United States.'; and

(2) in subsection (d)(1)(B)(i)(IX), by striking '(c)(1) of section 43' and inserting '(c)'.

## SECTION 3. CONFORMING AMENDMENTS.

(a) Marks Registrable on the Principal Register- Section 2(f) of the Trademark Act of 1946 (15 U.S.C. 1052(f)) is amended—

(1) by striking the last two sentences; and

(2) by adding at the end the following: 'A mark which would be likely to cause dilution by blurring or dilution by tarnishment under section 43(c), may be refused registration only pursuant to a proceeding brought under section 13. A registration for a mark which would be likely to cause dilution by blurring or dilution by tarnishment under section 43(c), may be canceled pursuant to a proceeding brought under either section 14 or section 24.'.

(b) Opposition- Section 13(a) of the Trademark Act of 1946 (15 U.S.C. 1063(a)) is amended in the first sentence by striking 'as a result of dilution' and inserting 'the registration of any mark which would be likely to cause dilution by blurring or dilution by tarnishment'.

(c) Cancellation- Section 14 of the Trademark Act of 1946 (15 U.S.C. 1064) is amended, in the matter preceding paragraph (1) by striking ', including as a result of dilution under section 43(c),' and inserting ', including as a result of a likelihood of dilution by blurring or dilution by tarnishment under section 43(c),'.

(d) Marks for the Supplemental Register- The second sentence of section 24 of the Trademark Act of 1946 (15 U.S.C. 1092) is amended to read as follows:

Whenever any person believes that such person is or will be damaged by the registration of a mark on the supplemental register—

(1) for which the effective filing date is after the date on which such person's mark became famous and which would be likely to cause dilution by blurring or dilution by tarnishment under section 43(c); or

(2) on grounds other than dilution by blurring or dilution by tarnishment, such person may at any time, upon payment of the prescribed fee and the filing of a petition

stating the ground therefor, apply to the Director to cancel
such registration.
(e) Definitions- Section 45 of the Trademark Act of 1946 (15 U.S.C.
1127) is amended by striking the definition relating to the term
'dilution'.

# TRIPs: Agreement on Trade-Related Aspects of Intellectual Property Rights

*Section 2 of Part II of TRIPs deals with trademarks. A comparison between the statute already presented and the treaty sections that follow should reveal whether the United States is in compliance (at least at the legislative level) with its international obligations under TRIPs.*

# Part II: Standards Concerning the Availability, Scope and Use of Intellectual Property Rights

## Section 2: Trademarks

### Article 15: Protectable Subject Matter

1. Any sign, or any combination of signs, capable of distinguishing the
goods or services of one undertaking from those of other undertakings,
shall be capable of constituting a trademark. Such signs, in particular
words including personal names, letters, numerals, figurative elements
and combinations of colours as well as any combination of such signs,
shall be eligible for registration as trademarks. Where signs are not
inherently capable of distinguishing the relevant goods or services,
Members may make registrability depend on distinctiveness acquired
through use. Members may require, as a condition of registration, that
signs be visually perceptible.
2. Paragraph 1 shall not be understood to prevent a Member from
denying registration of a trademark on other grounds, provided that
they do not derogate from the provisions of the Paris Convention
(1967).
3. Members may make registrability depend on use. However, actual
use of a trademark shall not be a condition for filing an application for
registration. An application shall not be refused solely on the ground
that intended use has not taken place before the expiry of a period of
three years from the date of application.

4. The nature of the goods or services to which a trademark is to be applied shall in no case form an obstacle to registration of the trademark.

5. Members shall publish each trademark either before it is registered or promptly after it is registered and shall afford a reasonable opportunity for petitions to cancel the registration. In addition, Members may afford an opportunity for the registration of a trademark to be opposed.

## Article 16: Rights Conferred

1. The owner of a registered trademark shall have the exclusive right to prevent all third parties not having the owner's consent from using in the course of trade identical or similar signs for goods or services which are identical or similar to those in respect of which the trademark is registered where such use would result in a likelihood of confusion. In case of the use of an identical sign for identical goods or services, a likelihood of confusion shall be presumed. The rights described above shall not prejudice any existing prior rights, nor shall they affect the possibility of Members making rights available on the basis of use.

2. Article 6*bis* of the Paris Convention (1967) shall apply, *mutatis mutandis*, to services. In determining whether a trademark is well-known, Members shall take account of the knowledge of the trademark in the relevant sector of the public, including knowledge in the Member concerned which has been obtained as a result of the promotion of the trademark.

3. Article 6*bis* of the Paris Convention (1967) shall apply, *mutatis mutandis*, to goods or services which are not similar to those in respect of which a trademark is registered, provided that use of that trademark in relation to those goods or services would indicate a connection between those goods or services and the owner of the registered trademark and provided that the interests of the owner of the registered trademark are likely to be damaged by such use.

## Article 17: Exceptions

Members may provide limited exceptions to the rights conferred by a trademark, such as fair use of descriptive terms, provided that such exceptions take account of the legitimate interests of the owner of the trademark and of third parties.

## Article 18: Term of Protection

Initial registration, and each renewal of registration, of a trademark shall be for a term of no less than seven years. The registration of a trademark shall be renewable indefinitely.

### Article 19: Requirement of Use

1. If use is required to maintain a registration, the registration may be cancelled only after an uninterrupted period of at least three years of non-use, unless valid reasons based on the existence of obstacles to such use are shown by the trademark owner. Circumstances arising independently of the will of the owner of the trademark which constitute an obstacle to the use of the trademark, such as import restrictions on or other government requirements for goods or services protected by the trademark, shall be recognized as valid reasons for non-use.

2. When subject to the control of its owner, use of a trademark by another person shall be recognized as use of the trademark for the purpose of maintaining the registration.

### Article 20: Other Requirements

The use of a trademark in the course of trade shall not be unjustifiably encumbered by special requirements, such as use with another trademark, use in a special form or use in a manner detrimental to its capability to distinguish the goods or services of one undertaking from those of other undertakings. This will not preclude a requirement prescribing the use of the trademark identifying the undertaking producing the goods or services along with, but without linking it to, the trademark distinguishing the specific goods or services in question of that undertaking.

### Article 21: Licensing and Assignment [omitted]
***

# Abercrombie & Fitch Co. v. Hunting World, Inc., 537 F.2d 4 (2d Cir. 1976)

*In this excerpt, Judge Friendly does a good job of explaining how and why certain words can become trademarks and others cannot. Along the way he takes a shot at the revered but often incomprehensible Judge Learned Hand. Learned Hand (whose full name was Billings Learned Hand) served on the Second Circuit before Henry Friendly; the former retired in 1951 while the latter started in 1959. The footnotes are from Judge Friendly's decision.*

Friendly, Circuit Judge:
***

I. [omitted]

II.

It will be useful at the outset to restate some basic principles of trademark law, which, although they should be familiar, tend to become lost in a welter of adjectives.

The cases, and in some instances the Lanham Act, identify four different categories of terms with respect to trademark protection. Arrayed in an ascending order which roughly reflects their eligibility to trademark status and the degree of protection accorded, these classes are (1) generic, (2) descriptive, (3) suggestive, and (4) arbitrary or fanciful. The lines of demarcation, however, are not always bright. Moreover, the difficulties are compounded because a term that is in one category for a particular product may be in quite a different one for another,[6] because a term may shift from one category to another in light of differences in usage through time,[7] because a term may have one meaning to one group of users and a different one to others, and because the same term may be put to different uses with respect to a single product. In various ways, all of these complications are involved in the instant case.

A generic term is one that refers, or has come to be understood as referring, to the genus of which the particular product is a species. At common law neither those terms which were generic nor those which were merely descriptive could become valid trademarks, see *Delaware & Hudson Canal Co. v. Clark*, 80 U.S. (13 Wall.) 311, 323, 20 L.Ed. 581 (1872) ("Nor can a generic name, or a name merely descriptive of an article or its qualities, ingredients, or characteristics, be employed as a trademark and the exclusive use of it be entitled to legal protection"). The same was true under the Trademark Act of 1905 . . ., except for marks which had been the subject of exclusive use for ten years prior to its enactment, 33 Stat. 726. While, as we shall see . . ., the Lanham Act makes an important exception with respect to those merely descriptive terms which have acquired secondary meaning . . ., it offers no such exception for generic marks. The Act provides for the cancellation of a registered mark if at any time it "becomes the common descriptive name of an article or substance," § 14(c). This means that even proof of secondary meaning, by virtue of which some "merely descriptive" marks may be registered, cannot transform a generic term into a subject for trademark. As explained in *J. Kohnstam, Ltd. v. Louis Marx and Company* . . . (1960), no matter how much money and effort the user of a generic term has poured into promoting the sale of its merchandise and what success it has achieved in securing public identification, it cannot deprive competing manufacturers of the product of the right to call an article by its name . . . We have recently had occasion to apply this doctrine of the impossibility of achieving trademark protection for a generic term . . . The pervasiveness of the principle is illustrated by a series of well known cases holding that when a suggestive or fanciful term has become generic as a result of a manufacturer's own advertising efforts, trademark protection will be denied save for those markets where the term still has not become generic and a secondary meaning has been shown to continue. . . . A term may thus be generic in one market and descriptive or suggestive or fanciful in another.

The term which is descriptive but not generic stands on a better basis. Although § 2(e) of the Lanham Act, 15 U.S.C. § 1052, forbids the registration of a mark which, when applied to the goods of the applicant, is "merely descriptive," § 2(f) removes a considerable part of the sting by providing that "except as expressly excluded in paragraphs (a)-(d) of this section, nothing in this chapter shall prevent the registration of a mark used by the applicant which has become distinctive of the applicant's goods in commerce" and that the Commissioner may accept, as prima facie evidence that the mark has become distinctive, proof of substantially exclusive and continuous use of the mark applied to the applicant's goods for five years preceding the application. As indicated in the cases cited in the discussion of the unregistrability of generic terms, "common descriptive name," as used in §§ 14(c) and 15(4), refers to generic terms applied to products and not to terms that are "merely descriptive." In the former case any claim to an exclusive right must be denied since this in effect would confer a monopoly not only of the mark but of the product by rendering a competitor unable effectively to name what it was endeavoring to sell. In the latter case the law strikes the balance, with respect to registration, between the hardships to a competitor in hampering the use of an appropriate word and those to the owner who, having invested money and energy to endow a word with the good will adhering to his enterprise, would be deprived of the fruits of his efforts.

The category of "suggestive" marks was spawned by the felt need to accord protection to marks that were neither exactly descriptive on the one hand nor truly fanciful on the other a need that was particularly acute because of the bar in the Trademark Act of 1905 . . ., (with an exceedingly limited exception noted above) on the registration of merely descriptive marks regardless of proof of secondary meaning . . . Having created the category the courts have had great difficulty in defining it. Judge Learned Hand made the not very helpful statement:

> It is quite impossible to get any rule out of the cases beyond this: That the validity of the mark ends where suggestion ends and description begins.

*Franklin Knitting Mills, Inc. v. Fashionit Sweater Mills, Inc.,* 297 F. 247, 248 (2 Cir. 1923), *aff'd per curiam,* 4 F.2d 1018 (2 Cir. 1925) . . . Another court has observed, somewhat more usefully, that:

> A term is suggestive if it requires imagination, thought and perception to reach a conclusion as to the nature of goods. A term is descriptive if it forthwith conveys an immediate idea of the ingredients, qualities or characteristics of the goods.

*Stix Products, Inc. v. United Merchants & Manufacturers Inc.,* 295 F.Supp. 479, 488 (S.D.N.Y.1968) . . . Also useful is the approach taken by this court in *Aluminum Fabricating Co. of Pittsburgh v. Season-All Window Corp.,* 259 F.2d 314 (2 Cir. 1958), that the reason for restricting the protection accorded descriptive terms, namely the undesirability of preventing an entrant from using a descriptive term for his product, is much less forceful when the trademark is a suggestive word since, as Judge Lumbard wrote, 259 F.2d at 317:

> The English language has a wealth of synonyms and related words with which to describe the qualities which manufacturers may wish to claim for their products and the ingenuity of the public relations profession supplies new words and slogans as they are needed.

If a term is suggestive, it is entitled to registration without proof of secondary meaning. Moreover, as held in the *Season-All* case, the decision of the Patent Office to register a mark without requiring proof of secondary meaning affords a rebuttable presumption that the mark is suggestive or arbitrary or fanciful rather than merely descriptive.

It need hardly be added that fanciful or arbitrary terms[12] enjoy all the rights accorded to suggestive terms as marks without the need of debating whether the term is "merely descriptive" and with ease of establishing infringement.

\*\*\*

# Patent

*To be patentable, an invention must be useful, novel, and nonobvious. Each of the first three sections of Chapter 10 of the Patent Code sets out one of these elements—or tries to. Congress here manages to be considerably less verbose than, for example, in its imposition of the aforementioned Macrovision copy-protection technology, but could these requirements have been set out more concisely?*

## Patent Act, 35 U.S.C. § 101. Inventions patentable

Whoever invents or discovers any new and useful process, machine, manufacture, or composition of matter, or any new and useful improvement thereof, may obtain a patent therefor, subject to the conditions and requirements of this title.

## Patent Act, 35 U.S.C. § 102. Conditions for patentability; novelty and loss of right to patent

A person shall be entitled to a patent unless—

(a) the invention was known or used by others in this country, or patented or described in a printed publication in this or a foreign country, before the invention thereof by the applicant for patent, or

(b) the invention was patented or described in a printed publication in this or a foreign country or in public use or on sale in this country, more than one year prior to the date of the application for patent in the United States, or

(c) he has abandoned the invention, or

(d) the invention was first patented or caused to be patented, or was the subject of an inventor's certificate, by the applicant or his legal representatives or assigns in a foreign country prior to the date of the application for patent in this country on an application for patent or inventor's certificate filed more than twelve months before the filing of the application in the United States, or

(e) the invention was described in (1) an application for patent, published under section 122(b), by another filed in the United States before the invention by the applicant for patent or (2) a patent granted on an application for patent by another filed in the United States before the invention by the applicant for patent, except that an international application filed under the treaty defined in section 351(a) shall have the effects for the purposes of this subsection of an application filed in the United States only if the international application designated the United States and was published under Article 21(2) of such treaty in the English language; or

(f) he did not himself invent the subject matter sought to be patented, or

(g)

(1) during the course of an interference conducted under section 135 or section 291, another inventor involved therein

establishes, to the extent permitted in section 104, that before such person's invention thereof the invention was made by such other inventor and not abandoned, suppressed, or concealed, or

(2) before such person's invention thereof, the invention was made in this country by another inventor who had not abandoned, suppressed, or concealed it. In determining priority of invention under this subsection, there shall be considered not only the respective dates of conception and reduction to practice of the invention, but also the reasonable diligence of one who was first to conceive and last to reduce to practice, from a time prior to conception by the other.

# Patent Act, 35 U.S.C. § 103. Conditions for patentability; non-obvious subject matter

(a) A patent may not be obtained though the invention is not identically disclosed or described as set forth in section 102 of this title, if the differences between the subject matter sought to be patented and the prior art are such that the subject matter as a whole would have been obvious at the time the invention was made to a person having ordinary skill in the art to which said subject matter pertains. Patentability shall not be negatived by the manner in which the invention was made.

(b)

(1) Notwithstanding subsection (a), and upon timely election by the applicant for patent to proceed under this subsection, a biotechnological process using or resulting in a composition of matter that is novel under section 102 and nonobvious under subsection (a) of this section shall be considered nonobvious if—

(A) claims to the process and the composition of matter are contained in either the same application for patent or in separate applications having the same effective filing date; and

(B) the composition of matter, and the process at the time it was invented, were owned by the same person or subject to an obligation of assignment to the same person.

(2) A patent issued on a process under paragraph (1)—

(A) shall also contain the claims to the composition of matter used in or made by that process, or

(B) shall, if such composition of matter is claimed in another patent, be set to expire on the same date as such other patent, notwithstanding section 154.

(3) For purposes of paragraph (1), the term "biotechnological process" means—
(A) a process of genetically altering or otherwise inducing a single- or multi-celled organism to—
(i) express an exogenous nucleotide sequence,
(ii) inhibit, eliminate, augment, or alter expression of an endogenous nucleotide sequence, or
(iii) express a specific physiological characteristic not naturally associated with said organism;
(B) cell fusion procedures yielding a cell line that expresses a specific protein, such as a monoclonal antibody; and
(C) a method of using a product produced by a process defined by subparagraph (A) or (B), or a combination of subparagraphs (A) and (B).
(c) Subject matter developed by another person, which qualifies as prior art only under one or more of subsections (e), (f), and (g) of section 102 of this title, shall not preclude patentability under this section where the subject matter and the claimed invention were, at the time the invention was made, owned by the same person or subject to an obligation of assignment to the same person.

# TRIPs: Agreement on Trade-Related Aspects of Intellectual Property Rights

*Section 5 of Part II of TRIPs deals with patent protection. Again, it may be interesting to compare the TRIPs requirements that follow with the aforementioned statute. Can you see how TRIPs was interpreted as requiring the United States (and other countries) to grant business method patents?*

# Part II: Standards Concerning the Availability, Scope and Use of Intellectual Property Rights

### Section 5: Patents

### Article 27: Patentable Subject Matter
1. Subject to the provisions of paragraphs 2 and 3, patents shall be available for any inventions, whether products or processes, in all fields of technology, provided that they are new, involve an inventive step

and are capable of industrial application. Subject to paragraph 4 of Article 65, paragraph 8 of Article 70 and paragraph 3 of this Article, patents shall be available and patent rights enjoyable without discrimination as to the place of invention, the field of technology and whether products are imported or locally produced.

2. Members may exclude from patentability inventions, the prevention within their territory of the commercial exploitation of which is necessary to protect *ordre public* or morality, including to protect human, animal or plant life or health or to avoid serious prejudice to the environment, provided that such exclusion is not made merely because the exploitation is prohibited by their law.

3. Members may also exclude from patentability:

(a) diagnostic, therapeutic and surgical methods for the treatment of humans or animals;

(b) plants and animals other than micro-organisms, and essentially biological processes for the production of plants or animals other than non-biological and microbiological processes. However, Members shall provide for the protection of plant varieties either by patents or by an effective *sui generis* system or by any combination thereof. The provisions of this subparagraph shall be reviewed four years after the date of entry into force of the WTO Agreement.

## Article 28: Rights Conferred

1. A patent shall confer on its owner the following exclusive rights:

(a) where the subject matter of a patent is a product, to prevent third parties not having the owner's consent from the acts of: making, using, offering for sale, selling, or importing for these purposes that product;

(b) where the subject matter of a patent is a process, to prevent third parties not having the owner's consent from the act of using the process, and from the acts of: using, offering for sale, selling, or importing for these purposes at least the product obtained directly by that process.

2. Patent owners shall also have the right to assign, or transfer by succession, the patent and to conclude licensing contracts.

## Article 29: Conditions on Patent Applicants

1. Members shall require that an applicant for a patent shall disclose the invention in a manner sufficiently clear and complete for the invention to be carried out by a person skilled in the art and may require the applicant to indicate the best mode for carrying out the invention known to the inventor at the filing date or, where priority is claimed, at the priority date of the application.

2. Members may require an applicant for a patent to provide information concerning the applicant's corresponding foreign applications and grants.

### Article 30: Exceptions to Rights Conferred
Members may provide limited exceptions to the exclusive rights conferred by a patent, provided that such exceptions do not unreasonably conflict with a normal exploitation of the patent and do not unreasonably prejudice the legitimate interests of the patent owner, taking account of the legitimate interests of third parties.

### Article 31: Other Use Without Authorization of the Right Holder [omitted]
***

### Article 32: Revocation/Forfeiture
An opportunity for judicial review of any decision to revoke or forfeit a patent shall be available.

### Article 33: Term of Protection
The term of protection available shall not end before the expiration of a period of twenty years counted from the filing date.

### Article 34: Process Patents: Burden of Proof [omitted]
***

# *In re Alappat,* 33 F.3d 1526 (Fed. Cir. 1994)

*In* In re Alappat, *the Federal Circuit (the U.S. court that handles patent appeals) completed the work of rehabilitating software patents in the United States, undoing the damage that was done by the U.S. Supreme Court in* Gottschalk v. Benson *and partially undone in Diamond v. Diehr (see Chapter 2). To do this, Judge Rich had to manage the difficult task of ensuring that Gottschalk would not be applied to software patent cases in the future—without overturning the decision, which he lacked the authority to do. Do you see how he did this?*

### Rich, Circuit Judge:
I. JURISDICTION [omitted]
***

II. THE MERITS
Our conclusion is that the appealed decision should be reversed
because the appealed claims are directed to a "machine" which is one
of the categories named in 35 U.S.C. § 101, as the first panel of the
Board held.

A. *Alappat's Invention*
Alappat's invention relates generally to a means for creating a
smooth waveform display in a digital oscilloscope. The screen of
an oscilloscope is the front of a cathode-ray tube (CRT), which is
like a TV picture tube, whose screen, when in operation, presents
an array (or raster) of pixels arranged at intersections of vertical
columns and horizontal rows, a pixel being a spot on the screen
which may be illuminated by directing an electron beam to that
spot, as in TV. Each column in the array represents a different time
period, and each row represents a different magnitude. An input
signal to the oscilloscope is sampled and digitized to provide a
waveform data sequence (vector list), wherein each successive
element of the sequence represents the magnitude of the waveform
at a successively later time. The waveform data sequence is then
processed to provide a bit map, which is a stored data array
indicating which pixels are to be illuminated. The waveform
ultimately displayed is formed by a group of vectors, wherein each
vector has a straight line trajectory between two points on the
screen at elevations representing the magnitudes of two successive
input signal samples and at horizontal positions representing the
timing of the two samples.
Because a CRT screen contains a finite number of pixels, rapidly
rising and falling portions of a waveform can appear
discontinuous or jagged due to differences in the elevation of
horizontally contiguous pixels included in the waveform. In
addition, the presence of "noise" in an input signal can cause
portions of the waveform to oscillate between contiguous pixel
rows when the magnitude of the input signal lies between values
represented by the elevations of the two rows. Moreover, the
vertical resolution of the display may be limited by the number of
rows of pixels on the screen. The noticeability and appearance of
these effects is known as *aliasing*.
To overcome these effects, Alappat's invention employs an anti-
aliasing system wherein each vector making up the waveform is
represented by modulating the illumination intensity of pixels
having center points bounding the trajectory of the vector. The
intensity at which each of the pixels is illuminated depends upon
the distance of the center point of each pixel from the trajectory of

the vector. Pixels lying squarely on the waveform trace receive maximum illumination, whereas pixels lying along an edge of the trace receive illumination decreasing in intensity proportional to the increase in the distance of the center point of the pixel from the vector trajectory. Employing this *anti-aliasing* technique eliminates any apparent discontinuity, jaggedness, or oscillation in the waveform, thus giving the visual appearance of a smooth continuous waveform. In short, and in lay terms, the invention is an improvement in an oscilloscope comparable to a TV having a clearer picture.

\*\*\*

D. *Analysis* [omitted]

\*\*\*

(b)

Given the foregoing, the proper inquiry in dealing with the so called mathematical subject matter exception to § 101 alleged herein is to see whether the claimed subject matter *as a whole* is a disembodied mathematical concept, whether categorized as a mathematical formula, mathematical equation, mathematical algorithm, or the like, which in essence represents nothing more than a "law of nature," "natural phenomenon," or "abstract idea." If so, *Diehr* precludes the patenting of that subject matter. That is not the case here.

Although many, or arguably even all, of the means elements recited in claim 15 represent circuitry elements that perform mathematical calculations, which is essentially true of all digital electrical circuits, the claimed invention as a whole is directed to a combination of interrelated elements which combine to form a machine for converting discrete waveform data samples into anti-aliased pixel illumination intensity data to be displayed on a display means. This is not a disembodied mathematical concept which may be characterized as an "abstract idea," but rather a specific machine to produce a useful, concrete, and tangible result.

The fact that the four claimed means elements function to transform one set of data to another through what may be viewed as a series of mathematical calculations does not alone justify a holding that the claim as a whole is directed to nonstatutory subject matter . . . Indeed, claim 15 as written is not "so abstract and sweeping" that it would "wholly pre-empt" the use of any apparatus employing the combination of mathematical calculations recited therein. *See Benson*, 409 U.S. at 68-72, 93 S.Ct. at 255-58 (1972). Rather, claim 15 is limited to the use of a particularly claimed combination of elements performing the particularly claimed combination of calculations to transform, i.e., rasterize, digitized waveforms (data) into anti-aliased, pixel illumination data to produce a smooth waveform.

Furthermore, the claim preamble's recitation that the subject matter for which Alappat seeks patent protection is a rasterizer for creating a smooth waveform is not a mere field-of-use label having no significance. Indeed, the preamble specifically recites that the claimed rasterizer converts waveform data into output illumination data for a display, and the means elements recited in the body of the claim make reference not only to the inputted waveform data recited in the preamble but also to the output illumination data also recited in the preamble. Claim 15 thus defines a combination of elements constituting a machine for producing an anti-aliased waveform.

The reconsideration Board majority also erred in its reasoning that claim 15 is unpatentable merely because it "reads on a general purpose digital computer 'means' to perform the various steps under program control." *Alappat*, 23 USPQ2d at 1345. The Board majority stated that it would "not presume that a stored program digital computer is not within the § 112 ¶ 6 range of equivalents of the structure disclosed in the specification." *Alappat*, 23 USPQ2d at 1345. Alappat admits that claim 15 would read on a general purpose computer programmed to carry out the claimed invention, but argues that this alone also does not justify holding claim 15 unpatentable as directed to nonstatutory subject matter. We agree. We have held that such programming creates a new machine, because a general purpose computer in effect becomes a special purpose computer once it is programmed to perform particular functions pursuant to instructions from program software. . . .

Under the Board majority's reasoning, a programmed general purpose computer could never be viewed as patentable subject matter under § 101. This reasoning is without basis in the law. The Supreme Court has never held that a programmed computer may never be entitled to patent protection. Indeed, the *Benson* court specifically stated that its decision therein did not preclude "a patent for any program servicing a computer." *Benson*, 409 U.S. at 71, 93 S.Ct. at 257. Consequently, a computer operating pursuant to software *may* represent patentable subject matter, provided, of course, that the claimed subject matter meets all of the other requirements of Title 35. In any case, a computer, like a rasterizer, is apparatus not mathematics.

CONCLUSION

For the foregoing reasons, the appealed decision of the Board affirming the examiner's rejection is REVERSED.

# Endnotes

### *Metro-Goldwyn-Mayer Studios, Inc. v. Grokster, Ltd.,* 125 S.Ct. 2764 (2005)

1. Peer-to-peer networks have disadvantages as well. Searches on peer-to-peer networks may not reach and uncover all available files because search requests may not be transmitted to every computer on the network. There may be redundant copies of popular files. The creator of the software has no incentive to minimize storage or bandwidth consumption, the costs of which are borne by every user of the network. Most relevant here, it is more difficult to control the content of files available for retrieval and the behavior of users.

2. The studios and recording companies and the songwriters and music publishers filed separate suits against the defendants that were consolidated by the District Court.

3. Subsequent versions of Morpheus, released after the record was made in this case, apparently rely not on Gnutella but on a technology called Neonet. These developments are not before us.

4. There is some evidence that both Grokster and StreamCast previously operated supernodes, which compiled indexes of files available on all of the nodes connected to them. This evidence, pertaining to previous versions of the defendants' software, is not before us and would not affect our conclusions in any event.

5. By comparison, evidence introduced by the plaintiffs in A & M Records, Inc. v. Napster, Inc., 239 F.3d 1004 (C.A.9 2001), showed that 87% of files available on the Napster filesharing network were copyrighted, id., at 1013.

6. The Grokster founder contends that in answering these e-mails he often did not read them fully. . . .

7. The record makes clear that StreamCast developed these promotional materials but not whether it released them to the public. Even if these advertisements were not released to the public and do not show encouragement to infringe, they illuminate StreamCast's purposes.

8. The mutual exclusivity of these values should not be overstated, however. On the one hand technological innovators, including those writing file-sharing computer programs, may wish for effective copyright protections for their work. See, e.g., Wu, When Code Isn't Law, 89 Va. L.Rev. 679, 750 (2003). (StreamCast itself was urged by an associate to "get [its] technology written down and [its intellectual property] protected." App. 866.) On the other hand the widespread distribution of creative works through improved technologies may enable the synthesis of new works or generate audiences for emerging artists. ***

9. We stated in Sony Corp. of America v. Universal City Studios, Inc., 464 U.S. 417, 104 S.Ct. 774, 78 L.Ed.2d 574 (1984), that "'the lines between direct infringement, contributory infringement and vicarious liability are not clearly drawn'. . . . [R]easoned analysis of [the Sony plaintiffs' contributory infringement claim] necessarily entails consideration of arguments and case law which may also be forwarded under the other labels, and indeed the parties . . . rely upon such arguments and authority in support of their respective positions on the issue of contributory infringement," id., at 435, n. 17, 104 S.Ct. 774 (quoting Universal City Studios, Inc. v. Sony Corp., 480 F.Supp. 429, 457-458 (C.D.Cal. 1979)). In the present case MGM has argued a vicarious liability theory, which allows imposition of liability when the defendant profits directly from the infringement and has a right and ability to supervise the direct infringer, even if the defendant initially lacks knowledge of the infringement. *** Because we resolve the case based on an inducement theory, there is no need to analyze separately MGM's vicarious liability theory.

10. Nor does the Patent Act's exemption from liability for those who distribute a staple article of commerce, 35

U.S.C. ß 271(c), extend to those who induce patent infringement, ß 271(b).

11. Inducement has been codified in patent law. Ibid.

### Abercrombie & Fitch Co. v. Hunting World, Inc., 537 F.2d 4 (2d Cir. 1976)

6. To take a familiar example "Ivory" would be generic when used to describe a product made from the tusks of elephants but arbitrary as applied to soap.

7. See, e. g., Haughton Elevator Co. v. Seeberger, 85 U.S.P.Q. 80 (1950), in which the coined word 'Escalator', originally fanciful, or at the very least suggestive, was held to have become generic.

### In re Alappat, 33 F.3d 1526 (Fed. Cir. 1994)

12. As terms of art, the distinctions between suggestive terms and fanciful or arbitrary terms may seem needlessly artificial. Of course, a common word may be used in a fanciful sense; indeed one might say that only a common word can be so used, since a coined word cannot first be put to a bizarre use. Nevertheless, the term "fanciful", as a classifying concept, is usually applied to words invented solely for their use as trademarks. When the same legal consequences attach to a common word, i.e., when it is applied in an unfamiliar way, the use is called "arbitrary."

# 7

# Directory of Organizations

Intellectual property is a huge global business, and it often excites considerable emotion. Far too many organizations are devoted to intellectual property to list here; this list is representative rather than comprehensive. It includes nongovernmental organizations and international organizations; groups focusing on copyright, groups focusing on patent, and groups focusing on trademark; groups from several countries and continents; groups representing content owners' interests, groups representing consumers' interests, groups representing legal practitioners' interests, a group representing equipment makers' interests, and groups that take no side in conflicts between these interests.

Many of these groups provide excellent resources for intellectual property research. The website of the World Intellectual Property Organization (WIPO) (www.wipo.org) is the best first stop for research in international intellectual property law. For U.S. intellectual property law, an excellent place to start is Bitlaw (www.bitlaw.com).

The websites listed here were functioning as of October 2006. Many of these groups also provide e-mail addresses or telephone contact numbers. E-mail is probably a more practical and efficient means of making contact than telephone, however. The telephone numbers listed here include area codes in parentheses (for United States and Canadian telephone numbers) or country codes separated from city codes and the remainder of the telephone number with a hyphen (for overseas telephone numbers). The "011" that appears at the beginning of each number is the international dialing prefix needed to call most overseas numbers from most U.S.

telephones. When calling from outside the United States, omit the 011 and use the appropriate dialing prefix.

**African Regional Intellectual Property Organization (ARIPO)**
11 Natal Road
Belgravia, Harare
Zimbabwe
Phone: 011-2634-794054
Fax: 011-2634-704072
E-mail: aripo@ecoweb.co.zw; mail@aripo.org
Website: http://www.aripo.org/

The ARIPO was founded as a regional international intellectual property law organization for anglophone Africa. (See also Organisation Africaine de la Propriété Intellectuelle.) In addition to administrative and harmonization efforts, a main concern of ARIPO has been to combat "dependent intellectual property legislation," a legacy of colonialism. This dependent legislation, found in many African countries until quite recently, provided no process for the grant or registration of an intellectual property right originating in the former colonies. Such intellectual property laws as existed served only to extend intellectual property rights acquired in another country (typically the United Kingdom) to the former colony's territory.

The ARIPO provides a single filing process for patent applications to ARIPO member states. The ARIPO website provides links to the text of several African regional intellectual property agreements.

**Alliance for Digital Progress (ADP)**
Bill Maguire, Executive Director
Phone: (202) 266-2537
E-mail: billm@adpcoalition.org
Website: http://www.alliancefordigitalprogress.org/

The ADP is a group of equipment manufacturers (including Apple, Cisco, Dell, Hewlett-Packard, IBM, Intel, Microsoft, and Motorola) and public interest organizations. The ADP was founded to oppose government-designed or government-mandated copyright protection technology. According to the organization's mission statement, "ADP believes that the best ways to meet consumer expectations and fight piracy include market-driven efforts to educate consumers, create digital distribution strategies, develop innovative technology, and enforce existing laws. ADP strongly opposes efforts to make the government design and mandate copy-protection technologies."

### American Bar Association Section of Intellectual Property Law
321 North Clark Street
Chicago, IL 60610-4714
Phone: (312) 988-5598
Fax: (312) 988-6800
E-mail: iplaw@abanet.org
Website: http://www.abanet.org/intelprop/

The American Bar Association Section of Intellectual Property Law, formed in 1894, claims to be the world's largest intellectual property law organization; its members include lawyers, law students, and others. Its website includes the Section newsletter and other publications, although the content of these can be arcane and are more likely to be of interest to attorneys than to the general public. The site also includes an excellent links page that contains links to many other intellectual property organizations and discussion groups on intellectual property law.

### American Intellectual Property Law Association (AIPLA)
241 Eighteenth Street South, Suite 700
Arlington, VA 22202
Phone: (703) 415-0780
Fax: (703) 415-0786
E-mail: AIPLA@aipla.org
Website: http://www.aipla.org/

The AIPLA, which was founded in 1897, is an association of more than 16,000 intellectual property lawyers. It publishes *The American Intellectual Property Law Association Quarterly Journal*, the *AIPLA Bulletin*, and the *Report of the Economic Survey*. The first of these is likely to be most useful to those who are not intellectual property lawyers but are interested in the subject. Some additional publications may be viewed for free on AIPLA's website under the heading "Publications Available for Viewing" in the "Educational Materials" section.

### American Society of Composers, Authors and Publishers (ASCAP)
7920 West Sunset Boulevard, Third Floor

Los Angeles, CA 90046
Phone: (323) 883-1000
Fax: (323) 883-1049
8 Cork Street
London W1X1PB
United Kingdom
Phone: 011-44-207-439-0909
Fax: 011-44-207-434-0073
E-mail: info@ascap.com
Website: http://www.ascap.com/

The ASCAP is a copyright clearinghouse with eight membership offices (in New York, Los Angeles, London, Miami, Nashville, Chicago, Puerto Rico, and Atlanta). It provides one-stop shopping for music copyright holders—composers, songwriters, performers, and music publishers—and those wishing to make lawful use of copyrighted music—bands, radio stations, and others. ASCAP members give blanket permission to ASCAP to license their work. The users pay a fee to ASCAP, which can grant a license to use the work without having to consult with the content creator or publisher. This is far simpler than, for example, having each radio station seek permission from each artist whose songs it wished to play, as well as those artists' publishing companies, the composer who wrote the music, the songwriter who wrote the lyrics, and perhaps others. While many of ASCAP's members may be concerned with music piracy (and disagree on how, or whether, it should be addressed), ASCAP itself is concerned with the day-to-day administration of music licensing; it is not an advocacy organization. That job is left to the Recording Industry Association of America (see entry in this chapter).

### Anti-DMCA
E-mail: anti-dmca@anti-dmca.org
Website: http://www.anti-dmca.org/

Anti-DMCA is, as the name says, a consumer advocacy group opposed to the Digital Millennium Copyright Act of 1998, especially the anticircumvention and digital rights management protection provisions of Sections 1201–1204. Anti-DMCA continues to oppose laws that would restrict consumer control over purchased content; the Anti-DMCA website is passionate and entertaining, but often slow to load.

**Arts and Humanities Research Board Shepherd and Wedderburn Research Centre in Intellectual Property and Technology (SCRIPT)**
School of Law
University of Edinburgh, Old College
Edinburgh EH8 9YL
Scotland
Phone: 011-44-131-650-2014
Fax: 011-44-131-662-0724
E-mail: itandip@ed.ac.uk
Website: http://www.law.ed.ac.uk/ahrb/

SCRIPT is a noteworthy academic center for the study of intellectual property law that addresses a somewhat broader scope of intellectual property concerns than the Berkman Center (see entry in this chapter). Materials available on its website include the online academic journal *SCRIPT-ed*.

**Association of Corporate Patent Counsel (ACPC)**
1255 Twenty-third Street, N.W., Suite 200
Washington, DC 20037
Website:
http://www.ipo.org/content/navigationmenu/acpc_site/acpc
_home_page_4.htm

The ACPC, which was founded in 1966, is an organization of corporate patent lawyers. Its membership includes persons working as chief intellectual property counsel, or the equivalent office, in companies operating in the United States.

**Association Internationale pour la Protection de la Propriété Intellectuelle (AIPPI)**
AIPPI General Secretariat
Tödistrasse 16
P.O. Box 8027
Zurich
Switzerland
Phone: 011-41-44-280-58-80
Fax: 011-41-44-280-58-85
E-mail: mail@aippi.org
Website: http://www.aippi.org/

The AIPPI (International Association for the Protection of Industrial Property), founded in 1897, is a nongovernmental organization dedicated to the study, development, and advancement of international intellectual property law. Although ostensibly neutral in disputes over intellectual property rights, its support for expanding intellectual property protection tends to favor the interests of content owners. The website provides copies of the Association's own materials and links to branches, other nongovernmental organizations, and governmental and international agencies worldwide.

**Association Littéraire et Artistique Internationale (ALAI)**
c/o Kimbrough & Associés
82, rue du Faubourg Saint-Honoré
75008 Paris
France
Phone: 011-33-1-53-30-24-24
Fax: 011-33-1-53-30-24-25
E-Mail: yves.gaubiac@kimbroughlaw.com;
paula.dionisio@kimbroughlaw.com
Website: http://www.alai.org/

The ALAI (International Literary and Artistic Association) was founded in 1878 by Victor Hugo and other writers who were concerned about international copying of their works. The ALAI grew out of the Société des Gens de Lettres, a writers' group founded in 1838 and still in existence (see the entry in this chapter). The ALAI's initial purpose was to push for an international copyright treaty, and its moment of triumph came just eight years after its founding, with the adoption of the Berne Convention. Today nearly every country in the world is a member of the Berne Convention, which creates a nearly seamless regime of international copyright protection, without formalities or the necessity of obtaining protection separately in each member country. The ALAI continues to act as an advocate for the interests of authors and artists. It has national affiliates in twenty-four countries, including the United States.

**Berkman Center for Internet & Society**
Harvard Law School
23 Everett Street, Second Floor
Cambridge, MA 02138

Phone: (617) 495-7547
Fax: (617) 495-7641
E-mail: cyber@law.harvard.edu
Website: http://cyber.law.harvard.edu/home/

The Berkman Center is one of the best known of the many university centers devoted in whole or part to the study of intellectual property law. According to its mission statement, the Center's mission is "to explore and understand cyberspace, its development, dynamics, norms, standards, and need or lack thereof for laws and sanctions." This includes intellectual property law (especially, but not only, copyright law) relating to the Internet as well as other areas of law, including First Amendment and privacy law. The Berkman Center's website provides a great many academic articles, podcasts, and other information available for free download.

**Bitlaw**
Beck & Tysver, PLLC
2900 Thomas Avenue South, Suite 100
Minneapolis, MN 55416
Phone: (612) 915-9633
Fax: (612) 915-9637
E-mail: info@bitlaw.com
Website: http://www.bitlaw.com/

Bitlaw, an excellent online research resource, is the project of Minneapolis intellectual property attorney Daniel A. Tysver. The entire body of U.S. statutory and regulatory law is available on the site, along with Tysver's informative explanations and commentary. It's an essential first stop in any online intellectual property research project.

**Budapest Open Access Initiative**
Melissa Hagemann
E-mail: mhagemann@sorosny.org
Website: http://www.soros.org/openaccess/

For academic authors, copyright protection is often more of a bane than a boon. The works themselves have little or no monetary value; their value to the authors depends on being widely read and cited by other scholars. Yet these articles are subject to the same term and scope of copyright protection as commercial works, and the authors often do not control the copyright. The copyright holder may be a journal or a university press. Many small journals keep poor copyright records or stop publishing without notice and without any formal distribution of assets (including intellectual property assets). Thus, locating the copyright holder may be difficult or sometimes impossible. When the copyright holder can be located, it may arbitrarily withhold permission to reprint an article even though the author wants to grant the permission.

The Budapest Open Access Initiative, created in 2002, attempts to address this problem through self-archiving (depositing articles in open-access electronic archives) and open-access journals. Open-access journals "will no longer invoke copyright to restrict access to and use of the material they publish. Instead they will use copyright and other tools to ensure permanent open access to all the articles they publish. Because price is a barrier to access, these new journals will not charge subscription or access fees, and will turn to other methods for covering their expenses" (Budapest Open Access Initiative 2002, http://www.soros.org/openaccess/).

Individual academic authors, to the extent that they are able to retain or control the copyright in their works, can achieve a similar result through the use of a license such as those available from Creative Commons (see entry in this chapter).

**Business Software Alliance (BSA)**
*BSA United States:*
1150 18th Street, N.W.
Suite 700
Washington, DC 20036
Phone: (202) 872-5500
Fax: (202) 872-5501
*BSA Europe:*
79 Knightsbridge
London, SW1X 7RB
United Kingdom
Phone: 011-44-207-245-0304
Fax: 011-44-207-245-0310
*BSA Asia:*
300 Beach Road
#25-08 The Concourse
Singapore 199555

Phone: 011-65-6292-2072
Fax: 011-65-6292-6369
Website: http://www.bsa.org/

The BSA is an organization representing the interests of software publishers. It pursues software patent and copyright violators and seeks to educate the public about the (possibly exaggerated) dangers of using pirated software.

**Campaign for Digital Rights (CDR)**
Martin Keegan
Phone: 011-0044-07779-296469
E-mail: mk@ukcdr.org
Website: http://ukcdr.org/

The CDR is a British consumers' rights organization. The scope of its advocacy and its ideological stance are similar to those of the Electronic Frontier Foundation (see entry in this chapter). The CDR opposes expansion of intellectual property protection under United Kingdom and European Union laws if such expansion would occur at the expense of the consumer. It also opposes attempts by the content industry to restrict consumers' use of legally purchased content.

**Canadian Motion Picture Distributors Association (CMPDA)**
P.O. Box 92033
7400 Taschereau Boulevard
Brossard, PQ J4W 3K8
Canada
Phone: (450) 672-1990; (800) 363-9166
Fax: (450) 672-1660
E-mail: gosmond@cmpda.org
Website: http://www.cmpda.org/

The CMPDA, like the Motion Picture Association of America (see entry in this chapter), is a movie industry group representing the interests of content owners. Its Anti-Piracy Operations department tracks down and seeks criminal prosecution of makers and distributors of illegally copied DVDs, file sharers, and makers and distributors of illegal descramblers and other devices that allow free access to pay-per-view, cable, and satellite TV networks.

**Center for Intellectual Property Studies (CIP)**
Chalmers University of Technology/Göteborg University
Vera Sandbergs Allé 8A
412 96 Göteborg
Sweden
Phone: 011-46-31-772-8247
Fax: 011-46-31–772-1917
E-mail: info@cip.chalmers.se
Website: http://www.cip.chalmers.se/

The CIP, like the Centre for International Industrial Property Studies (see the entry in this chapter), is an academic study program in intellectual property. The CIP is a joint project of two Swedish universities, Chalmers University of Technology and Göteborg University. Some CIP publications are available on the website; most are in English.

**Centre d'Etudes Internationales de la Propriété Industrielle (CEIPI)**
11, rue du Maréchal Juin
BP 68
67046 Strasbourg Cedex
France
Phone: 011-03-88-14-45-86
Fax: 011-03-88-14-45-94
E-mail : ceipi@urs.u-strasbg.fr
Website: http://www.ceipi.edu/

The CEIPI (Center for International Industrial Property Studies), which was founded in 1963, is a graduate study program in intellectual property law at the Université Robert Schuman in Strasbourg, France. In addition to information about graduate studies, CEIPI makes the students' papers available on its website (in French).

**Copyright Clearance Center**
222 Rosewood Drive
Danvers, MA 01923
Phone: (978) 750-8400
Fax: (978) 646-8600
E-mail: info@copyright.com
Website: http://www.copyright.com/

The Copyright Clearance Center, like ASCAP (see entry in this chapter), is a copyright clearinghouse. While the latter is a clearinghouse for music copyrights, the former is a clearinghouse for copyrights in text. It is a member of the International Federation of Reproduction Rights Organizations (see entry in this chapter). Like other clearinghouses, it provides a single location for content owners to license their work and for those seeking to make use of that content.

**The Copyright Society of the United States of America (CSUSA)**
352 Seventh Avenue, Suite 739
New York, NY 10001
Phone: (212) 354-6401
E-mail: amy@csusa.org
Website: http://www.csusa.org/

The CSUSA is a nonpartisan organization of copyright lawyers, academics, and others in the copyright industry. It publishes the *Journal of the Copyright Society of the USA,* which can be found in law libraries. The CSUSA's website includes a useful links page under the "Research" button.

**Creative Commons**
543 Howard Street, 5th Floor
San Francisco, CA 94105-3013
Phone: (415) 946-3070
Fax: (415) 946-3001 (include "Attn: Creative Commons" on cover sheet)
E-mail: info@creativecommons.org
Website: http://creativecommons.org

For many authors, the main reason for creating a work is to have it distributed as widely as possible, rather than to control all possible uses of the work. The traditional copyright approach, reserving all of the rights granted to authors under 17 U.S.C. § 106, is designed to protect commercially valuable works. However, in some cases this may hinder rather than help the distribution of noncommercial works. Even some commercial works, especially by new entrants to a field (such as aspiring musicians), may benefit more from enhanced distribution than from enhanced protection.

Many of these authors want to preserve some rights in their work; for an example, an author might want to allow free noncommercial distribution of an e-novel but retain the right to profit from that novel if it is ever printed, bound, and sold in hard copy. Yet few authors know how to create such a license. Creative Commons provides a library of licenses to suit every purpose, along with tools for selecting the proper license. Its website declares "We work to offer creators a best-of-both-worlds way to protect their works while encouraging certain uses of them—to declare 'some rights reserved.'"

### DigitalConsumer.org
Melissa Walia
Phone: (650) 208-4523
E-mail: info@digitalconsumer.org; press@digitalconsumer.org
Website: http://www.digitalconsumer.org/

DigitalConsumer.org is a consumer rights group dedicated to protecting the traditional fair-use exception to copyright protection (and related rights, including the right to make backup copies) against encroachment by the anticircumvention provisions of Section 1201 and related laws. It advocates a six-point Consumer Technology Bill of Rights:

1. Users have the right to "time-shift" content that they have legally acquired.
2. Users have the right to "space-shift" content that they have legally acquired.
3. Users have the right to make backup copies of their content.
4. Users have the right to use legally acquired content on the platform of their choice.
5. Users have the right to translate legally acquired content into comparable formats.
6. Users have the right to use technology in order to achieve the rights previously mentioned.

The first five of these are already legal for non–copy-protected content; item 6 would make them legal for copy-protected content as well.

**Electronic Frontier Foundation (EFF)**
454 Shotwell Street
San Francisco, CA 94110-1914
Phone: (415) 436-9333
Fax: (415) 436-9993
E-mail: information@eff.org
Website: http://www.eff.org/

The EFF, founded in 1990, is perhaps the best known of the many consumers' rights groups dedicated to Internet and electronic intellectual property issues. Its website lists thirty-two topics of concern, of which seventeen—more than half—are partly or entirely intellectual property concerns. The remaining topics are mostly related to First Amendment rights, privacy rights, and other civil rights. On all of these issues EFF's stance is consistently in favor of individual rights. EFF seeks to protect individual rights against infringement by governments and corporations. The EFF has taken an active role in many intellectual property lawsuits and debates over pending legislation. The EFF website includes a great deal of useful information on these.

**Eurasian Patent Organization (EAPO)**
Staroalexeevskaya ulica 21
Moscow, 129626
Russian Federation
Phone: 011-7-495-411-61-50
Fax: 011-7-495-616-22-53
E-mail: info@eapo.org
Website: http://www.eapo.org/ (the site is in Russian, but there is a link to an English translation)

The EAPO is a regional patent organization covering nine states that were formerly part of the Soviet Union. The EAPO created a single-application patent system for these nine states. Patents granted by EAPO provide protection in all nine states. The EAPO website provides legal documents and information about the patent process in Russian and English.

**European Digital Rights (EDRI)**
Kandelaarsstraat 23
B1000 Brussels

Belgium
E-mail: press@edri.org
Website: http://www.edri.org/

The EDRI, which was founded in 2002, is a consumers' rights group along the lines of the EFF in the United States (and worldwide) and the Campaign for Digital Rights in the United Kingdom. The EDRI opposes attempts to expand intellectual property protection when that expansion would infringe on other individual rights. The "EDRI-grams" on the website include a great deal of useful information about current issues in European Union intellectual property law.

**European Patent Office (EPO)**
80298 Munich
Germany
Phone: 011-49-89-2399-4636
Fax: 011-49-89-2399-4465
Website: http://www.european-patent-office.org

The EPO, an organ of the European Patent Organization, was established by the Convention on the Grant of European Patents in 1973. It reviews and grants (or denies) applications for European patents. These patents protect an invention in the territories of all of the member states. The EPO's parent, the European Patent Organization, has also concluded bilateral patent agreements with Albania, Croatia, Latvia, Lithuania, and Macedonia, bringing those countries within the European patent system. The EPO's website includes legal documents, patent documents, and descriptive information about European patent law and the patent process.

**Fédération Internationale des Conseils en Propriété Industrielle (FICPI)**
Holbeinstrasse 36-38
4003 Basel
Switzerland
Phone: 011-33-1-44-20-7776-7302
Fax: 011-33-1-44-20-7726-0055
E-mail: JRCrump@mintz.com
Website: http://www.ficpi.org/

The FICPI (International Federation of Intellectual Property Attorneys), founded in 1906, is an organization of intellectual property attorneys in private practice in eighty countries. The FICPI newsletter and papers are available on the website.

**The Institute of Patentees and Inventors**
P.O. Box 39296
London SE3 7WH
United Kingdom
Phone: 011-44-0871-226-2091
Fax: 011-44-0208-293-5920
E-mail: ipi@invent.org.uk
Website: http://www.invent.org.uk/

The Institute of Patentees and Inventors is an organization of inventors and patent attorneys in the United Kingdom. It provides information and advice on United Kingdom patent law and the patent process, and its website offers links to other useful sites, including sites of United Kingdom copyright and trademark groups.

**Institute of Professional Representatives before the European Patent Office (epi)**
Tal 29
80331 Munich
Germany
Phone: 011-49-89-242052-0
Fax: 011-49-89-242052-20
E-mail: info@patentepi.com
Website: http://www.patentepi.com/

The epi is the European Patent Convention bar. Its members are attorneys who are eligible to practice before the European Patent Office (see entry in this chapter). The website provides information about examinations and other requirements for admission to practice before the European Patent Office.

**Institute of Trade Mark Attorneys (ITMA)**
Canterbury House
2-6 Sydenham Road
Croydon, Surrey, CRO 9XE

United Kingdom
Phone: 011-44-020-8686-2052
Fax: 011-44-020-8680-5723
E-mail: tm@itma.org.uk
Website: http://www.itma.org.uk/

The ITMA, which was founded in 1934, is a professional organization for trademark attorneys practicing in the United Kingdom. Its website includes information on the trademark registration process in the United Kingdom.

**Intellectual Property Owners Association (IPO)**
1255 23rd Street NW
Suite 200
Washington, DC 20037
Phone: (202) 466-2396
Website: http://www.IPO.org

The IPO is a content industry group that lobbies state, national, and international legislative and rule-making bodies for rules more favorable to intellectual property owners. Its website provides analysis of current intellectual property issues and general background information. Particularly useful to aspiring intellectual property attorneys is its Corporate IP Career Bank, which provides job listings and a resume bank.

**International Anticounterfeiting Coalition (IACC)**
1725 K Street, N.W., Suite 411
Washington, DC 20006
Phone: (202) 223-6667
Fax: (202) 223-6668
E-mail: rwynne@iacc.org
Website: http://www.iacc.org/

The IACC is an organization representing the interests of copyright and trademark owners. It seeks to prevent the manufacture and sale of counterfeit goods, from Adidas sneakers to Zippo lighters, in the United States and around the world. It carries out its work through education and outreach, through lobbying, and through collecting information about counterfeit goods.

**International Association for the Advancement of Teaching and Research in Intellectual Property (ATRIP)**
Professor Dr. Ysolde Gendreau, President

Faculte de droit
Universite de Montreal
C.P. 6128 Succursale A. Centre-Ville
Montreal, Quebec
Canada H3C 3J7
Phone: (514) 343-6062
Fax: (514) 343-2030
E-mail: ysolde.gendreau@umontreal.ca
Website: http://www.atrip.org/

The ATRIP is an organization of intellectual property law professors and researchers. The group organizes an annual academic conference, and some documents from past conferences are available on the ATRIP website.

**International Association of Entertainment Lawyers**
Duncan Calow
DLA Piper Rudnick Gray Cary UK LLP
3 Noble Street
London EC2V 7EE
United Kingdom
Phone: 011-44-8700-111-111
Website: http://www.iael.org/

The International Association of Entertainment Lawyers, founded in 1977, is, as the name says, an organization of entertainment attorneys. Each year it publishes a book on current issues in entertainment law; these often include intellectual property issues.

**International Federation of Inventors' Associations (IFIA)**
IFIA Secretariat
P.O. Box 319
H-1591 Budapest
Hungary
Phone: 011-36-20-945-8078
Fax: 011-36-1-422-09-36
E-mail: ifia@inventor.hu
Website: http://www.invention-ifia.ch/

The IFIA is an umbrella organization for inventors' associations in eighty-two countries. Its member organizations provide a variety of assistance to inventors, including help in navigating the patent law system.

**International Federation of Reproduction Rights
Organizations (IFRRO)**
Rue du Prince Royal 87
B-1050 Brussels
Belgium
Phone: 011-32-2-551-08-99
Fax: 011-32-2-551-08-95
E-mail: secretariat@ifrro.be
Website: http://www.ifrro.org

The IFRRO represents the interests of copyright holders. Its mission statement declares "IFRRO works to increase on an international basis the lawful use of copyright works and eliminate *unauthorised copying* by promoting efficient *Collective Management of rights* through RROs" (emphasis in original; "RROs" are reproduction rights organizations). Individual copyright holders usually lack the resources to detect and seek redress for copyright violations. Persons wishing to make lawful copies of copyrighted material may be unable to locate individual authors to obtain permission, so RROs seek to solve both problems by locating and suing copyright violators and by acting as clearinghouses to authorize reproduction of the copyrighted material. The IFRRO is an umbrella organization uniting and coordinating the activities of more than 100 RROs and similar organizations.

**International Intellectual Property Alliance (IIPA)**
1747 Pennsylvania Avenue, N.W., Suite 825
Washington, DC 20006-4637
Phone: (202) 833-4198
Fax: (202) 872-0546
E-mail: info@iipa.com
Website: http://www.iipa.com/

The IIPA is a content industry coalition whose goal is to expand the reach of the global copyright regime and combat piracy of copyrighted content. Despite its name, it focuses solely on copyright, rather than on other forms of intellectual property. The website provides IIPA press releases and other IIPA documents.

**International Intellectual Property Institute (IIPI)**
1100 H Street, N.W., Suite 1100
Washington, DC 20005
Telephone: (202) 544-6610

Fax: (202) 478-1955
Website: http://www.iipi.org/

The IIPI is a Washington, DC, think tank advocating the spread of intellectual property regimes on the U.S. or developed-world model to developing countries. Its website provides many of the Institute's policy and research papers as well as some legal materials.

**International Law Association (ILA)**
Charles Clore House
17 Russell Square
London WC1B 5DR
United Kingdom
Phone: 011-44-20-7323-2978
Fax: 011-44-20-7323-3580
E-mail: info@ila-hq.org
Website: http://www.ila-hq.org

The ILA was founded in 1873 for "the study, clarification and development of international law, both public and private, and the furtherance of international understanding and respect for international law." Its International Law on Biotechnology Committee and International Trade Law Committee deal with concerns related to international intellectual property law. The ILA website includes conference reports and resolutions of these committees.

**International Trademark Association (INTA)**
655 Third Avenue, 10th Floor
New York, NY 10017-5617
Phone: (212) 642-1700
Fax (212) 768-7796
E-mail: info@inta.org
Website: www.inta.org

The INTA, founded in 1878 and has members in more than 180 countries, represents the interests of trademark owners. In addition to its advocacy efforts on behalf of the owners of trademarks and other marks, the INTA gathers information to be used by its members. Most INTA publications are available online only to members, but the FAQs section of the INTA website provides a great deal of useful basic information about marks and trademark law.

**Internet Corporation for Assigned Names and Numbers (ICANN)**
*Marina del Rey Office:*
4676 Admiralty Way, Suite 330
Marina del Rey, CA 90292
Phone: (310) 823-9358
Fax: (310) 823-8649
*Brussels Office:*
6 Rond Point Schuman, Bt. 5
Brussels B-1040
Belgium
Tel: 011-32-2-234-7870
Fax: 011-32-2-234-7848
E-mail: press@icann.org; info@icann.org
Website: http://www.icann.org/

The ICANN administers the Internet domain name system. It was created in 1998 as a nonprofit organization under the laws of California, by agreement between the Internet Assigned Numbers Authority and the U.S. Department of Commerce. ICANN directly administers the top-level domain name system. (Top-level domains are the parts of a domain name that appear after the last dot in the URL, such as ".com," ".edu," ".cn," and ".ca.") It authorizes national or private registrars, as appropriate, to assign domain names within the top-level domains. The assignment of domain names has trademark implications, and ICANN also resolves disputes regarding rights to domain names under its Uniform Domain Name Dispute Resolution Policy (see Chapter 2).

**Japan Intellectual Property Association (JIPA)**
Asahi Seimei Otemachi Building 18F
6-1 Ohtemachi 2-chome
Chiyoda-ku
Tokyo, 100-0004
Japan
Phone: 011-81-03-5205-3321
Fax: 011-81-03-5205-3391
E-mail: info@jipa.or.jp
Website: http://www.jipa.or.jp/ (in Japanese);
http://www.jipa.or.jp/content/english/ (in English)

The JIPA, founded in 1938, is an organization of lawyers, academics, government employees, and other workers in the field of Japanese intellectual property law. It publishes policy statements, some of which are available online in English, and the *Journal of the Japan Intellectual Property Association.* The journal's table of contents is available in English, as are some, but not all, of the articles.

**Max-Planck-Institut für Geistiges Eigentum, Wettbewerbs-und Steuerrecht**
Marstallplatz 1
80539 Munich, Germany
Phone: 011-49-89-24246-0
Fax: 011-49-89-24246-501
E-mail: Institut@ip.mpg.de
Website: http://www.ip.mpg.de/ww/en/pub/news.cfm
(in German and English)

The Max-Planck-Institut für Geistiges Eigentum, Wettbewerbs-und Steuerrecht (Max Planck Institute for Intellectual Property, Competition and Tax Law) is a research institute within Germany's famed Max Planck Institute. It does not offer courses or professional degrees, but exists solely for advanced research in areas including intellectual property law. Some Institute publications, many of them in English, are available through the website.

**Motion Picture Association of America (MPAA)**
*Los Angeles Office:*
15503 Ventura Boulevard
Encino, CA 91436
Phone: (818) 995-6600
Fax: (818) 382-1795
*International Offices:*
108 rue du Trône
B-1050 Brussels
Belgium
Phone: 011-32-2-778-2711
Fax: 011-32-2-778-2700

Rua Sergipe 475, 10th Floor
Higienópolis
São Paulo, SP 01243-001

Brazil
Phone: 011-5511-3667-2080
Fax: 011-5511-3825-5544

No. 1 Magazine Road
Central Mall #04-07
Singapore 059571
Phone: 011-65-6253-1033
Fax: 011-65-6255-1838
Website: http://www.mpaa.org

The MPAA is one of the two most influential content-industry organizations in the United States, the other being the Recording Industry Association of America (see entry in this chapter). For nearly four decades, from 1966 to 2004, the MPAA was headed by the legendary Jack Valenti (see Chapter 5). The MPAA performs a wide variety of functions, including administering the movie content rating system in use in the United States (G, PG, PG-13, R, NC-17). In recent years, however, the MPAA's attentions and efforts have been largely focused on video piracy.

Piracy of films does not pose quite the threat to the industry's business model that piracy of music poses to the music content industry's business model. The amount of money invested in each film, however, is much greater than the amount invested in each song. The MPAA tries to combat piracy at every level, from education and outreach aimed at young Internet users to lawsuits and criminal prosecutions against copyright infringers and incessant lobbying of Congress, international organizations, the World Trade Organization (WTO), and foreign governments for greater intellectual property protection.

**Music Publishers' Association (MPA)**
243 5th Avenue, Suite 236
New York, NY 10016
Phone: (212) 327-4044
E-mail: admin@mpa.org
Website: http://www.mpa.org/

The MPA, founded in 1895, deals with all aspects of music publishing but focuses particularly on publishing of printed music. Its Copyright Resource Center provides copyright search and clearance services, as well as information about copyright law and the licensing process.

**National Association of Patent Practitioners (NAPP)**
4680-18-i Monticello Avenue, PMB101
Williamsburg, VA 23188
Phone: (800) 216-9588
Fax: (757) 220-3928
Website: www.napp.org

The NAPP, founded in 1996, focuses on the actual practice of patent law before the U.S. Patent and Trademark Office, rather than on broader issues of intellectual property policy. Its website provides useful links.

**Office for Harmonization in the Internal Market (Trade Marks and Designs) (OHIM)**
Avenida de Europa, 4
E-03008 Alicante
Spain
Phone: 011-34-96-513-9100
Fax: 011-34-96-513-1344
Website: http://oami.eu.int/en/default.htm

The OHIM is the European Union's trademark office. It can grant trademarks that are valid in all member states of the European Union. The website provides links to legal documents related to the trademark process.

**Open Society Institute (OSI)**
400 West 59th Street
New York, NY 10019
Phone: (212) 548-0600
Website: http://www.soros.org/initiatives/information

The OSI, with the Soros Foundations Network, declares in its mission statement that its goal is "to shape public policy to promote democratic governance, human rights, and economic, legal, and social reform." In furtherance of these goals, the OSI's Information Program has called for a critical reexamination of intellectual property laws. It is a major driving force behind the Open Access movement and sponsors conferences such as the 2006 Brussels Conference on the Politics and Ideology of Intellectual Property.

**Organisation Africaine de la Propriété Intellectuelle (OAPI)**
BP 887 Yaoundé
Cameroun
Phone: 011-237-220-57-00
Fax: 011-237-220-57-27
E-mail: oapi.oa@oapi.oa.wipo.net
Website: http://www.oapi.wipo.net

The OAPI is the francophone counterpart of the ARIPO (see entry in this chapter), and it shares many of ARIPO's concerns and goals. Its members are fourteen former French colonies, plus Equatorial Guinea and Guinea-Bissau. Most, although not all, of the documents on its website are available in English as well as French.

**Patent Office of the Cooperation Council for the Arab States of the Gulf**
Riyadh, Saudi Arabia
Website: http://www.gcc-sg.org/ (in Arabic only; partial English translation at http://www.gcc-sg.org/index_e.html)

The Patent Office of the Cooperation Council for the Arab States of the Gulf provides a single-filing, unitary patent process under which patents may be granted for six Persian Gulf states. Translations of many legal documents are available from the English-language version of the website.

**Project Gutenberg**
809 North 1500 West
Salt Lake City, UT 84116
E-mail: help@pglaf.org
Website: http://www.gutenberg.org

Project Gutenberg is concerned not so much with intellectual property as with its absence. The oldest and perhaps the largest public domain literary archive, Project Gutenberg makes electronic versions of public domain works available to the public, free of charge. Many of these works are difficult or impossible to find elsewhere; the duration of copyright is so long that by the time the copyright expires, the work has often been out of print for decades.

More than 18,000 e-books are now available through Project Gutenberg, with more being added constantly. Most are uncopyrighted works, at least under U.S. law; a few are copyrighted works that the copyright holders have licensed Project Gutenberg to distribute. Note that works that are in the public domain in the United States may still be protected by copyright in other countries; a particularly notorious example is J.M. Barrie's *Peter Pan.*

**Public Knowledge**
1875 Connecticut Avenue, N.W., Suite 650
Washington, DC 20009
Phone: (202) 518-0020
Fax: (202) 986-2539
E-mail: pk@publicknowledge.org
Website: http://www.publicknowledge.org/

Public Knowledge is a consumer rights organization that is concerned with intellectual property law, especially copyright law. Its mission statement sets forth four goals: (1) "Ensuring that U.S. intellectual property law . . . [provides] an incentive to creators and innovators while benefiting the public through the free flow of information and ideas"; (2) "Preserving an Internet that is built upon open standards and protocols"; (3) "Protecting consumers of digital technology from market practices designed to erode competition, choice and fairness"; and (4) "Ensuring that international intellectual property policies are adopted through democratic processes and with public interest participation." In furtherance of these goals, Public Knowledge engages in advocacy and reports on legislation potentially affecting consumers' rights.

Public Knowledge also engages in special projects. Empowering Creators in the Digital Age is an attempt to determine the ideal balance between the need of content creators to make use of prior copyrighted works and the need of those same content creators for protection for their created content. The Global Knowledge Initiative strives to represent the interests of the public, particularly as consumers, in the ongoing international intellectual property rule-making process. The Open Access Project promotes open-access publishing of scholarly works (see the Budapest Open Access Initiative and Open Society Institute entry). The Wi-Fi Project is not an intellectual property project; it is dedicated to bringing wireless Internet access to the National Mall in Washington, D.C.

**Recording Industry Association of America (RIAA)**
1330 Connecticut Avenue, N.W.
Washington, DC 20036
Fax: (202) 775-7253
Website: http://www.riaa.com

The best known of all content owners' groups, the RIAA represents music content industry companies. It has taken an extremely high-profile, adversarial approach to the threat digital music piracy poses to its members' business models. In doing so, it has made many enemies and has alienated some consumers. Inasmuch as there is a single target for consumer rage arising from intellectual property issues, that target is the RIAA.

To judge from its website, the RIAA sees itself as fighting a battle for its members' survival. Digital copying and sharing of compressed music files is easy; there is little or no incentive for consumers to pay sixteen dollars or more to buy an album on CD to obtain a single desired song. For years, the RIAA attempted to preserve the bundling of songs in albums as the primary model for delivery of music content to the public; it was not until the advent of iTunes that a means of delivering single songs directly to consumers gained widespread acceptance.

To protect its business model, and now to protect the paid-download model against the free alternatives offered by P2P (peer-to-peer) networks, the RIAA has engaged in incessant litigation and lobbying. It has sued to force Internet service providers to disclose the names of their allegedly file-sharing subscribers. It has sued equipment makers for making MP3 players, file-sharing services as third-party copyright infringers, and individual consumers as direct infringers. It has lobbied for increased copyright protection, particularly against online file sharing.

These often heavy-handed tactics have brought some negative media attention. The suits against individual Internet users, particularly when those users are children or the elderly, have been particularly unpopular. The RIAA is a frequent target of cartoonists and op-ed columnists. It has shown some tentative signs of willingness to compromise with file-sharing networks, but it seems unlikely to change its litigation and lobbying strategies in the near future. Its website is a valuable resource for intellectual property researchers, and it contains a wealth of information on the RIAA's positions and policies.

**Société des Gens de Lettres (SGDL)**
Hôtel de Massa
38, rue du Faubourg Saint-Jacques
75014 Paris
France
Phone: 011-33-1-53-10-12-13
E-mail: sgdl@sgdl.org
Website: http://www.sgdl.org

The Société des Gens de Lettres, which was founded in 1838, advises and represents the interests of writers in a variety of areas, particularly on intellectual property issues. It gave rise to the Association Littéraire et Artistique Internationale, which in turn gave rise to the Berne Convention and the current international copyright law regime. Its website includes a great deal of practical information (in French) on French copyright law.

**Trade Marks, Patents and Designs Federation (TMPDF)**
Fifth Floor, 63-66 Hatton Garden
London EC1N 8LE
United Kingdom
Phone: 011-44-020-7242-3923
Fax: 011-44-020-7242-3924
E-mail: admin@tmpdf.org.uk
Website: http://www.tmpdf.org.uk/

The TMPDF, founded in 1920, is an industry organization that provides input representing its members' interests in the United Kingdom and international intellectual property rule-making process.

**Tufts Multilaterals Project**
Edwin Ginn Library
The Fletcher School
160 Packard Avenue
Medford, MA 02155-7082
Phone: (617) 627-3273
Fax: (617) 627-3736
E-mail: ginnref@tufts.edu
Website: http://fletcher.tufts.edu/multi/trade.html

The Tufts Multilaterals Project is an online treaty database. Under the heading "Trade and Commercial Relations" it provides the full text of several intellectual property treaties. It also provides general information on treaty research and links to other online international law resources.

**United States Copyright Office**
Library of Congress
Copyright Office
101 Independence Avenue, S.E.
Washington, DC 20559-6000
Website: http://www.copyright.gov/

The U.S. Copyright Office is an essential resource for anyone interested in intellectual property law. In addition to registering U.S. copyrights, the Copyright Office provides access to copyright registration records, information about the registration process, and information on copyright licensing. It also provides the full and updated text of copyright laws, regulations, cases, treaties, and other materials, as well as detailed information about these sources. For example, Copyright Office Circular 38a, which is available on the website, contains complete information on U.S. copyright relations with other countries. From Circular 38a, it is easy to determine that U.S. copyright relations with, say, Canada are governed by treaties including a bilateral treaty dated 1 January 1924; the Berne Convention; the Geneva version of the Universal Copyright Convention; and Trade-Related Aspects of Intellectual Property (TRIPs). Copyright Office circulars also address a wide variety of specific types of content, from cartoons to recipes. Copyright Office reports and studies provide more detailed examinations of some topics and of the effects of changes in U.S. copyright laws.

**United States Patent and Trademark Office (USPTO)**
600 Dulany Street
Alexandria, VA 22314
Phone: (800) 786-9199 or (571) 272-1000
Fax: (571) 273-8300
E-mail: usptoinfo@uspto.gov (put "Patents" or "Trademarks" in subject line)
Website: http://www.uspto.gov/

Like the Copyright Office for copyright law, the USPTO is an essential resource for anyone interested in patent or trademark law. In addition to its primary functions of registering trademarks and granting (or denying) patents, the USPTO provides a wealth of information on its website. This includes information about the various types of intellectual property protection available and the process for obtaining each. The site provides links to U.S. and international legal materials. Employees of the USPTO are eligible for active membership in the Patent and Trademark Society, which publishes the influential *Journal of the Patent and Trademark Society.* (Nonemployees are eligible only for associate membership.)

**World Intellectual Property Organization (WIPO)**
34, chemin des Colombettes
Geneva, Switzerland
Phone: 011-41-22-338-95-47; 011-41-22-338-91-11
Fax: 011-41-22-733-54-28
E-mail: publicinf@wipo.int
Website: http://www.wipo.int

The WIPO is responsible for administering most of the treaties upon which the international intellectual property law regime is based. WIPO's origins can be traced to 1893, when the administrative organizations of the 1883 Paris Convention and the 1886 Berne Convention united to form the Bureaux Internationaux Réunis pour la Protection de la Propriété Intellectuelle (BIRPI). BIRPI grew over the years and in 1967 became WIPO. Among the most important of the two dozen treaties now administered by WIPO are the Berne and Paris Conventions, the Madrid Agreement and Protocol (trademark), and the Patent Cooperation Treaty. Multilateral treaties not administered by WIPO (such as the Universal Copyright Convention and the Buenos Aires Convention) are relatively unimportant, with one significant exception—TRIPs, administered by the WTO (see entry in this chapter).

For intellectual property researchers, WIPO's website is perhaps the single most valuable site listed in this chapter. It includes the full text of all of the treaties administered by WIPO, as well as lists of parties to each treaty and the dates that those countries became parties. It also includes information about the copyright laws of member states and links to those laws online, where available; WIPO documents, many with analysis of intellectual property treaties and legislation; and links to documents from other international organizations, including the WTO.

**World Trade Organization (WTO)**
Centre William Rappard
Rue de Lausanne 154
CH-1211 Geneva 21
Switzerland
Phone: 011-41-22-739-51-11
Fax: 011-41-22-731-42-06
E-mail: enquiries@wto.org
Website: http://www.wto.org/

After decades of negotiations under the General Agreement on Tariffs and Trade, in 1995 the countries of the world succeeded in establishing the WTO. In the Uruguay Round of negotiations (1986–1994) leading up to formation of the WTO, some countries, including the United States, advocated inclusion of an intellectual property agreement in the WTO treaty package. Advocates of this intellectual property agreement were motivated in part by concerns that the existing WIPO regime provided inadequate protections for pharmaceutical patents; however, the agreement that was ultimately adopted was the most comprehensive intellectual property agreement yet created, covering nearly every aspect of intellectual property.

This agreement, the Agreement on TRIPs, created a separate international intellectual property protection system outside the WIPO regime; the WTO and WIPO harmonized the two systems with the 1995 Agreement Between the World Intellectual Property Organization and the World Trade Organization. TRIPs serves more to bring about uniformity in intellectual property law than to deal with day-to-day administrative matters such as multinational patent applications, which are handled by WIPO. However, TRIPs provides a valuable dispute resolution mechanism: The WTO dispute resolution body can resolve intellectual property disputes between WTO members arising under TRIPs.

The WTO website provides the full text of TRIPs and a considerable body of information about the treaty.

# 8

# Resources

A great many works on intellectual property law have been published and continue to be published daily. The books, articles, journals, and other resources in this chapter provide a sampling of materials for further research, as do the cases. The listed statutes and treaties provide a fairly comprehensive guide to the legal regime governing copyright, patent, and trademark law in the United States and internationally.

## Books

**Elias, Stephen R., and Richard Stim. 2006.** *Patent, Copyright and Trademark: An Intellectual Property Desk Reference.* **8th ed. Berkeley, CA: Nolo Press.**

**Stim, Richard. 2004.** *Getting Permission: How to License and Clear Copyrighted Materials Online and Off.* **2nd ed. Berkeley, CA: Nolo Press.**

These two books, both from Nolo Press, are aimed at nonlawyers. Nolo Press (www.nolo.com) publishes do-it-yourself legal guides; Nolo declares that "Our goal is to help people handle their own everyday legal matters—or learn enough about them to make working with a lawyer a more satisfying experience." The two works listed here, like most Nolo publications, are practical guides; they are useful in dealing with immediate intellectual property issues, but provide less theoretical depth, historical background, or policy analysis than some of the other reference works available. *Getting Permission* deals specifically with copyright, focusing on the use of materials copyrighted by others. *An Intellectual Property Desk Reference* provides definitions of intellectual property law terms, in more accessible form but with less detail than *McCarthy's Desk Encyclopedia of Intellectual Property* (also listed in this section).

**Garner, Bryan A., ed. 2006. *Black's Law Dictionary*. 8th ed. St. Paul, MN: West Publishing.**

Intellectual property law, like any area of law, involves the use of fairly specialized terminology. For lawyers as well as nonlawyers, terms like "constructive knowledge" or "equitable remedy" often require definition; they do not mean what the everyday English meaning of the words might suggest. *Black's Law Dictionary* is a standard legal reference used by attorneys, judges, academics, law students, and others in the legal profession. When planning to spend any amount of time reading legal materials, it is a good idea to keep a copy of *Black's* (or a similar work) at hand.

## Similar Works

**Kohn, Al, and Bob Kohn.  2000. *Kohn on Music Licensing*. 3rd ed. New York: Aspen Publishers.**

Music copyright involves a web of overlapping and intertwined copyright interests. Separate persons may hold copyrights to the melody, the lyrics, and the performance of a single song. Some or all of these copyright holders may have rights to control the reproduction of the performed work, the reproduction of the lyrics or sheet music in printed form, the broadcast of the recorded work, the live performance of the work by other artists, the recording of a performance of the work by other artists, the licensing of the melody to other artists who wish to put different words to it, and other uses. Figuring out who has the right to control what often pits composers, songwriters, performers, and recording companies against each other. *Kohn on Music Licensing* is perhaps the best guide to untangling this mess. (The third edition comes with a helpful e-documents supplement on CD.)

**Leaffer, Marshall A. 2005. *Understanding Copyright Law*. 4th ed. New York: LexisNexis Matthew Bender.**

*Understanding Copyright Law* is an entry in the Understanding series from the Matthew Bender division of LexisNexis. The Understanding series is similar to the Nutshell series (see Miller and Davis); like the Nutshell series, it is aimed at legal professionals and law students. *Understanding Copyright Law* provides, as the title suggests, a comprehensive overview of U.S. copyright law, including historical background, and international law affecting U.S. copyright law.

**Lessig, Lawrence. 2004.** *Free Culture: How Big Media Uses Technology and the Law to Lock Down Culture and Control Creativity.* **New York: Penguin.**

**Lessig, Lawrence. 2001.** *The Future of Ideas: The Fate of the Commons in a Connected World.* **New York: Random House.**

**Lessig, Lawrence. 1999.** *Code and Other Laws of Cyberspace.* **New York: Basic Books.**

Intellectual property is a field in crisis, largely, but not entirely, as a result of the advent of home computing and the Internet. A library could be filled with books written about intellectual property and the digital information revolution; Lawrence Lessig is among the best-known and most influential commentators. In the three books listed here, Lessig presents his thesis that the expansion of intellectual property protection is stifling innovation, causing economic and social harm.

His prediction in *Code and Other Laws of Cyberspace* that "we will see the Net move to an architecture of control" has proved accurate. In the intellectual property field, improved digital rights management technology and loss of online privacy, together with enhanced legal rights for content owners, have made online copyright infringement a more difficult and risky business, without managing to stop the practice. *The Future of Ideas* develops Lessig's thesis further, warning that control of the Internet by content-owning corporations will stifle creativity. In *Free Culture,* Lessig examines the intellectual property battles over file sharing and his own involvement in the court battle against the Sonny Bono Copyright Term Extension Act, a battle that ended in defeat with the Supreme Court's decision in *Eldred v. Ashcroft.*

McCarthy, J. Thomas, Roger E. Schechter, and David J. Franklyn. 2004. *McCarthy's Desk Encyclopedia of Intellectual Property.* 3rd ed. **Washington, DC: Bureau of National Affairs.**

Where *Black's* and other law dictionaries leave off, *McCarthy's* begins. *McCarthy's Desk Encyclopedia of Intellectual Property* is a more specialized reference work with definitions of arcane terms from all areas of intellectual property. The definitions include detailed explanations and references to statutes, cases, and other sources. It covers both U.S. and international intellectual property law.

Miller, Arthur Raphael, and Michael H. Davis. 2000. *Intellectual Property: Patents, Trademarks, and Copyright in a Nutshell.* St. Paul, MN: West Publishing.

*Intellectual Property: Patents, Trademarks, and Copyright in a Nutshell* is an entry in the Nutshell series from West Publishing, one of the largest and oldest legal publishing companies in the United States. The Nutshell series is designed with law students in mind, although Nutshells are often used by practicing attorneys and other legal professionals as well. This makes Nutshells somewhat more accessible than works aimed entirely at practicing attorneys or legal academics, although they are still somewhat more challenging than works aimed at the general public, such as those from Nolo Press or the "For Dummies" series. *Intellectual Property in a Nutshell* covers the three traditional areas: copyright, patents, and trademarks.

Vaidhyanathan, Siva. 2004. *The Anarchist in the Library: How the Clash Between Freedom and Control Is Hacking the Real World and Crashing the System.* New York: Basic Books.

Vaidhyanathan, Siva. 2001. *Copyrights and Copywrongs: The Rise of Intellectual Property and How It Threatens Creativity.* New York: New York University Press.

Professor Vaidhyanathan, like Professor Lessig (see earlier listing), is a well-known commentator on intellectual property law and the Internet. Vaidhyanathan, a former journalist who teaches communications, approaches the issues from a somewhat different perspective, but reaches a similar conclusion: The current expansion of intellectual property rights is strangling creativity and has the potential for dire economic and political consequences. In

*Copyrights and Copywrongs* he warns that the stifling effect of the current copyright law is unevenly distributed, so that the cultural expression of minority cultures is disproportionately affected. (See also Greene 1999.) In *The Anarchist in the Library* he relates this problem to a broader political problem, describing the ways in which attempts to control information and attempts to evade that control are related to the global problems of totalitarianism and terrorism, respectively.

*Everybody's Legal Glossary.* http://www.nolo.com/glossary.cfm.

Gifis, Steven, ed. 2003. *Law Dictionary.* 5th ed. Hauppauge, NY: Barron's Educational Series.

Handler, Jack. 1993. *Ballentine's Law Dictionary: Legal Assistant Edition.* Clifton Park, NY: Thomson Delmar Learning.

*Law.com Dictionary.* http://dictionary.law.com/.

*Legal Dictionary.* http://dictionary.lp.findlaw.com.

Merriam-Webster. 1996. *Merriam-Webster's Dictionary of Law.* Springfield, MA: Merriam-Webster

## Other Titles

Biegel, Stuart. 2001. *Beyond Our Control? Confronting the Limits of Our Legal System in the Age of Cyberspace.* Cambridge, MA: MIT Press.

Buergenthal, Thomas, and Sean D. Murphy. 2002. *Public International Law in a Nutshell.* 3rd ed. St. Paul, MN: West Publishing.

Charmasson, Henri. 2004. *Patents, Copyrights & Trademarks for Dummies.* Hoboken, NJ: Wiley Publishing.

Chused, Richard, ed. 1998. *A Copyright Anthology: The Technology Frontier.* Cincinnati, OH: Anderson Publishing.

D'Amato, Anthony, and Doris Estelle Long, eds. 1996. *International Intellectual Property Anthology.* Cincinnati, OH: Anderson Publishing.

Dinwoodie, Graeme B., William O. Hennessey, and Shira Perlmutter. 2002. *International and Comparative Patent Law.* Newark, NJ: LexisNexis Matthew Bender.

Fishman, Stephen. 2001. *Copyright Your Software.* 3rd ed. Berkeley, CA: Nolo Press.

Goldstein, Paul. 2001. *International Copyright: Principles, Law, and Practice.* Oxford: Oxford University Press.

Menn, Joseph. 2003. *All the Rave: The Rise and Fall of Shawn Fanning's Napster.* New York: Crown Business.

Nimmer, David. 2004. *Copyright: Sacred Text, Technology, and the DMCA.* The Hague: Kluwer Academic/Plenum Publishers.

Pires de Carvalho, Nuno. 2005. *The TRIPS Regime of Patent Rights.* 2nd ed. The Hague: Kluwer Law International.

Samuels, Edward. 2000. *The Illustrated History of Copyright.* New York: St. Martin's Press.

Schechter, Frank I. 1925. *Historical Foundations of the Law Relating to Trade-marks.* New York: Columbia University Press.

# Journal, Magazine, and News Website Articles and Pamphlets

Intellectual property law is a field of controversy and rapid change. Much of the controversy takes place on, or is reported in, the pages of academic journals, which are also often among the first to report and explain changes in the law. A list of recent articles that have been particularly informative, influential, or both is provided below, followed by a list of journals specializing in intellectual property law and the closely related fields of technology and entertainment law.

Law libraries and some other libraries will have copies of these journals; the articles are also available through the proprietary databases listed at the end of this chapter, and sometimes, though not always, from the websites of the journals that published them; these website addresses, where available, are given in the "Journals" section.

Austin, Graeme W. 2004. "Trademarks and the Burdened Imagination." *Brooklyn Law Review* 69: 827.

BBC. "EU Software Patent Law Faces Axe." February 17, 2005. http://news.bbc.co.uk/1/hi/technology/4274811.stm.

BBC. "Patents: Gone but Not Forgotten." July 15, 2005. http://news.bbc.co.uk/2/hi/technology/4685731.stm.

Berger, Eric. 2004. "Traffix Devices, Inc. v. Marketing Displays, Inc.: Intellectual Property in Crisis: Rubbernecking the Aftermath of the United States Supreme Court's Traffix Wreck." *Arkansas Law Review* 57: 383.

Byerly, Lisa M. 1998. "Look and Feel Protection of Web Site User Interfaces: Copyright or Trade Dress?" *Santa Clara Computer and High Technology Law Journal* 14: 221.

Choi, Yunjeong. 2003. "Development of Copyright Protection in Korea: Its History, Inherent Limits, and Suggested Solutions." *Brooklyn Journal of International Law* 28: 643.

Cole, Rodger R. 1995. "Substantial Similarity in the Ninth Circuit: A 'Virtually Identical' 'Look and Feel'?" *Santa Clara Computer and High Technology Law Journal* 11: 417.

Conley, John M. 2003. "The International Law of Business Method Patents." *U.S. Patent and Trademark Office Economic Review,* October. http://ideas.repec.org/a/fip/fedaer/y2003p15-33nv.88no.4.html.

"Dancing with Google's Spiders." 2006. *Economist Technology Quarterly,* March 11, 14–15.

"Face Value: The Quiet Iconoclast—With KaZaA, Niklas Zennstrom Undermined the Music Industry." 2004. *The Economist,* July 3, 54.

Froomkin, A. Michael. 2000. "Wrong Turn in Cyberspace: Using ICANN to Route Around the APA and the Constitution." *Duke Law Journal* 50: 17.

Gilwit, Dara B. 2003. "The Latest Cybersquatting Trend: Typosquatters, their Changing Tactics, and How to Prevent Public Deception and Trademark Infringement." *Washington University Journal of Law and Policy* 11: 267.

Ginsburg, Jane C. 1990. "A Tale of Two Copyrights: Literary Property in Revolutionary France and America." *Tulane Law Review* 64: 991.

Greene, Kevin J. 2004. "Abusive Trademark Litigation and the Incredible Shrinking Confusion Doctrine—Trademark Abuse in the Context of Entertainment Media and Cyberspace." *Harvard Journal of Law and Public Policy* 27: 609.

Greene, Kevin J. 1999. "Copyright, Culture, and Black Music: A Legacy of Unequal Protection." *Hastings Communication & Entertainment Law Journal* 20: 339.

Hasan, Amar A. 2005. "Sweating in Europe: The European Union Database Directive." *Computer Law Review and Technology Journal* 9: 479.

"I Want My P2P: Record Labels Are Trying to Do Deals with File-Sharing Networks." 2004. *The Economist,* November 20, 65.

Kellner, Lauren Fisher. 1994. "Trade Dress Protection for Computer User Interface 'Look and Feel.'" *University of Chicago Law Review* 61: 1011.

Leaffer, Marshall. 1990. "International Copyright from an American Perspective." *Arkansas Law Review* 43: 373.

Lee, Ilhyung. 2001. "Culturally-Based Copyright Systems? The U.S. and Korea in Conflict." *Washington University Law Quarterly* 79: 1103.

Likourezos, George. 1995. "Trademark Law in the Computer Age: Applying Trademark Principles to the 'Look and Feel' of Software." *Journal of the Patent and Trademark Office Society* 77: 451.

McMillan, Robert. 2006. "DHS: Sony Rootkit May Lead to Regulation: U.S. Officials Aim to Avoid Future Security Threats Caused by Copy Protection." *ComputerWorld,* February 16. http://www.computerworld.com/governmenttopics/govern ment/policy/story/0,10801,108793,00.html.

Nard, Craig Allen, and Andrew P. Morriss. 2004. *Constitutionalizing Patents: From Venice to Philadelphia.* Case Research Paper Series in Legal Studies, Working Paper 04-12. http://ssrn.com/abstract =585661.

Nguyen, Xuan-Thao N. 2000. "Should It Be a Free for All? The Challenge of Extending Trade Dress Protection to the Look and Feel of Web Sites in the Evolving Internet." *American University Law Review* 49: 1233.

Robert, Daphne. 1996. "Commentary on the Lanham Trade-Mark Act." *Trademark Reporter* 6: 373.

Rosenoer, Jonathan. "Apple Loses." *Cyberlaw.* 1994. http://www.cyberlaw.com/cylw994.html.

Samuelson, Pamela. 1997. "The U.S. Digital Agenda at WIPO." *Virginia Journal of International Law* 37: 369.

Samuelson, Pamela, Randall Davis, Mitchell D. Kapor, and J. H. Reichman. 1994. "A Manifesto Concerning the Legal Protection of Computer Programs." *Columbia Law Review* 94: 2308.

Schneider, Mark. 1998. "The European Union Database Directive." *Berkeley Technology Law Journal* 13: 551.

Schortgen, Steven. 1994. "'Dressing' up Software Interface Protection: The Application of Two Pesos to 'Look and Feel.'" *Cornell Law Review* 80: 158.

Smith, Seagrumn. 2003. "From Napster to KaZaA: The Battle Over Peer-to-Peer Filesharing Goes International." *Duke Law & Technology Review* 2003: 8.

Sorgen, Rebecca S. 2001. "Trademark Confronts Free Speech on the Information Superhighway: 'Cybergripers' Face a Constitutional Collision." *Loyola of Los Angeles Entertainment Law Review* 22: 115.

Stagnone, Lauren A. 1997. "Copyright Law—Computer Program Menu Command Hierarchy: An Uncopyrightable Method of Operation? *Lotus Development Corporation v. Borland International, Inc.*, 49 F.3rd 807 (1995), aff'd, 116 S. Ct. 804 (1996)." *Suffolk University Law Review* 30: 939.

Sunder, Madhavi. 1996. "Authorship and Autonomy as Rites of Exclusion: The Intellectual Propertization of Free Speech in *Hurley v. Irish-American Gay, Lesbian, and Bisexual Group of Boston*." *Stanford Law Review* 49: 143.

Takenaka, Toshiko. 2003. "The Best Patent Practice or Mere Compromise? A Review of the Current Draft of the Substantive Patent Law Treaty and a Proposal for a First-to-Invent Exception for Domestic Applicants." *Texas Intellectual Property Law Journal* 11: 259.

Terry, Nicolas P. 1994. "GUI Wars: The Windows Litigation and the Continuing Decline of 'Look and Feel.'" *Arkansas Law Review* 47: 93.

Tiefenbrun, Susan. 1999. "A Hermeneutic Methodology and How Pirates Misread the Berne Convention." *Wisconsin International Law Journal* 17: 1.

"Unexpected Harmony: The Music and Computer Industries Make Peace, but Differences Remain." 2003. *The Economist*, January 23.

Wells, Matthew G. 2001. "Internet Business Method Patent Policy." *Virginia Law Review* 87: 729.

Withers, Kay. 2006. "Copyright Sings to a Different Tune." February 17. http://news.bbc.co.uk/2/hi/technology/4724664.stm.

Woodford, Chad. 2004. "Trusted Computing or Big Brother? Putting the Rights Back in Digital Rights Management." *University of Colorado Law Review* 75: 253.

World Intellectual Property Organization. *About WIPO*. WIPO Publication No. 400(E). June 2001. http://www.wipo.int/about-wipo/en/gib.htm#P9_1980.

"World v Web: America Does Not Want the United Nations to Run the Internet." 2004. *The Economist*, November 20, 65.

Younge, Gary. 2003. "US Music Industry Sues 261 for Online Song Copying." *The Guardian*, September 10. http://www.guardian.co.uk/online/news/0,12597,1038979,00.html.

# Journals

Universities across the United States publish many journals on intellectual property law, as well as journals on topics such as entertainment law and technology law that include many articles on intellectual property issues. Most of these journals are available in law libraries and online through Westlaw (www.westlaw.com), Lexis (www.lexis.com), and HeinOnline (www.heinonline.org). All of these services charge a fee for access, but some journals may also be available, often for free, from the journals' own websites. Where available, website addresses are given below; unless otherwise noted, these addresses were functional as of October 2006.

*Albany Law Journal of Science & Technology*
Albany Law School
80 New Scotland Avenue
Albany, NY 12208
Phone: (518) 472-5855
E-mail: lawjournal@mail.als.edu
Website: http://www.albanylawjournal.org/

*The American Intellectual Property Law Association*
*Quarterly Journal*
George Washington University Law School
2002 G Street, N.W.
Washington, DC 20052
Phone: (202) 994-8620
E-mail: jschaf@law.gwu.edu
Website: http://www.aipla.org/Content/NavigationMenu/
Publications/Quarterly_Journal1/Default800.htm

*The Berkeley Technology Law Journal*
University of California at Berkeley
Boalt Hall School of Law
587 Simon Hall
Berkeley, CA 94720
Phone: (510) 643-6454
Fax: (510) 643-6816
E-mail: btlj@law.berkeley.edu
Website: http://www.btlj.boalt.org/

*Buffalo Intellectual Property Law Journal*
University at Buffalo Law School
State University of New York
John Lord O'Brian Hall, North Campus, Box 60110
Buffalo, NY 14260-1100
Phone: (716) 645-2749

Fax: (716) 645-2064
E-mail: buffaloipjournal@gmail.com
Website: http://wings.buffalo.edu/law/biplj/

*Cardozo Arts & Entertainment Law Journal*
Yeshiva University

Benjamin N. Cardozo School of Law
55 Fifth Avenue
New York, NY 10003
Phone: (212) 790-0292
Fax: (212) 790-0345
E-mail: cardozoaelj@gmail.com
Website: http://www.cardozo.yu.edu/aelj/

*Columbia Journal of Law & the Arts*
Columbia Law School
435 West 116th Street
New York, NY 10027
Phone: (212) 854-1607
E-mail: columbiajla@gmail.com
Website: http://www.columbia.edu/cu/jla/

*Computer Law Review and Technology Journal*
Southern Methodist University Dedman School of Law
P.O. Box 750116
Dallas, TX 75275-0116
Phone: (214) 768-4391
E-mail: complrev@mail.smu.edu
Website: http://www.smu.edu/csr/

*DePaul–LCA Journal of Art & Entertainment Law*
DePaul University College of Law
25 East Jackson Boulevard
Room 712
Chicago, IL 60604
Phone: (312) 362-5635
Fax: (312) 362-5448
E-mail: journae@condor.depaul.edu
Website: http://condor.depaul.edu/~journae/entmain.html

*Entertainment and Sports Lawyer*
425 Market Street, Suite 2200

San Francisco, CA 94105
Phone: (415) 955-2641
Fax: (415) 651-8817
E-mail: bob@rgpimm.com
Website: http://www.abanet.org/forums/entsports/esl.html

*Fordham Intellectual Property, Media & Entertainment*
*Law Journal*
Fordham University School of Law
140 West 62nd Street
New York, NY 10023
Phone: (212) 636-6948
Fax: (212) 636-6582
E-mail: iplj@fordham.edu
Website: http://www.fordham.edu/law/student/Journals.htm#1

*Harvard Journal of Law & Technology*
Harvard Law School Publications Center
28 Pound Hall
Cambridge, MA 02138
Phone: (617) 495-3606
Fax: (617) 495-8828
E-mail: jolt@law.harvard.edu
Website: http://jolt.law.harvard.edu/

*Hastings Communications and Entertainment Law Journal*
*(COMM/ENT)*
University of California, Hastings College of the Law
200 McAllister Street
San Francisco, CA 94102-4978
Phone: (415) 581-8970
Fax: (415) 551-4110
E-mail: comment@uchastings.edu
Website: http://w3.uchastings.edu/comment/

*Idea: The Intellectual Property Law Review*
Franklin Pierce Law Center
Two White Street
Concord, NH 03301
Phone: (603) 228-1541
E-mail: idea@piercelaw.edu

Website: http://www.idea.piercelaw.edu/

*Intellectual Property Law Journal*
University of Baltimore School of Law
1420 North Charles Street
Baltimore, MD 21201-5779

Phone: (410) 837-4372
Fax: (410) 837-4487
E-mail: ubiplj@ubalt.edu
Website: http://law.ubalt.edu/iplj/

*The John Marshall Journal of Computer & Information Law*
The John Marshall Law School
315 South Plymouth Court
Chicago, IL 60604
Phone: (312) 987-2354
Fax: (312) 427-8307
E-mail: 5jcil@stu.jmls.edu
Website: http://www.jcil.org/

*The Journal of Arts Management, Law, and Society*
Helen Dwight Reid Educational Foundation
Heldref Publications
1319 Eighteenth Street, N.W.
Washington, DC 20036-1802
Phone: (202) 296-6267
Fax: (202) 296-5149
Website: http://www.heldref.org/jamls.php

*The Journal of BioLaw & Business*
P.O. Box 650222
West Newton, MA 02465
Phone: (617) 244-4762
Fax: (617) 964-0971
E-mail: editor@biolawbusiness.com
Website: http://www.biolawbusiness.com/

*The Journal of High Technology Law*
Suffolk University Law School
Suite 450B, 120 Tremont Street
Boston, MA 02108
Phone: (617) 305-1695

Fax: (617) 305-6288
E-mail: jhtl@suffolk.edu
Website: http://www.jhtl.org/

*Journal of Intellectual Property Law*
University of Georgia School of Law
Athens, GA 30602-6012
Phone: (706) 542-7288
E-mail: jipl@uga.edu
Website: http://www.law.uga.edu/jipl/

*Journal of Law, Technology, and Policy*
University of Illinois at Urbana-Champaign College of Law
504 East Pennsylvania Avenue
Champaign, IL 61820
Phone: (217) 244-6757
E-mail: jltp@law.uiuc.edu
Website: http://www.jltp.uiuc.edu/

*Journal of Science & Technology Law*
Boston University School of Law
765 Commonwealth Avenue
Boston, MA 02215
Phone: (617) 353-8368
E-mail: jstl@bu.edu
Website: http://www.bu.edu/law/scitech/

*Journal of Technology Law & Policy*
University of Florida Levin College of Law
141 Bruton-Geer Hall
Gainesville, FL 32611-7637
Phone: (352) 273-0906
Website: http://grove.ufl.edu/~techlaw/

*Journal of Technology Law & Policy*
University of Pittsburgh School of Law
3900 Forbes Avenue
Pittsburgh, PA 15260
Phone: (412) 648-1400
Website: http://tlp.law.pitt.edu/

*Journal of the Copyright Society of the U.S.A.*
352 Seventh Avenue, Suite 307
New York, NY 10001
Phone: (212) 354-6401

Fax: (212) 354-2847
E-mail: amy@csusa.org
Website: http://www.csusa.org/html/publications/journal/
journal.htm

*Journal of the Patent and Trademark Office Society*
P.O. Box 2600
Arlington, VA 22202
Website: http://www.jptos.org/

*Journal on Telecommunications and High Technology*
University of Colorado
Campus Box 401
Boulder, CO 80309-0401
Phone: (303) 735-1032
E-mail: jthtl@colorado.edu
Website: http://www.colorado.edu/law/jthtl/

*Jurimetrics: The Journal of Law, Science, and Technology*
Arizona State University
Sandra Day O'Connor College of Law
McAllister & Orange Streets
P.O. Box 877906
Tempe, AZ 85287-7906
Phone: (480) 965-6181
Fax: (480) 965-2427
E-mail: jurimetrics@asu.edu
Website: http://www.law.asu.edu/Programs/Jurimetrics

*Law/Technology*
World Jurist Association
1000 Connecticut Avenue, N.W., Suite 202
Washington, DC 20036
Phone: (202) 466-5428
Fax: (202) 452-8540
E-mail: wja@worldjurist.org
Website: http://www.worldjurist.org/publications.html
(description only)

*Loyola of Los Angeles Entertainment Law Review*
Loyola Law School

919 South Albany Street
Los Angeles, CA 90015
Phone: (213) 736-1403
Fax: (213) 385-6149
E-mail: elr@lls.edu
Website: http://elr.lls.edu/

*Marquette Intellectual Property Law Review*
Marquette University Law School
Sensenbrenner Hall, Room 146
P.O. Box 1881
Milwaukee, WI 53201-1881
Phone: (414) 288-7090
Fax: (414) 288-6403
E-mail: iplawrev@marquette.edu
Website: http://204.11.208.101/cgi-
bin/site.pl?2130&pageID=158

*Michigan Telecommunications and Technology Law Review*
University of Michigan Law School
625 South State
Ann Arbor, MI 48109-1215
Phone: (734) 764-4181
Fax: (734) 764-6100
E-mail: mttlr@umich.edu
Website: http://www.mttlr.org/html/home.html

*Minnesota Journal of Law, Science & Technology*
University of Minnesota Law School
Walter F. Mondale Hall
229 19th Avenue South
Minneapolis, MN 55455
Phone: (612) 626-0224
E-mail: mipr@umn.edu
Website: http://mipr.umn.edu/common/index.htm

*North Carolina Journal of Law & Technology*
University of North Carolina at Chapel Hill
School of Law
Van-Hecke Wettach Hall, CB #3380

Chapel Hill, NC 27599-3380
E-mail: info@ncjolt.com
Website: http://www.jolt.unc.edu/

*Northwestern Journal of Technology and Intellectual Property*
Northwestern University School of Law
357 East Chicago Avenue
Chicago, IL 60611-3069
Website: http://www.law.northwestern.edu/njtip/

*Oklahoma Journal of Law & Technology*
University of Oklahoma College of Law
300 Timberdell Road
Norman, OK 73019
E-mail: okjolt@ou.edu
Website: http://www.okjolt.org/

*Richmond Journal of Law & Technology*
T.C. Williams School of Law
University of Richmond
Richmond, VA 23173
Phone: (804) 289-8202
Fax: (804) 289-8968
E-mail: jolt@richmond.edu
Website: http://law.richmond.edu/jolt/index.asp

*Rutgers Computer and Technology Law Journal*
Rutgers University School of Law–Newark
123 Washington Street, Suite 312
Newark, NJ 07102
Phone: (973) 353-5549
E-mail: rctlj@pegasus.rutgers.edu
Website: http://pegasus.rutgers.edu/~rctlj/

*Santa Clara Computer & High Technology Law Journal*
Santa Clara University School of Law
500 El Camino Real
Santa Clara, CA 95053
Phone: (408) 554-4197
E-mail: chtlj@scu.edu
Website: http://www.scu.edu/techlaw/

*Seton Hall Journal of Sports and Entertainment Law*
Seton Hall University School of Law
One Newark Center
Newark, NJ 07102
Phone: (973) 642-8239
E-mail: sportslaw@shu.edu
Website: http://law.shu.edu/journals/sportslaw/

*Stanford Technology Law Review*
Crown Quadrangle
Stanford Law School
Stanford University
Stanford, CA 94305-8610
E-mail: stlr-editors@lists.stanford.edu
Website: http://stlr.stanford.edu/STLR/Core_Page/index.htm

*Texas Intellectual Property Law Journal*
University of Texas School of Law
727 East 26th Street, Suite 2.130
Austin, TX 78705-3299
Phone: (512) 232-1399
Fax: (512) 471-6988
E-mail: tiplj@mail.law.utexas.edu
Website: http://www.utexas.edu/law/journals/tiplj/

*Texas Review of Entertainment and Sports Law*
University of Texas School of Law
The University of Texas at Austin
727 East Dean Keeton Street
Austin, TX 78705-3299
Phone: (512) 232-2816
Fax: (512) 471-6988
E-mail: tresl@mail.law.utexas.edu
Website: http://www.utexas.edu/law/journals/tresl/

*The Trademark Reporter*
International Trademark Association
655 Third Avenue, 10th Floor
New York, NY 10017
Phone: (212) 768-9887
Fax: (212) 768-7796
E-mail: tmr@inta.org

Website: https://www.inta.org/index.php?option=com_content
&task=view&id=54&Itemid=237&getcontent=4
(or http://www.inta.org and navigate from there)

*Tulane Journal of Technology & Intellectual Property*
Tulane University Law School
6329 Freret Street
John Giffen Weinmann Hall
New Orleans, LA 70118-5670
Website: http://www.law.tulane.edu/tuexp/journals/jtip/links
.html

*UCLA Entertainment Law Review*
UCLA School of Law
P.O. Box 951476
Los Angeles, CA 90095-1476
Phone: (310) 825-3712
E-mail: elr@lawnet.ucla.edu
Website: http://www.law.ucla.edu/elr/public_html/

*University of Miami Business Law Review*
University of Miami School of Law, Suite E260
P.O. Box 248087
Coral Gables, FL 33124-8087
Phone: (305) 284-6885
Fax: (305) 284-4765

*Vanderbilt Journal of Entertainment and Technology Law*
Vanderbilt Law School
131 21st Avenue South
Nashville, TN 37212
Phone: (615) 322-5600
E-mail: jetl@vanderbilt.edu
Website: http://law.vanderbilt.edu/jetl/

*Virginia Journal of Law and Technology*
University of Virginia School of Law
580 Massie Road
Charlottesville, VA 22903
Phone: (434) 924-7090
E-mail: vjolt@vjolt.net
Website: http://www.vjolt.net/

*Wake Forest Intellectual Property Law Journal*
Wake Forest University School of Law
P.O. Box 7206, Reynolds Station
Winston-Salem, NC 27109
Phone: (336) 758-5430
Website: http://www.law.wfu.edu/ipjournal.xml

# U.S. Materials

In the United States, copyright law and patent law are entirely (or so close to entirely as to make no practical difference) governed by federal law. Trademark is governed by both federal and state law, as are trade secrets.

The U.S. legal system is perhaps the most complex and comprehensive set of rules ever created. Congress and fifty state legislatures enact statutes; the president and fifty state governors issue various proclamations, orders, and decrees, many of which are later reviewed for possible conflict with the statutes authorizing them. This reviewing is done by several hundred state and federal courts; these courts also review statutes for possible conflict with the Constitution or, in the case of state statutes, for possible preemption by federal statutes or treaties. Most of the time, however, courts are simply deciding disputes between parties, which often requires them to interpret or explain the language of statutes, regulations, treaties, and so forth. These courts may issue reported decisions, which then become part of our common law. Lawyers spend years in law school learning how all of these pieces fit together; it would be a mistake to focus on a single statute, case, or regulation in isolation.

Complexity is only the first aspect of the problem; the second is mutability. Old statutes are constantly being revised or repealed, while new ones spring into existence whenever the legislature is in session. Regulations and proclamations are similarly changeable, while reported cases may be overturned, superseded, depublished, or otherwise rendered obsolete. Lawyers keep track of these changes in a number of ways, including citator services such as Shepard's Citations and West's Keycite. Using these services correctly is itself a skill requiring special training, however, and it is best to ask a law librarian for assistance.

# Federal Statutes

Statutes enacted by Congress are first organized in chronological order. Locating one of these statutes is not, by itself, particularly helpful. The Copyright Act of 1976, for example, as originally enacted, would include requirements for copyright protection and terms of protection quite different from those in force today. A determined legal researcher could, over many years, go through every statute enacted by Congress during the past two centuries or more, locate all of the law affecting a particular topic, and determine the current state of law. Fortunately, however, there is no need to do this: This service is already provided by the United States Code (U.S.C.).

The U.S.C. divides the statutes enacted by Congress into fifty "titles," or subjects, with hundreds or thousands of subdivisions within each title. Copyright law and related intellectual property rights occupy all of Title 17 of the U.S.C. Patent law occupies all of Title 35, and trademark law occupies part of Title 15. Updated versions of the U.S.C. are available online, in all law libraries, and in many other libraries. Two privately published versions of the code, the United States Code Annotated and the United States Code Service, are even more useful; these versions provide not only the updated text of the statute itself, but also information about cases, academic articles, and other materials that interpret, discuss, or apply the statute.

A list of federal intellectual property statutes, in the order in which they appear in the U.S.C., follows. (Repealed, relocated, or otherwise no longer effective sections have been omitted.) Space does not permit reproducing the entire statute, although some crucial sections are reproduced in Chapter 6. Any of the individual statutes listed below can be easily located in a law library or by typing the citation (e.g., "17 U.S.C. § 102" or simply "17 U.S.C. 102") into Google or another search engine.

## Trademark
Chapter 22: Trademarks
    Subchapter I: The Principal Register
        15 U.S.C. § 1051. Application for registration; verification
        15 U.S.C. § 1052. Trademarks registrable on principal register; concurrent registration
        15 U.S.C. § 1053. Service marks registrable

15 U.S.C. § 1054. Collective marks and certification marks registrable

15 U.S.C. § 1055. Use by related companies affecting validity and registration

15 U.S.C. § 1056. Disclaimer of unregistrable matter

15 U.S.C. § 1057. Certificates of registration

15 U.S.C. § 1058. Duration

15 U.S.C. § 1059. Renewal of registration

15 U.S.C. § 1060. Assignment

15 U.S.C. § 1061. Execution of acknowledgments and verifications

15 U.S.C. § 1062. Publication

15 U.S.C. § 1063. Opposition to registration

15 U.S.C. § 1064. Cancellation of registration

15 U.S.C. § 1065. Incontestability of right to use mark under certain conditions

15 U.S.C. § 1066. Interference; declaration by Director

15 U.S.C. § 1067. Interference, opposition, and proceedings for concurrent use registration or for cancellation; notice; Trademark Trial and Appeal Board

15 U.S.C. § 1068. Action of Director in interference, opposition, and proceedings for concurrent use registration or for cancellation

15 U.S.C. § 1069. Application of equitable principles in inter partes proceedings

15 U.S.C. § 1070. Appeals to Trademark Trial and Appeal Board from decisions of examiners

15 U.S.C. § 1071. Appeal to courts

15 U.S.C. § 1072. Registration as constructive notice of claim of ownership

Subchapter II: The Supplemental Register

15 U.S.C. § 1091. Supplemental register

15 U.S.C. § 1092. Publication; not subject to opposition; cancellation

15 U.S.C. § 1093. Registration certificates for marks on principal and supplemental registers to be different

15 U.S.C. § 1094. Provisions of chapter applicable to registrations on supplemental register

15 U.S.C. § 1095. Registration on principal register not precluded

15 U.S.C. § 1096. Registration on supplemental register not used to stop importations
Subchapter III: General Provisions
15 U.S.C. § 1111. Notice of registration; display with mark; recovery of profits and damages in infringement suit
15 U.S.C. § 1112. Classification of goods and services; registration in plurality of classes
15 U.S.C. § 1113. Fees
15 U.S.C. § 1114. Remedies; infringement; innocent infringement by printers and publishers
15 U.S.C. § 1115. Registration on principal register as evidence of exclusive right to use mark; defenses
15 U.S.C. § 1116. Injunctive relief
15 U.S.C. § 1117. Recovery for violation of rights
15 U.S.C. § 1118. Destruction of infringing articles
15 U.S.C. § 1119. Power of court over registration
15 U.S.C. § 1120. Civil liability for false or fraudulent registration
15 U.S.C. § 1121. Jurisdiction of Federal courts; State and local requirements that registered trademarks be altered or displayed differently; prohibition
15 U.S.C. § 1122. Liability of United States and States, and instrumentalities and officials thereof
15 U.S.C. § 1123. Rules and regulations for conduct of proceedings in Patent and Trademark Office
15 U.S.C. § 1124. Importation of goods bearing infringing marks or names forbidden
15 U.S.C. § 1125. False designations of origin, false descriptions, and dilution forbidden
15 U.S.C. § 1126. International conventions
15 U.S.C. § 1127. Construction and definitions; intent of chapter
15 U.S.C. § 1128. National Intellectual Property Law Enforcement Coordination Council
15 U.S.C. § 1129. Cyberpiracy protections for individuals
Subchapter IV: The Madrid Protocol
15 U.S.C. § 1141. Definitions
15 U.S.C. § 1141a. International applications based on United States applications or registrations

15 U.S.C. § 1141b. Certification of the international application

15 U.S.C. § 1141c. Restriction, abandonment, cancellation, or expiration of a basic application or basic registration

15 U.S.C. § 1141d. Request for extension of protection subsequent to international registration

15 U.S.C. § 1141e. Extension of protection of an international registration to the United States under the Madrid Protocol

15 U.S.C. § 1141f. Effect of filing a request for extension of protection of an international registration to the United States

15 U.S.C. § 1141g. Right of priority for request for extension of protection to the United States

15 U.S.C. § 1141h. Examination of and opposition to request for extension of protection; notification of refusal

15 U.S.C. § 1141i. Effect of extension of protection

15 U.S.C. § 1141j. Dependence of extension of protection to the United States on the underlying international registration

15 U.S.C. § 1141k. Affidavits and fees

15 U.S.C. § 1141l. Assignment of an extension of protection

15 U.S.C. § 1141m. Incontestability

15 U.S.C. § 1141n. Rights of extension of protection

### Copyright and Other Rights
(Note that Chapters 9 and 13 protect forms of intellectual property that have aspects of copyright and of patent [both] and trademark [Chapter 13].)

Chapter 1: Subject Matter and Scope of Copyright

17 U.S.C. § 101. Definitions

17 U.S.C. § 102. Subject matter of copyright: In general

17 U.S.C. § 103. Subject matter of copyright: Compilations and derivative works

17 U.S.C. § 104. Subject matter of copyright: National origin

17 U.S.C. § 104A. Copyright in restored works

17 U.S.C. § 105. Subject matter of copyright: United States Government works

17 U.S.C. § 106. Exclusive rights in copyrighted works

17 U.S.C. § 106A. Rights of certain authors to attribution and integrity

17 U.S.C. § 107. Limitations on exclusive rights: Fair use

17 U.S.C. § 108. Limitations on exclusive rights: Reproduction by libraries and archives

17 U.S.C. § 109. Limitations on exclusive rights: Effect of transfer of particular copy or phonorecord

17 U.S.C. § 110. Limitations on exclusive rights: Exemption of certain performances and displays

17 U.S.C. § 111. Limitations on exclusive rights: Secondary transmissions

17 U.S.C. § 112. Limitations on exclusive rights: Ephemeral recordings

17 U.S.C. § 113. Scope of exclusive rights in pictorial, graphic, and sculptural works

17 U.S.C. § 114. Scope of exclusive rights in sound recordings

17 U.S.C. § 115. Scope of exclusive rights in nondramatic musical works: Compulsory license for making and distributing phonorecords

17 U.S.C. § 116. Negotiated licenses for public performances by means of coin-operated phonorecord players

17 U.S.C. § 117. Limitations on exclusive rights: Computer programs

17 U.S.C. § 118. Scope of exclusive rights: Use of certain works in connection with noncommercial broadcasting

17 U.S.C. § 119. Limitations on exclusive rights: Secondary transmissions of superstations and network stations for private home viewing

17 U.S.C. § 120. Scope of exclusive rights in architectural works

17 U.S.C. § 121. Limitations on exclusive rights: Reproduction for blind or other people with disabilities

17 U.S.C. § 122. Limitations on exclusive rights: Secondary transmissions by satellite carriers within local markets

Chapter 2: Copyright Ownership and Transfer

17 U.S.C. § 201. Ownership of copyright

17 U.S.C. § 202. Ownership of copyright as distinct from ownership of material object

17 U.S.C. § 203. Termination of transfers and licenses granted by the author

17 U.S.C. § 204. Execution of transfers of copyright ownership

17 U.S.C. § 205. Recordation of transfers and other documents

Chapter 3: Duration of Copyright

17 U.S.C. § 301. Preemption with respect to other laws

17 U.S.C. § 302. Duration of copyright: Works created on or after January 1, 1978

17 U.S.C. § 303. Duration of copyright: Works created but not published or copyrighted before January 1, 1978

17 U.S.C. § 304. Duration of copyright: Subsisting copyrights

17 U.S.C. § 305. Duration of copyright: Terminal date

Chapter 4: Copyright Notice, Deposit, and Registration

17 U.S.C. § 401. Notice of copyright: Visually perceptible copies

17 U.S.C. § 402. Notice of copyright: Phonorecords of sound recordings

17 U.S.C. § 403. Notice of copyright: Publications incorporating United States Government works

17 U.S.C. § 404. Notice of copyright: Contributions to collective works

17 U.S.C. § 405. Notice of copyright: Omission of notice on certain copies and phonorecords

17 U.S.C. § 406. Notice of copyright: Error in name or date on certain copies and phonorecords

17 U.S.C. § 407. Deposit of copies or phonorecords for Library of Congress

17 U.S.C. § 408. Copyright registration in general

17 U.S.C. § 409. Application for copyright registration

17 U.S.C. § 410. Registration of claim and issuance of certificate

17 U.S.C. § 411. Registration and infringement actions

17 U.S.C. § 412. Registration as prerequisite to certain remedies for infringement

Chapter 5: Copyright Infringement and Remedies

17 U.S.C. § 501. Infringement of copyright

17 U.S.C. § 502. Remedies for infringement: Injunctions

17 U.S.C. § 503. Remedies for infringement: Impounding and disposition of infringing articles

17 U.S.C. § 504. Remedies for infringement: Damages and profits

17 U.S.C. § 505. Remedies for infringement: Costs and attorney's fees

17 U.S.C. § 506. Criminal offenses

17 U.S.C. § 507. Limitations on actions

17 U.S.C. § 508. Notification of filing and determination of actions

17 U.S.C. § 509. Seizure and forfeiture

17 U.S.C. § 510. Remedies for alteration of programming by cable systems

17 U.S.C. § 511. Liability of States, instrumentalities of States, and State officials for infringement of copyright

17 U.S.C. § 512. Limitations on liability relating to material online

17 U.S.C. § 513. Determination of reasonable license fees for individual proprietors

Chapter 6: Manufacturing Requirements and Importation

17 U.S.C. § 601. Manufacture, importation, and public distribution of certain copies

17 U.S.C. § 602. Infringing importation of copies or phonorecords

17 U.S.C. § 603. Importation prohibitions: Enforcement and disposition of excluded articles

Chapter 7: Copyright Office

17 U.S.C. § 701. The Copyright Office: General responsibilities and organization

17 U.S.C. § 702. Copyright Office regulations

17 U.S.C. § 703. Effective date of actions in Copyright Office

17 U.S.C. § 704. Retention and disposition of articles deposited in Copyright Office

17 U.S.C. § 705. Copyright Office records: Preparation, maintenance, public inspection, and searching

17 U.S.C. § 706. Copies of Copyright Office records

17 U.S.C. § 707. Copyright Office forms and publications

17 U.S.C. § 708. Copyright Office fees

17 U.S.C. § 709. Delay in delivery caused by disruption of postal or other services

Chapter 8: Copyright Arbitration Royalty Panels

17 U.S.C. § 801. Copyright arbitration royalty panels: Establishment and purpose

17 U.S.C. § 802. Membership and proceedings of copyright arbitration royalty panels

17 U.S.C. § 803. Institution and conclusion of proceedings

Chapter 9: Protection of Semiconductor Chip Products

17 U.S.C. § 901. Definitions

17 U.S.C. § 902. Subject matter of protection

17 U.S.C. § 903. Ownership, transfer, licensing, and recordation

17 U.S.C. § 904. Duration of protection

17 U.S.C. § 905. Exclusive rights in mask works

17 U.S.C. § 906. Limitation on exclusive rights: Reverse engineering; first sale

17 U.S.C. § 907. Limitation on exclusive rights: Innocent infringement

17 U.S.C. § 908. Registration of claims of protection

17 U.S.C. § 909. Mask work notice

17 U.S.C. § 910. Enforcement of exclusive rights

17 U.S.C. § 911. Civil actions

17 U.S.C. § 912. Relation to other laws

17 U.S.C. § 913. Transitional provisions

17 U.S.C. § 914. International transitional provisions

Chapter 10: Digital Audio Recording Devices and Media

Subchapter A: Definitions

17 U.S.C. § 1001. Definitions

Subchapter B: Copying Controls

17 U.S.C. § 1002. Incorporation of copying controls

Subchapter C: Royalty Payments

17 U.S.C. § 1003. Obligation to make royalty payments

17 U.S.C. § 1004. Royalty payments

17 U.S.C. § 1005. Deposit of royalty payments and deduction of expenses

17 U.S.C. § 1006. Entitlement to royalty payments

17 U.S.C. § 1007. Procedures for distributing royalty payments

Subchapter D: Prohibition on Certain Infringement Actions, Remedies, and Arbitration

17 U.S.C. § 1008. Prohibition on certain infringement actions

17 U.S.C. § 1009. Civil remedies

17 U.S.C. § 1010. Arbitration of certain disputes

Chapter 11: Sound Recordings and Music Videos

17 U.S.C. § 1101. Unauthorized fixation and trafficking in sound recordings and music videos

Chapter 12: Copyright Protection and Management Systems

17 U.S.C. § 1201. Circumvention of copyright protection systems

17 U.S.C. § 1202. Integrity of copyright management information

17 U.S.C. § 1203. Civil remedies

17 U.S.C. § 1204. Criminal offenses and penalties

17 U.S.C. § 1205. Savings clause

Chapter 13: Protection of Original Designs

17 U.S.C. § 1301. Designs protected

17 U.S.C. § 1302. Designs not subject to protection

17 U.S.C. § 1303. Revisions, adaptations, and rearrangements

17 U.S.C. § 1304. Commencement of protection

17 U.S.C. § 1305. Term of protection

17 U.S.C. § 1306. Design notice

17 U.S.C. § 1307. Effect of omission of notice

17 U.S.C. § 1308. Exclusive rights

17 U.S.C. § 1309. Infringement

17 U.S.C. § 1310. Application for registration

17 U.S.C. § 1311. Benefit of earlier filing date in foreign country

17 U.S.C. § 1312. Oaths and acknowledgments

17 U.S.C. § 1313. Examination of application and issue or refusal of registration

17 U.S.C. § 1314. Certification of registration

17 U.S.C. § 1315. Publication of announcements and indexes

17 U.S.C. § 1316. Fees
17 U.S.C. § 1317. Regulations
17 U.S.C. § 1318. Copies of records
17 U.S.C. § 1319. Correction of errors in certificates
17 U.S.C. § 1320. Ownership and transfer
17 U.S.C. § 1321. Remedy for infringement
17 U.S.C. § 1322. Injunctions
17 U.S.C. § 1323. Recovery for infringement
17 U.S.C. § 1324. Power of court over registration
17 U.S.C. § 1325. Liability for action on registration
    fraudulently obtained
17 U.S.C. § 1326. Penalty for false marking
17 U.S.C. § 1327. Penalty for false representation
17 U.S.C. § 1328. Enforcement by Treasury and Postal
    Service
17 U.S.C. § 1329. Relation to design patent law
17 U.S.C. § 1330. Common law and other rights
    unaffected
17 U.S.C. § 1331. Administrator; Office of the
    Administrator
17 U.S.C. § 1332. No retroactive effect

## Patent
Part I: United States Patent and Trademark Office
    Chapter 1: Establishment, Officers and Employees,
        Functions
        35 U.S.C. § 1. Establishment
        35 U.S.C. § 2. Powers and duties
        35 U.S.C. § 3. Officers and employees
        35 U.S.C. § 4. Restrictions on officers and employees as
            to interest in patents
        35 U.S.C. § 5. Patent and Trademark Office Public
            Advisory Committees
        35 U.S.C. § 6. Board of Patent Appeals and
            Interferences
        35 U.S.C. § 7. Library
        35 U.S.C. § 8. Classification of patents
        35 U.S.C. § 9. Certified copies of records
        35 U.S.C. § 10. Publications
        35 U.S.C. § 11. Exchange of copies of patents and
            applications with foreign countries

35 U.S.C. § 12. Copies of patents and applications for public libraries

35 U.S.C. § 13. Annual report to Congress

Chapter 2: Proceedings in the Patent and Trademark Office

35 U.S.C. § 21. Filing date and day for taking action

35 U.S.C. § 22. Printing of papers filed

35 U.S.C. § 23. Testimony in Patent and Trademark Office cases

35 U.S.C. § 24. Subpoenas, witnesses

35 U.S.C. § 25. Declaration in lieu of oath

35 U.S.C. § 26. Effect of defective execution

Chapter 3: Practice Before Patent and Trademark Office

35 U.S.C. § 32. Suspension or exclusion from practice

35 U.S.C. § 33. Unauthorized representation as practitioner

Chapter 4: Patent Fees; Funding; Search Systems

35 U.S.C. § 41. Patent fees; patent and trademark search systems

35 U.S.C. § 42. Patent and Trademark Office funding

Part II: Patentability of Inventions and Grant of Patents

Chapter 10: Patentability of Inventions

35 U.S.C. § 100. Definitions

35 U.S.C. § 101. Inventions patentable

35 U.S.C. § 102. Conditions for patentability; novelty and loss of right to patent

35 U.S.C. § 103. Conditions for patentability; non-obvious subject matter

35 U.S.C. § 104. Invention made abroad

35 U.S.C. § 105. Inventions in outer space

Chapter 11: Application for Patent

35 U.S.C. § 111. Application

35 U.S.C. § 112. Specification

35 U.S.C. § 113. Drawings

35 U.S.C. § 114. Models, specimens

35 U.S.C. § 115. Oath of applicant

35 U.S.C. § 116. Inventors

35 U.S.C. § 117. Death or incapacity of inventor

35 U.S.C. § 118. Filing by other than inventor

35 U.S.C. § 119. Benefit of earlier filing date; right of priority

35 U.S.C. § 120. Benefit of earlier filing date in the United States

35 U.S.C. § 121. Divisional applications

35 U.S.C. § 122. Confidential status of applications; publication of patent applications

Chapter 12: Examination of Application

35 U.S.C. § 131. Examination of application

35 U.S.C. § 132. Notice of rejection; reexamination

35 U.S.C. § 133. Time for prosecuting application

35 U.S.C. § 134. Appeal to the Board of Patent Appeals and Interferences

35 U.S.C. § 135. Interferences

Chapter 13: Review of Patent and Trademark Office Decisions

35 U.S.C. § 141. Appeal to Court of Appeals for the Federal Circuit

35 U.S.C. § 142. Notice of appeal

35 U.S.C. § 143. Proceedings on appeal

35 U.S.C. § 144. Decision on appeal

35 U.S.C. § 145. Civil action to obtain patent

35 U.S.C. § 146. Civil action in case of interference

Chapter 14: Issue of Patent

35 U.S.C. § 151. Issue of patent

35 U.S.C. § 152. Issue of patent to assignee

35 U.S.C. § 153. How issued

35 U.S.C. § 154. Contents and term of patent; provisional rights

35 U.S.C. § 155. Patent term extension

35 U.S.C. § 155A. Patent term restoration

35 U.S.C. § 156. Extension of patent term

35 U.S.C. § 157. Statutory invention registration

Chapter 15: Plant Patents

35 U.S.C. § 161. Patents for plants

35 U.S.C. § 162. Description, claim

35 U.S.C. § 163. Grant

35 U.S.C. § 164. Assistance of Department of Agriculture

Chapter 16: Designs

35 U.S.C. § 171. Patents for designs

35 U.S.C. § 172. Right of priority

35 U.S.C. § 173. Term of design patent

Chapter 17: Secrecy of Certain Inventions and Filing Applications in Foreign Country

35 U.S.C. § 181. Secrecy of certain inventions and withholding of patent
35 U.S.C. § 182. Abandonment of invention for unauthorized disclosure
35 U.S.C. § 183. Right to compensation
35 U.S.C. § 184. Filing of application in foreign country
35 U.S.C. § 185. Patent barred for filing without license
35 U.S.C. § 186. Penalty
35 U.S.C. § 187. Nonapplicability to certain persons
35 U.S.C. § 188. Rules and regulations, delegation of power
Chapter 18: Patent Rights in Inventions Made with Federal Assistance
35 U.S.C. § 200. Policy and objective
35 U.S.C. § 201. Definitions
35 U.S.C. § 202. Disposition of rights
35 U.S.C. § 203. March-in rights
35 U.S.C. § 204. Preference for United States industry
35 U.S.C. § 205. Confidentiality
35 U.S.C. § 206. Uniform clauses and regulations
35 U.S.C. § 207. Domestic and foreign protection of federally owned inventions
35 U.S.C. § 208. Regulations governing Federal licensing
35 U.S.C. § 209. Licensing federally owned inventions
35 U.S.C. § 210. Precedence of chapter
35 U.S.C. § 211. Relationship to antitrust laws
35 U.S.C. § 212. Disposition of rights in educational awards
Part III: Patents and Protection of Patent Rights
Chapter 25: Amendment and Correction of Patents
35 U.S.C. § 251. Reissue of defective patents
35 U.S.C. § 252. Effect of reissue
35 U.S.C. § 253. Disclaimer
35 U.S.C. § 254. Certificate of correction of Patent and Trademark Office mistake
35 U.S.C. § 255. Certificate of correction of applicant's mistake
35 U.S.C. § 256. Correction of named inventor
Chapter 26: Ownership and Assignment
35 U.S.C. § 261. Ownership; assignment
35 U.S.C. § 262. Joint owners

Chapter 27: Government Interests in Patents
    35 U.S.C. § 267. Time for taking action in government
        applications
Chapter 28: Infringement of Patents
    35 U.S.C. § 271. Infringement of patent
    35 U.S.C. § 272. Temporary presence in the United
        States
    35 U.S.C. § 273. Defense to infringement based on
        earlier inventor
Chapter 29: Remedies for Infringement of Patent, and Other
    Actions
    35 U.S.C. § 281. Remedy for infringement of patent
    35 U.S.C. § 282. Presumption of validity; defenses
    35 U.S.C. § 283. Injunction
    35 U.S.C. § 284. Damages
    35 U.S.C. § 285. Attorney fees
    35 U.S.C. § 286. Time limitation on damages
    35 U.S.C. § 287. Limitation on damages and other
        remedies; marking and notice
    35 U.S.C. § 288. Action for infringement of a patent
        containing an invalid claim
    35 U.S.C. § 289. Additional remedy for infringement of
        design patent
    35 U.S.C. § 290. Notice of patent suits
    35 U.S.C. § 291. Interfering patents
    35 U.S.C. § 292. False marking
    35 U.S.C. § 293. Nonresident patentee; service and
        notice
    35 U.S.C. § 294. Voluntary arbitration
    35 U.S.C. § 295. Presumption: Product made by
        patented process
    35 U.S.C. § 296. Liability of States, instrumentalities of
        States, and State officials for infringement of
        patents
    35 U.S.C. § 297. Improper and deceptive invention
        promotion
Chapter 30: Prior Art Citations to Office and Ex Parte
    Reexamination of Patents
    35 U.S.C. § 301. Citation of prior art
    35 U.S.C. § 302. Request for reexamination
    35 U.S.C. § 303. Determination of issue by Director
    35 U.S.C. § 304. Reexamination order by Director

35 U.S.C. § 305. Conduct of reexamination proceedings
35 U.S.C. § 306. Appeal
35 U.S.C. § 307. Certificate of patentability, unpatentability, and claim cancellation
Chapter 31: Optional Inter Partes Reexamination Procedures
35 U.S.C. § 311. Request for inter partes reexamination
35 U.S.C. § 312. Determination of issue by Director
35 U.S.C. § 313. Inter partes reexamination order by Director
35 U.S.C. § 314. Conduct of inter partes reexamination proceedings
35 U.S.C. § 315. Appeal
35 U.S.C. § 316. Certificate of patentability, unpatentability, and claim cancellation
35 U.S.C. § 317. Inter partes reexamination prohibited
35 U.S.C. § 318. Stay of litigation
Part IV: Patent Cooperation Treaty
Chapter 35: Definitions
35 U.S.C. § 351. Definitions
Chapter 36: International Stage
35 U.S.C. § 361. Receiving Office
35 U.S.C. § 362. International Searching Authority and International Preliminary Examining Authority
35 U.S.C. § 363. International application designating the United States: Effect
35 U.S.C. § 364. International stage: Procedure
35 U.S.C. § 365. Right of priority; benefit of the filing date of a prior application
35 U.S.C. § 366. Withdrawn international application
35 U.S.C. § 367. Actions of other authorities: Review
35 U.S.C. § 368. Secrecy of certain inventions; filing international applications in foreign countries
Chapter 37: National Stage
35 U.S.C. § 371. National stage: Commencement
35 U.S.C. § 372. National stage: Requirements and procedure
35 U.S.C. § 373. Improper applicant
35 U.S.C. § 374. Publication of international application
35 U.S.C. § 375. Patent issued on international application: Effect
35 U.S.C. § 376. Fees

# Federal Cases

The United States, like most of the English-speaking countries of the world, follows the common law legal tradition. In the common law tradition, opinions issued by judges deciding reported cases become part of the body of the law; in other words, judges can make law. Finding this judge-made or common law can be difficult; lawyers spend many years in law school learning how to do so. The reported court decisions that make up the common law, after being issued by courts, are collected in bound volumes called reporters. Any law library, and many other libraries, will have a full set of federal case reporters, as well as reporters for the state in which the library is located. Most law libraries will have case reporters covering all fifty states. These reporters are commonly referred to by abbreviations such as those appearing in the citations that follow. "U.S." stands for "United States Reports," a reporter of decisions of the U.S. Supreme Court. "S.Ct." stands for "Supreme Court Reporter," another reporter of U.S. Supreme Court decisions. "F.2d" and "F.3d" stand for "Federal Reporter, Second Series" and "Federal Reporter, Third Series," respectively; these reporters contain decisions from federal appellate (circuit) courts. "F. Supp." and "F. Supp.2d" stand for "Federal Supplement" and "Federal Supplement, Second Series," reporters of cases from federal trial (district) courts. "U.S.P.Q." and "U.S.P.Q.2d" stand for "United States Patent Quarterly" and "United States Patent Quarterly, Second Series," reporters of patent decisions. All of this may seem complicated, and it is, but any lawyer or law librarian looking at the citation will be familiar with these abbreviations and will be able to find the case or statute instantly.

*A & M Records, Inc. v. Napster, Inc.*, 239 F.3d 1004 (9th Cir. 2001), *on remand*, 2001. WL 227083 (N.D. Cal. 2001), *affirmed*, 284 F.3d 1091 (9th Cir. 2002).

*Abercrombie & Fitch Co. v. Hunting World, Inc.*, 537 F.2d 4 (2d Cir. 1976).

*Albie's Foods, Inc. v. Menusaver, Inc.*, 170 F. Supp.2d 736 (E.D. Mich. 2001).

*Amazon.com, Inc. v. Barnesandnoble.com, Inc.*, 239 F.3d 1343 (Fed. Cir. 2001).

*America Online, Inc. v. AT&T Corp.,* 64 F. Supp.2d 549 (E.D. Va. 1999).

*AMF Inc. v. Sleekcraft Boats,* 599 F.2d 341, 348-49 (9th Cir. 1979).

*Apple Computer, Inc. v. Franklin Computer,* 714 F.2d 1240 (3d Cir. 1983).

*Apple Computer, Inc. v. Microsoft Corp.,* 35 F.3d 1435 (9th Cir. 1994).

*Apple Computer, Inc. v. Microsoft Corp.,* 799 F. Supp. 1006, 1020-21 (N.D. Cal. 1992).

*Apple Computer, Inc. v. Microsoft Corp.,* 779 F. Supp. 133 (N.D. Cal. 1991).

*Atari, Inc. v. JS & A Group, Inc.,* 747 F.2d 1422 (Fed. Cir. 1984).

*Baker v. Selden,* 101 U.S. 99 (1880).

*Bihari v. Gross,* 119 F. Supp.2d 309 (S.D. N.Y. 2000).

*Building Officials & Code Administration v. Code Technology, Inc.,* 628 F.2d 730 (1st Cir. 1980).

*Campbell v. Acuff-Rose Music, Inc.,* 510 U.S. 569 (1994).

*Coca-Cola Co. v. Gemini Rising, Inc.,* 346 F. Supp. 1183 (E.D. N.Y. 1972).

*Data East USA v. Epyx,* 862 F.2d 204 (9th Cir. 1988).

*Diamond v. Diehr,* 450 U.S. 175 (1981).

*Effects Associates v. Cohen,* 908 F.2d 555 (9th Cir. 1990).

*Eldred v. Ashcroft,* 123 S.Ct. 769 (2003).

*Feist Publications v. Rural Telephone Service Co.,* 499 U.S. 340 (1991).

*Fonovisa, Inc. v. Cherry Auction, Inc.,* 76 F.3d 259 (9th Cir. 1996).

*Georgia v. The Harrison Co.,* 548 F. Supp. 110, *vacated by agreement between the parties,* 559 F. Supp. 37 (N.D. Ga. 1983).

*Gershwin Publishing Corporation v. Columbia Artists Management, Inc.,* 443 F.2d 1159 (2d Cir. 1971).

*Gold Seal Co. v. Weeks,* 129 F. Supp. 928 (D.C. Cir. 1956), *affirmed,* 230 F.2d 832, *certiorari denied,* 328 U.S. 829 (1956).

*Goodis v. United Artists Television, Inc.,* 425 F.2d 397 (2d Cir. 1070).

*Gottschalk v. Benson*, 409 U.S. 63 (1972).

*Hoehling v. Universal City Studios, Inc.*, 618 F.2d 972 (2d Cir. 1980).

*Hotel Security Checking Co. v. Lorraine Co.*, 160 F. 467 (2d Cir. 1908).

*In re Aimster Copyright Litigation (Aimster II)*, 252 F. Supp.2d 634 (N.D. Ill. 2002); *affirmed in part*, 334 F.3d 643 (7th Cir. 2003); *certiorari denied sub nom Deep v. Recording Industry Association of America, Inc.*, 124 S.Ct. 1069 (2004).

*In re Alappat*, 33 F.3d 1526 (Fed. Cir. 1994).

*In re Budge Manufacturing Co.*, 857 F.2d 773 (Fed. Cir. 1988).

*In re Clarke*, 17 U.S.P.Q.2d 1238 (T.T.A.B. 1990).

*In re Old Glory Condom Corp.*, 26 U.S.P.Q.2d 1216 (T.T.A.B. 1993).

*In re Trade-Mark Cases*, 100 U.S. 82 (1879).

*Inwood Labs, Inc. v. Ives Labs, Inc.*, 456 U.S. 844, 853-53 (1982).

*Lotus Development Corporation v. Borland International, Inc.*, 49 F.3d 807 (1st Cir. 1995), *affirmed*, 516 U.S. 233 (1996).

*Lucent Technologies, Inc. v. Lucentsucks.com*, 95 F. Supp.2d 528 (E.D. Va. 2000).

*MAI Systems Corp. v. Peak Computer*, 991 F.2d 511 (9th Cir. 1993).

*Manville Sales Co. v. Paramount Systems, Inc.*, 917 F.2d 544 (Fed. Cir. 1990).

*Mead Data Central, Inc. v. Toyota Motor Sales, Inc.*, 875 F.2d 1026 (2d Cir. 1989).

*Metro-Goldwyn-Mayer Studios, Inc. v. Grokster, Ltd.*, 259 F. Supp.2d 1029 (C.D. Cal. 2003); *affirmed*, 380 F.3d 1154 (9th Cir. 2004); *vacated & remanded*, 125 S.Ct. 2764 (2005).

*Midway Manufacturing Co. v. Arctic International*, 704 F.2d 1009 (7th Cir. 1982).

*NEC v. Intel*, 10 U.S.P.Q.2d 1177 (N.D. Cal. 1989).

*New Kids on the Block v. News America Publishing, Inc.*, 971 F.2d 302 (9th Cir. 1992).

*Niton Corp. v. Radiation Monitoring Devices, Inc.*, 27 F. Supp.2d 102 (D. Mass. 1998).

*Oasis Publishing Co. v. West Publishing Co.*, 924 F. Supp. 918 (D. Minn. 1996).

*Playboy Enterprises, Inc. v. Welles*, 279 F.3d 796 (9th Cir. 2002).

*Polaroid Corp. v. Polarad Electronics Corp.*, 287 F.2d 492 (2d Cir. 1961).

*ProCD, Inc. v. Zeidenberg*, 86 F.3d 1447 (7th Cir. 1996).

*Qualitex Co. v. Jacobson Products Co.*, 514 U.S. 159 (1995).

*Recording Industry Association of America v. Diamond Multimedia Systems, Inc.*, 180 F.3d 1072 (9th Cir. 1999).

*Recording Industry Association of America, Inc. v. Verizon Internet Services*, 240 F. Supp.2d 24 (D.D.C. 2003); *reversed*, 351 F.3d 1229 (D.C. Cir. 2003); *certiorari denied*, 125 S.Ct. 309 and 125 S. Ct. 347 (2004).

*Religious Technology Center v. Netcom On-Line Communication Services, Inc.*, 907 F. Supp. 1361 (N.D. Cal. 1995).

*Sega Enterprises v. Accolade*, 977 F.2d 1510 (9th Cir. 1992).

*Sony Computer Entertainment, Inc. v. Connectix Corp.*, 203 F.3d 596 (9th Cir. 2000).

*Sony Corp. of America v. Universal City Studios, Inc.*, 464 U.S. 417 (1984).

*Sporty's Farm L.L.C. v. Sportsman's Market, Inc.*, 202 F.3d 489 (2nd Cir. 2000).

*State of Ohio v. Perry*, 83 Ohio St. 3d 41, 697 N.E.2d 624 (1998).

*State Street Bank & Trust v. Signature Financial Group, Inc.*, 149 F.3d 1368 (Fed. Cir. 1999).

*Sunmark, Inc. v. Ocean Spray Cranberries, Inc.*, 64 F.3d 1055 (7th Cir. 1995).

*Two Pesos, Inc. v. Taco Cabana, Inc.*, 505 U.S. 763 (1992).

*UMG Recordings, Inc. v. MP3.com, Inc.*, 92 F. Supp.2d 349 (S.D. N.Y. 2000).

*United States v. LaMacchia*, 871 F. Supp. 535 (D. Mass. 1994).

*Universal City Studios, Inc. v. Reimerdes*, 111 F. Supp.2d 294 (S.D. N.Y. 2000), *affirmed by Universal City Studios, Inc. v. Corley*, 273 F.3d 429 (2nd Cir. 2001).

*Vault Corporation v. Quaid Software Ltd.*, 847 F.2d 255 (5th Cir. 1988).

*White v. Dunbar*, 119 U.S. 47 (1886).

*Williams Electronics v. Arctic International*, 685 F.2d 870 (3d Cir. 1982).

## State Case

*DVD Copy Control Association, Inc. v. Bunner*, 113 Cal. Rptr.2d 338 (2001), *reversed*, 4 Cal. Rptr.3d 69 (2003).

# Treaties and Other International Agreements

The treaties to which the United States is a party have legal effect within the United States under Article VI, clause 2 of the U.S. Constitution. Even treaties to which the United States is not a party may have some domestic and international effect as evidence of customary international law. The treaties are collected in a variety of print and online sources; however, the easiest way to find the treaties listed here is online. Most are available in multiple locations; nearly all are available on the website of the World Intellectual Property Organization (www.wipo.org).

In the citations that follow, U.N.T.S. stands for United Nations Treaty Series, L.N.T.S. stands for League of Nations Treaty Series, U.S.T. stands for United States Treaties and Other International Agreements, I.L.M. stands for International Legal Materials, and Y.B.U.N. stands for Yearbook of the United Nations. All are available in law libraries and from proprietary databases.

"Agreement between the United Nations and the World Intellectual Property Organization." December 17, 1974. General Assembly Res. 3346, U.N. GAOR, 29th Sess., U.N. Doc. A/RES/3346 (XXIX).

"Agreement Between the World Intellectual Property Organization and the World Trade Organization." December 22, 1995. 35 I.L.M. 754.

"Agreement on Trade-Related Aspects of Intellectual Property Rights (TRIPs), Marrakesh Agreement Establishing the World Trade Organization, Annex 1C." April 15, 1994. 33 I.L.M. 81.

"Brussels Convention Relating to the Distribution of Programme-Carrying Signals Transmitted by Satellite." May 21, 1974. 13 I.L.M. 1444.

"Budapest Treaty on the International Recognition of the Deposit of Microorganisms for the Purposes of Patent Procedure." April 28, 1977, as amended on September 26, 1980. 32 U.S.T. 1241, 1861 U.N.T.S. 361.

Buenos Aires Convention. August 20, 1910. 38 Stat. 1785, 155 L.N.T.S. 179.

"Convention Concerning the Creation of an International Union for the Protection of Literary and Artistic Works (Berne Convention)." September 9, 1886, as last revised at Paris, July 24, 1971 (amended 1979). 25 U.S.T. 1341, 828 U.N.T.S. 221.

"Convention Establishing the World Intellectual Property Organization." July 14, 1967, as amended on September 28, 1979 (WIPO Convention). 21 U.S.T. 1749, 828 U.N.T.S. 3.

"Convention for the Protection of Producers of Phonograms Against Unauthorized Duplication of Their Phonograms." October 29, 1971. 25 U.S.T. 309.

"Convention on the Grant of European Patents." October 5, 1973. 13 I.L.M. 276. Text as amended through December 10, 1998. http://www.european-patent-office.org/legal/epc/e/ma1.html.

"Hague Agreement Concerning the International Deposit of Industrial Designs." November 6, 1925. 74 L.N.T.S. 343, revised at London, June 2, 1934, 205 L.N.T.S. 179, revised at The Hague, November 28, 1960; supplemented by the Additional Act of Monaco, November 18, 1961, the Complementary Act of Stockholm, July 14, 1967, and the Protocol of Geneva, April 10, 1975, 26 U.S.T. 571; and as amended, September 1979.

"Inter-American Convention for the Protection of Industrial Property." August 20, 1910. 39 Stat. 1675; T.S. 626; 1 Bevans 772. Replaced by General Inter-American Convention for Trademark and Commercial Protection. February 20, 1929. 46 Stat. 2907, T.S. 833, 2 Bevans 751, 124 L.N.T.S. 357.

"Lisbon Agreement for the Protection of Appellations of Origin and their International Registration." October 31, 1958. As revised at Stockholm on July 14, 1967, and as amended on September 28, 1979. 923 U.N.T.S. 205.

"Locarno Agreement Establishing an International Classification for Industrial Designs." October 8, 1968. As amended September 28, 1979, 23 U.S.T. 1389.

"Madrid Agreement Concerning the International Registration of Marks." April 14, 1891. As revised at Brussels on December 14, 1900, at Washington on June 2, 1911, at The Hague on November 6, 1925, at London on June 2, 1934, at Nice on June 15, 1957, and at Stockholm on July 14, 1967, and as amended on September 28, 1979. 828 U.N.T.S. 389.

"Madrid Agreement for the Repression of False or Deceptive Indications of Source on Goods." April 14, 1891, as revised at Washington on June 2, 1911, at The Hague on Nov. 6, 1925, at London on June 2, 1934, and at Lisbon on October 31, 1958. Additional Act, Stockholm. July 14, 1967. 828 U.N.T.S. 389.

"Nairobi Treaty on the Protection of the Olympic Symbol." September 26, 1981. 1863 U.N.T.S. 367.

"Nice Agreement Concerning the International Classification of Goods and Services for the Purposes of the Registration of Marks." June 15, 1957. As revised at Stockholm on July 14, 1967, and at Geneva on May 13, 1977, and amended on September 28, 1979. 23 U.S.T. 1336, 550 U.N.T.S. 45.

"Paris Convention for the Protection of Industrial Property." March 20, 1883. As revised at Brussels on December 14, 1900, at Washington on June 2, 1911, at The Hague on November 6, 1925, at London on June 2, 1934, at Lisbon on October 31, 1958, and at Stockholm on July 14, 1967, and as amended on September 28, 1979. 21 U.S.T. 1583, 828 U.N.T.S. 305.

"Patent Cooperation Treaty." Washington. June 19, 1970. As amended on September 28, 1979, and as modified on February 3, 1984, and October 3, 2001. 28 U.S.T. 7645, 9 I.L.M. 978.

"Patent Law Treaty." June 1, 2000. 39 I.L.M. 1047.

"Protocol Relating to the Madrid Agreement Concerning the International Registration of Marks." June 27, 1989. http://www

.wipo.int/madrid/en/legal_texts/.

"Rome Convention for the Protection of Performers, Producers of Phonograms and Broadcasting Organizations." October 26, 1961. 496 U.N.T.S. 43.

"Statute of the International Court of Justice." Art. 38(1), 59 Stat. 1055, 1060 (1945), T.S. No. 993, 3 Bevans 1153, 1976 Y.B.U.N. 1052.

"Strasbourg Agreement Concerning the International Patent Classification." March 24, 1971. As amended on September 28, 1979. 26 U.S.T. 1793.

"Trademark Law Treaty." October 27, 1994. http://www.wipo .int/clea/docs/en/wo/wo027en.htm.

"Treaty on the International Registration of Audiovisual Works." April 20, 1989. http://www.wipo.int/treaties/en/ip/frt/trt docs_wo004.html.

"Treaty on Intellectual Property in Respect of Integrated Circuits." Washington. May 26, 1989. 28 I.L.M. 1477 (not in force).

"Universal Copyright Convention." September 6, 1952. 6 U.S.T. 2731. Revised at Paris. July 24, 1971. 25 U.S.T. 1341.

"Vienna Agreement Establishing an International Classification of the Figurative Elements of Marks." June 12, 1973. As amended October 1, 1985. http://www.wipo.int/clea/docs/en/wo/ wo031en.htm.

"WIPO Copyright Treaty." December 20, 1996. 36 I.L.M. 65 (1997).

"WIPO Performance and Phonograms Treaty." December 20, 1996. 36 I.L.M. 76 (1997).

# Other International and Foreign Materials

*Buma & Stemra v. KaZaA.* Amsterdam Court of Appeal (2002). Unofficial English translation. www.eff.org/IP/P2P/BUMA_v _Kazaa/20020328_kazaa_appeal_judgment.html.

Council Directive 93/98/EEC of 29 October 1993 Harmonizing

the Term of Protection of Copyright and Certain Related Rights, 1993 O.J. (L290) 9.

EU Directive 2001/29/EC on the Harmonisation of Certain Aspects of Copyright and Related Rights in the Information Society. 2001 O.J. (L167) 10.

*International Business Machines Corporation.* Technical Board of Appeal of the European Patent Office, Case No. T 0935/97–3.5.1 (1999).

*Sunde (for Norway) v. Johansen.* Oslo First Instance Trial Court. January 7, 2003. No. 02-507 M/94. English translation by Professor Jon Bing. http://www.eff.org/IP/Video/Johansen_DeCSS_case/20030109_johansen_decision.html (visited March 11, 2006). *On appeal,* Borgarting Appellate Court, December 22, 2003. No. LB-2003-00731. Unofficial English translation by Professor Jon Bing. http://www.efn.no/DVD-dom-20031222-en.html.

# Internet Corporation for Assigned Names and Numbers (ICANN) Materials

ICANN, a nonprofit organization created by agreement between the Internet Assigned Numbers Authority and the U.S. Department of Commerce, is perhaps the closest thing to a governing authority that the Internet has. Its decisions and other documents exert enormous influence over the Internet, and thus over intellectual property, especially, in the case of domain names, trademark. All of the documents listed here are available online.

"Articles of Incorporation of Internet Corporation for Assigned Names and Numbers." Revised Noveember 21, 1998. http://www.icann.org/general/articles.htm.

"Bylaws for Internet Corporation for Assigned Names and Numbers, a California Nonprofit Public-Benefit Corporation." As amended effective April 19, 2004. http://www.icann.org/general/archive-bylaws/bylaws-13oct03.htm.

"ICANN Uniform Domain Name Dispute Resolution Policy." August 26, 1999. http://www.icann.org/udrp/udrp-policy-24oct99.htm.

"Internet Domain Name System Structure and Delegation (ccTLD Administration and Delegation)." May 1999. http://www .icann.org/icp/icp-1.htm.

"Memorandum of Understanding between the U.S. Department of Commerce and the Internet Corporation for Assigned Names and Numbers." November 1998. http://www.icann.org/general/ icann-mou-25nov98.htm.

# Other Web Resources

While most treaties, statutes, and cases can be located in a variety of locations online, accurate, up-to-date legal research requires a dedicated database and a staff of legal professionals to maintain it. Creating and maintaining such a database is expensive, and is usually done for profit. The websites listed here are commercial database providers; they store a wide variety of legal materials, which they make available in the expectation of profit from subscriber fees, advertising, or both. In addition to these sites, the websites of the organizations listed in Chapter 7 are valuable research tools.

*Findlaw (www.findlaw.com)*

Findlaw offers articles and summaries on a wide variety of legal topics. It is the only one of the databases listed here that can be accessed without paying a fee.

*Hein Online (heinonline.org)*

Hein Online is a useful database for academic journals, treaties, and federal administrative materials. Access requires payment of a fee.

*LexisNexis (www.lexis.com)*

Lexis is one of the two leading providers of comprehensive online legal research databases in the United States and several other countries. Its chief competitor is Westlaw. Lexis offers databases covering every area of U.S. law, including specialized intellectual property databases. Access requires payment of a fee.

*Westlaw (www.westlaw.com)*

Westlaw is one of the two leading providers of comprehensive online legal research databases in the United States. Its chief competitor is LexisNexis. Like LexisNexis, Westlaw's databases cover every area of U.S. law and include specialized intellectual property databases. The coverage and organization of the two services is similar but not identical, and professional legal researchers generally prefer the one that best suits their individual research styles and needs. A fee is charged for access.

# Glossary

**adhesion contract:** A contract made between parties with highly unequal bargaining power, usually presented as a form prepared by the party with greater bargaining power. Shrink-wrap and click-wrap agreements are often (or may often contain) adhesion contracts, as the purchaser has no opportunity to negotiate the terms of the contract, but must accept it as is. Adhesion contracts are sometimes called take-it-or-leave-it contracts.

**affirmative defense:** A defense that must be raised by a defendant and that, if proved, will enable the defendant to avoid conviction (in a criminal case) or liability (in a civil case) even though the defendant did, in fact, do all of the acts alleged by the prosecutor or plaintiff. Invalidity of the underlying patent is an affirmative defense to a patent infringement suit: Even if the defendant did, in fact, infringe on the patent, he or she will avoid liability if he or she can prove that the patent should not have been issued in the first place. In *Harper & Row Pub. v. Nation Enterprises*, 471 U.S. 539 (1985), the U.S. Supreme Court stated that fair use is an affirmative defense to copyright infringement.

**alienable:** Able to be sold, given away, devised (left by will), or otherwise transferred to another person.

**assignment:** A transfer of one or more rights or property interests.

**blanket license:** A license allowing the licensee to use all of the works of the licensor; particularly the ASCAP blanket license, which allows the licensee to perform any or all of the musical works in the ASCAP catalog.

**blurring:** One of the two ways in which a famous mark can be diluted; the mark is blurred by a use that causes it to lose its distinctive quality.

**caching:** Local storage of frequently used information for quicker and easier access.

**certiorari:** A writ issued by a higher court that directs a lower court to deliver the record in a particular case for review. Certiorari is the procedural mechanism by which most of the cases reviewed by the U.S. Supreme Court come before the court.

**click-wrap agreement:** A licensing contract for downloaded or installed software, appearing on the screen, to which the customer may consent by clicking "I agree" or something similar on the screen. Click-wrap agreements are rarely read in their entirety by consumers and may constitute or contain adhesion contracts.

**common law:** In the United States, the United Kingdom, and most other English-speaking countries, the body of law based on reported judicial opinions.

**compulsory license:** A license allowing the licensee to use a protected intellectual property right (patent, copyright, or trademark) without the owner's consent, so long as the licensee pays a specified fee.

**cybergriping:** Complaining, usually about a company, using a website created specifically for that purpose.

**cybersquatting:** Registering another's trademark as a domain name for the purpose of obtaining money from the trademark owner.

**damages:** Money sought or awarded at law as compensation for an injury; they are paid or to be paid by the person causing the injury.

**de minimis:** Minimal; insignificant.

**dead letter:** A treaty, law, or practice that has not been abolished, overturned, or repealed but is no longer applied.

**derivative work:** A work based on a preexisting work but adding some original element to that work.

**design patent:** A patent for an ornamental industrial design.

**dilution:** The blurring or tarnishing of a famous mark.

**encryption:** A method of arranging the contents of a document in such a way as to render the document unintelligible until the encryption process is reversed with the aid of a decryption key.

**ephemeral:** Of short duration.

**estoppel:** A legal bar to the assertion of a particular claim, right, or argument.

**exclusive license:** A license granted to only one person; the licensor is prohibited from granting the license to additional licensees.

**file sharing:** Sharing files on one computer with other computers to which the computer is linked through a network.

**in personam:** An action in personam is a lawsuit brought against a particular person. Jurisdiction in personam is jurisdiction over a particular person.

**in rem:**   An action in rem is a lawsuit brought "against" (that is, to determine the ownership and status of) a thing. The thing may be tangible (a jar of peanut butter) or intangible (a domain name). Jurisdiction in rem is jurisdiction over a thing. An action brought to determine the rights and responsibilities of a particular party in relation to a thing is called an action quasi in rem.

**injunction; injunctive relief:**   An order from a court that something be done or not be done.

**metatag:**   Text inserted near the top of an HTML document that is invisible when the document is viewed as a Web page.

**peer-to-peer (P2P):**   A form of file-sharing network in which files are exchanged directly between users without passing through any central server.

**plant patent:**   A patent for a variety of plant; in the United States plant patents are governed by the 1930 Plant Patent Act and the 1970 Plant Variety Protection Act.

**plurality:**   The largest share, even if not a majority. If nine people vote on three options, for example, and four vote for Option A, three for Option B, and two for Option C, Option A has received a plurality of the votes cast, even though a majority (five in all) have not voted for Option A.

**prima facie:**   On first appearance; sufficient to establish a presumption, and thus requiring the opposing party to disprove or rebut the presumption.

**public domain:**   Inventions and original works unprotected by patent and copyright, respectively, and thus available for the use of the public. Inventions may be in the public domain because they were never patented or because the patent has expired or has otherwise terminated. Original works may be in the public domain because they are original U.S. government works or because the copyright has expired.

**remanded:**   Sent back to the originating court for further action.

**rootkit:**   Software intended to conceal traces of an intruder on a system; allowing the intruder undetected root access.

**search-engine spamming:**   Using unethical or questionable methods to mislead search engines into giving a website a higher search-result ranking than it would otherwise have.

**shareware:**   Computer programs distributed free of charge, usually on condition that after a trial period the user will pay for the program if he or she chooses to keep using it.

**shrink-wrap agreement:** A software licensing contract to which the customer consents by opening the shrink-wrap packaging of the disks or other media containing the software. Like click-wrap agreements, shrink-wrap agreements are rarely read in their entirety by the consumers and may constitute or contain adhesion contracts.

**spamming:** A form of abuse of e-mail, search engines, instant messaging, newsgroups, text messaging, and other forms of communication in which a very large number of unsolicited messages are sent, or an illusorily high search-engine rank is created, usually for the financial benefit of the spammer or the spammer's clients.

**statutory:** Appearing in or related to an act passed by a legislature (a statute).

**supernode:** A computer connected to a peer-to-peer (P2P) network and acting as a relayer and proxy server for the network. The supernode computer is not ordinarily under the control of anyone involved in creating the P2P network or the software enabling it; any connected computer with sufficient bandwidth can become a supernode, and supernodes can change frequently.

**tarnishment:** One of the two ways in which a famous mark can be diluted: The mark is tarnished by a use that decreases the positive mental associations connected with the mark or creates negative associations. Association of a mark with illegal drug use or pornography may constitute tarnishment.

**trade dress:** Nonfunctional elements of the packaging or presentation of goods or services that combine to create a visual image that identifies the goods or services to consumers; trade dress may be protected as a trademark or service mark.

**utility patent:** The right granted to the inventor of a useful, novel, and nonobvious invention allowing the inventor to prevent others from making, using, or selling the invention.

**vacated:** Nullified.

**webcasting:** Noninteractive linear transmission of audio or video content over the World Wide Web.

**works for hire:** A work created by an employee within the scope of his or her employment, or pursuant to a commission or agreement under which the parties agree to treat the work as a work for hire.

# Index

*A&M Records v. Napster,*
71–72
*Abercrombie & Fitch Co. v.
Hunting World, Inc.,*
28–29, 224n.
decision in (text), 210–213
ACPA. *See*
Anticybersquatting
Consumer Protection
Act of 1999
African Regional Intellectual
Property Organization
(ARIPO), 226
Agreement on Trade-Related
Aspects of Intellectual
Property Rights. *See*
TRIPs
AHRA. *See* Audio Home
Recording Act of 1992
Aimster, 72–73
Alliance for Digital Progress
(ADP), 226–227
*Amazon.com, Inc. v.
Barnesandnoble.com,
Inc.,* 60–61
American Bar Association
Section of Intellectual
Property Law, 227
American Intellectual
Property Law
Association (AIPLA),
227

American Society of
Composers, Authors
and Publishers,
227–228
Anti-DMCA, 228
Anticounterfeiting Consumer
Protection Act of 1996,
10, 11
Anticybersquatting
Consumer Protection
Act of 1999, 10, 11,
90–92
*Apple Computer, Inc. v.
Microsoft Corp.,* 53–55
Apple Corporation. *See Apple
Computer, Inc. v.
Microsoft Corp.;* Lisa
computer; Macintosh
computers and
operating system;
iTunes
ARPANET, 104–105
Arts and Humanities
Research Board
Shepherd and
Wedderburn Research
Centre in Intellectual
Property and
Technology, 229
ASCAP. *See* American Society
of Composers, Authors
and Publishers

Association Internationale
pour la Protection de la
Propriété Intellectuelle
(AIPPI), 229–230
Association Littéraire et
Artistique International
(ALAI), 230
Association of Corporate
Patent Counsel
(ACPC), 229
*Atari v. JS & A*, 75
ATRIP. *See* International
Association for the
Advancement of
Teaching and Research
in Intellectual Property
Audio Home Recording Act
of 1992, 67–68

Bakers' marks, 8–9
Barnes & Noble. *See Amazon
.com, Inc. v. Barnesand
noble.com, Inc.*
Barton, Clara, 149–151
Berkman Center for Internet
& Society, 230–231
Berne Convention, 5, 8,
107–108
on copyrightable subject
matter, 110–111
and duration of copyright,
111, 112
on exclusive rights, 111
and national treatment, 110
on notice and registration,
17, 18
and U.S., 5–6, 108–109
Berne Convention
Implementation Act of
1988, 18, 24, 109
Berners-Lee, Tim, 105
Bi Sheng, 2
Bitlaw, 225, 231

Borland software. *See Lotus
Development v. Borland*
Bourget, Ernest, 151–152
Britain
early development of
printing, 3
Stationer's Company, 3–4
Statute of Anne, 3–4
Brunelleschi, Filippo, 12,
153–155
Budapest Open Access
Initiative, 231–232
Buenos Aires Convention,
108–109
Bunner, Andrew, 86
Business methods, and
patents, 58–62, 93
Business Software Alliance
(BSA), 232–233

Cailliau, Robert, 105
Campaign for Digital Rights
(CDR), 233
Canadian Motion Picture
Distributors
Association (CMPDA),
233
*Canterbury Tales*, 3
Caxton, William, 3
Center for Intellectual
Property Studies (CIP),
234
Centre d'Etudes
Internationales de la
Propriété Industrielle
(CEIPI), 234
CERN. *See* European
Organization for
Nuclear Research
Certification marks, 26
Chaucer, Geoffrey, 3
Coca-Cola, 120
Collective marks, 26

Computer Maintenance
 Competition Assurance
 Act, 7
Computer programs
 and copyright, 51–58
 look-and-feel infringement
  (and menu command
  hierarchy), 53–58, 93
 and patents, 50–51, 52, 93
 and shrink-wrap
  agreements, 64
 and trade dress, 57–58
Computers. *See* Lisa
 computer; Macintosh
 computers and operating
 system; Semiconductor
 manufacturing mask
 works
Consumer Empowerment, 74
Content Scramble System, 84,
 86
Copy protection, 82, 87, 93
 Content Scramble System,
  84, 86
 and DeCSS, 84–87
 and DMCA, 82–83
 Macrovision, 83–84
Copying devices, 49, 66–68
  *See also* Digital copying
Copyleft, 24
Copyright, 1, 41
 authorship, 15–16
 Britain, 3–4
 collective works, 24
 compulsory licensing, 25–26
 of computer programs,
  51–58
 and copy protection, 82–87
 and copying devices, 49,
  66–68
 duration, 21–23
 economic rights, 14–15,
  18–19

and electronic databases,
 62–66
fair use, 19–20
France, 4–5
international, 106–114. *See
 also* Berne Convention
and Internet, 6–8
joint works, 24
moral rights, 5, 15, 112
notice and registration,
 17–18
originality, 15
ownership, 24
and printing, 1–6
and public domain, 23–24
right of first sale, 18–19
*scènes a fàire*, 16, 17
tangible medium of
 expression, 15, 16
transfers of, 25
U.S. acts, 4, 5–8
works for hire, 24
*See also* Berne Convention;
 Buenos Aires
 Convention; Copyright
 infringement; Digital
 Millennium Copyright
 Act of 1998; File
 sharing; Open-source
 licensing; Statute of
 Anne; Universal
 Copyright Convention
Copyright Act of 1790, 4
Copyright Act of 1909, 5,
 108–109, 112
Copyright Act of 1976, 5–6,
 109
 on exclusive rights (text),
  176–177
 on fair use (text), 177–178
 preemption clause, 63–65
 on subject matter of
  copyright (text), 176

Copyright Clearance Center, 234–235
Copyright infringement
  contributory, 21, 70–74, 77
  direct, 20, 70
  indirect (third-party), 20–21, 70–72
  inducing, 21, 70, 76
  vicarious, 21, 70–76
Copyright Renewal Act of 1992, 22
The Copyright Society of the Untied States of America (CSUSA), 235
Corley, Eric, 84–86
Coster, Laurens, 3, 155–156
Creative Commons, 235–236
CSS. *See* Content Scramble System
Cybergriping, 92
Cybersquatting, 49, 90–92, 93
  15 U.S.C. Sec. 1125 on, 198–203
  *See also* Anticybersquatting Consumer Protection Act of 1999

DAT. *See* Digital audio tape
DeCSS, 84–87
*Dépôt légale*, 4, 5
Diamond Rio MP3 player, 68
*Diamond Sutra*, 2
*Diamond v. Diehr*, 52
Dickens, Charles, 107
Digital audio tape, 67–68
Digital copying, 6–8, 67–68
  *See also* Copying devices
Digital Millennium Copyright Act of 1998, 6, 7–8
  on circumvention of copyright protection systems, 82–83, 178–185

DigitalConsumer.org, 236
DMCA. *See* Digital Millennium Copyright Act of 1998
*Domaine publique*, 24
*Donaldson v. Beckett*, 4
*DVD Copy Control Association, Inc. v. Bunner*, 86

Economic Espionage Act of 1996, 122
EFF. *See* Electronic Frontier Foundation
Electronic databases, and copyright, 62–66
Electronic Frontier Foundation, 84, 237
Ellsworth, Annie, 156–157
epi. *See* Institute of Professional Representatives before the European Patent Office
Eurasian Patent Organization (EAPO), 237
European Digital Rights (EDRI), 237–238
European Organization for Nuclear Research, 105
European Patent Convention
  and business methods, 62
  and computer programs, 51, 52
European Patent Office (EPO), 51, 238
European Union
  and copyright duration, 8
  Database Directive, 66

Fair use, 19, 20
  and copyright, 19–20
  and parody, 20

and reverse engineering,
20
space shifting, 19, 68
as statutory right, 83
time shifting, 19
and trademarks, 33, 88–89
and TRIPs, 113–114
*See also* File sharing
FastTrack software, 74
Federal Trademark Dilution
Act of 1995, 10, 11,
32–33
Fédération Internationale des
Conseils en Propriété,
238–239
*Feist Publications v. Rural
Telephone Service Co.*,
15, 62–63
File sharing, 69
and Aimster, 72–73
and books, 80
and dissatisfaction with
music industry's
business model, 78–79
and equipment
manufacturers, 81
and Grokster, 74–78
and Internet service
providers, 81
and KaZaA, 73–74
and movies, 80–81
and MP3.com, 69–70
and music, 69–78
and Napster, 70–72
First Inventor Defense Act of
1999, 61–62
First4Internet rootkit, 87
Francis I, King of France, 4

*Gottschalk v. Benson*, 50–51
Grokster, 74–78
Gutenberg, Johannes, 3,
158–159

Henry VI, King of England, 13
Hewlett-Packard, 54
Hoshi Ryokan, 8
Hugo, Victor, 107, 159–160

IANA. *See* Internet Assigned
Numbers Authority
ICANN. *See* Internet
Corporation for
Assigned Names and
Numbers
*In re Aimster Copyright
Litigation*, 72–73
*In re Alappat*, 52, 224n.
decision in (text), 218–222
*In re Trade-Mark Cases*, 9–10
Industrial designs, 120
Information technology
and intellectual property
law, 41–42, 49
*See also* Computer
programs
The Institute of Patentees
and Inventors, 239
Institute of Professional
Representatives before
the European Patent
Office, 239
Institute of Trade Mark
Attorneys (ITMA),
239–240
Intellectual property, 1, 41–42
and international law,
99–104, 119–123
specialized categories,
119–120
*See also* Copyright; Patents;
Trademarks
Intellectual Property Owners
Association (IPO), 240
Inter-American Convention
for the Protection of
Industrial Property, 10

International
  Anticounterfeiting
  Coalition (IACC), 240
International Association of
  Entertainment
  Lawyers, 241
International Association for
  the Advancement of
  Teaching and Research
  in Intellectual Property,
  240–241
International Court of Justice,
  Statue of the, 99–100
International Federation of
  Inventors' Associations
  (IFIA), 241
International Federation of
  Reproduction Rights
  Organizations (IFRRO),
  242
International Intellectual
  Property Alliance
  (IIPA), 242
International Intellectual
  Property Institute
  (IIPI), 242–243
International Law
  Association (ILA), 243
International Trademark
  Association (INTA),
  243
Internet
  development of, 104–105
  distinguished from World
    Wide Web, 104
  and intellectual property
    law, 42
  metatags, 12, 88
  *See also* Business methods;
    Electronic databases;
    World Wide Web
Internet Assigned Numbers
  Authority, 106

Internet Corporation for
  Assigned Names and
  Numbers, 92, 106, 244
iTunes, 79

Japan Intellectual Property
  Association (JIPA),
  244–245
Jenks, Joseph, 173–174
Johansen, Jon Lech, 84,
  160–162
Johnson, Lyndon, 50

KaZaA, 73–74
Kazan, Roman, 84–86
Kies, Mary, 162–163
Kongo Gumi, 8

Lanham Trademark Act of
  1946, 10
Lefèvre, Raoul, 3
Lisa computer, 54
*Lotus Development v. Borland*,
  55–57
Lotus 1-2-3 software, 56
Lowenbrau, 8

Macintosh computers and
  operating system,
  53–55
Macrovision, 83–84
Madrid Agreement
  Concerning the
  International
  Registration of Marks,
  114
Madrid Union and Protocol,
  114–115
*MAI Systems v. Peak
  Computer*, 7
Manufacturing Clause, 108
Marrakesh Agreement on
  Trade-Related Aspects

of Intellectual Property
Rights. *See* TRIPs
Max-Planck-Institut für
Geistiges Eigentum,
Wettbewerbs-und
Steuerrecht, 245
*Metro-Goldwyn-Mayer Studios,
Inc. v. Grokster, Ltd.,*
74–78, 93, 222n.–224n.
Supreme Court opinion
(text), 186–198
Meucci, Antonio, 163–164
*MGM v. Grokster. See Metro-
Goldwyn-Mayer Studios,
Inc. v. Grokster, Ltd.*
Microsoft Corporation
Internet Explorer, 105–106
MS-DOS operating system,
53
Windows operating
system, 54–55
*See also Apple Computer, Inc.
v. Microsoft Corp.*
Mosaic browser, 105
Most favored nation
treatment, 104
Motion Picture Association of
America (MPAA),
245–246
MP3 files, 68
MP3.com, 69–70
Music Publishers'
Association (MPA),
246
Muybridge, Eadweard,
164–167

Napster, 70–72
National Association of
Patent Practitioners
(NAPP), 247
National treatment, 104, 110
Netscape Navigator, 105

Network Solutions, Inc., 106
*The New Code of Etiquette,* 2
NewWave software, 54
Niton Corporation, 89
No Electronic Theft Act of
1997, 6–7

Office for Harmonization in
the Internal Market
(Trade Marks and
Designs), 247
*Ohio v. Perry,* 64–65
Online Copyright
Infringement Liability
Limitation Act, 7
Open Society Institute (OSI),
247
Open-source licensing, 24, 26,
51
Organisation Africaine de la
Propriété Intellectuelle
(OAPI), 248

P2P networks. *See* Peer-to-
peer networks
Paris Convention for the
Protection of Industrial
Property, 14, 114,
116–117
Paris Union, 114, 116–117
Parker, Sean, 71
Patent Act (35 U.S.C. Sec.
101)
on non-obvious subject
matter (text), 215–216
on novelty and loss of right
to patent (text),
214–215
Patent Act of 1836, 14
Patent Act of 1870, 14
Patent Cooperation Treaty,
38, 103, 117–118
Patent Law Treaty, 118

Patent Office of the
Cooperation Council
for the Arab States of
the Gulf, 248
Patents, 1, 34, 42
application process, 35–38
of business methods,
58–62, 93
for computer programs,
50–51, 52, 93
drawings, 35
duration, 40–41
England, 13
exclusive rights of holders,
38
fees, 35, 37–38
filing date, 37
first-to-invent rule, 118
induced infringement, 40
infringement, 38–40,
198–203
international agreements,
13–14, 116–119, 123
invention date, 36–37
licensing, 41
"nose of wax rule," 38
ownership, 41
priority date, 37
and reduction to practice,
61–62
specifications, 35
as territorial grants, 117
and third-party liability,
39–40
transfer, 41
U.S., 13, 14
Venetian statute of 1421,
12–13
what is covered, 34–35
wrapper estoppel
(prosecution history
estoppel), 38–39
Peer-to-peer networks, 70, 78

and Voluntary Collective
License, 80
*See also* Aimster; Grokster;
KaZaA; Napster
Plant Patent Act of 1930, 14
*Playboy Enterprises, Inc. v.
Welles*, 88–89
Postel, Jon, 106
President's Commission on
the Patent System, 50
Printing
early development in
China and Korea, 2
government monopolies, 2,
3, 4
Stationer's Company, 3–4
*ProCD, Inc. v. Zeidenberg*, 65
Project Gutenberg, 248–249
Public domain, 23–24
Public Knowledge, 249

Quattro Pro software, 56

Radiation Monitoring
Devices, Inc., 89
Recording Industry
Association of
America, 78, 79, 250
*Recording Industry Association
of America v. Verizon
internet services*, 81
*The Recuyell of the Historyes of
Troye*, 3
Reimerdes, Shawn, 84–86
RIAA. *See* Recording
Industry Association of
America

*Scènes a fàire*, 16, 17, 55
SCMS. *See* Serial Copy
Management System
SCRIPT. *See* Arts and
Humanities Research

Board Shepherd and Wedderburn Research Centre in Intellectual Property and Technology

Search-engine spamming, 12, 49, 87–89

Semiconductor manufacturing mask works, 119–120

Serial Copy Management System, 67

Service marks, 8, 26, 30

Sharman Networks, 74

Signature Financial Group. *See State Street Bank & Trust v. Signature Financial Group*

Sklyarov, Dmitri, 167–168

Société des Gens de Lettres (SGDL), 251

Software. *See* Computer programs

Sonny Bono Copyright Term Extension Act of 1998, 6, 8, 21

Sony, 87

*Sony Corp. of America v. Universal City Studios, Inc.*, 66, 68, 93

*Southern v. How*, 9

Spam. *See* Search-engine spamming

*State Street Bank & Trust Co. v. Signature Financial Group*, 14, 59

Stationer's Company, 3–4

Statute of Anne, 3–4, 109

Statue of the International Court of Justice, 99–100

Statute of Monopolies of 1623 (England), 13

Stella Artois, 8

Stowe, Harriet Beecher, 107

*Sunde (for Norway) v. Johansen*, 84

TESS. *See* Trademark Electronic Search System

TLT. *See* Trademark Law Treaty

Trade dress, 57–58, 93

Trade Marks, Patents and Designs Federation (TMPDF), 251

Trade secrets, 120–123

Trademark Act of 1870, 9

Trademark Dilution Revision Act of 2006, 10, 11 text, 203–208

Trademark Electronic Search System, 30

Trademark Law Revision Act of 1988, 10

Trademark Law Treaty, 115

Trademark Law Treaty Act of 1998, 115

Trademarks, 1, 8, 26–27, 42
  blurring, 30, 32
  defined, 26
  dilution, 11, 30, 31–33, 198–203
  duration, 33–34
  England, 8–9
  fair use, 33, 88–89
  15 U.S.C. Sec. 1125 (text), 198–203
  infringement, 30–31
  international agreements, 10–11, 114–116, 123
  items covered and not covered, 27–29
  and metatags, 12, 88
  notice, 30
  registration, 29–30, 34
  and state law, 10, 29

Trademarks *(cont.)*
  and third-party liability, 33
  tarnishment, 30, 32–33
  transfer of, 33
  U.S., 9–10
  *See also* Certification
    marks; Collective
    marks;
    Cybersquatting;
    Federal Trademark
    Dilution Act of 1995;
    Search-engine
    spamming; Service
    marks; Trade dress;
    Trademark Dilution
    Revision Act of 2006
Treaty on Trade-Related
    Aspects of Intellectual
    Property Rights. *See*
    TRIPs
TRIPs, 14, 59, 101, 103, 123
  and Berne Convention, 112
  as comprehensive treaty on
    intellectual property,
    104
  on copyright (text),
    185–186
  on database protection,
    112–113
  and fair use, 113–114
  and most favored nation
    treatment, 104, 112
  and national treatment,
    104, 112
  and patent law, 117
  on patents (text), 216–218
  on performance and
    recording rights, 113
  on software and movie
    rentals, 113
  and trade secrets, 122
  and trademark law,
    115–116

  on trademarks (text),
    208–210
  *See also* World Intellectual
    Property Organization;
    World Trade
    Organization
Trollope, Anthony, 107
Tufts Multilaterals Project,
    251–252

*UMG Recordings v. MP3.com*,
    69–70
*Uncle Tom's Cabin*, 107
Uniform Domain Name
    Dispute Resolution
    Policy, 92
Uniform Trade Secrets Act
    (U.S. states), 121–122
*Universal City Studios, Inc. v.*
    *Corley*, 7, 86
*Universal City Studios, Inc. v.*
    *Reimerdes*, 86
Universal Copyright
    Convention, 5, 108
U.S. Constitution
  and international law, 100
  Patent and Copyright
    Clause, 4, 13
U.S. Copyright Office, 252
U.S. Patent Office (before
    1975), 14
U.S. Patent and Trademark
    Office (since 1975), 14,
    30, 34, 252–253
USPTO. *See* U.S. Patent and
    Trademark Office
UTSA. *See* Uniform Trade
    Secrets Act
Utynam, John of, 13

Valenti, Jack, 169–171
*Vault Corporation v. Quaid*
    *Software*, 64

Verizon, 81
Vessel Hull Design Protection
    Act, 120
Virtual private networks, 72
Voluntary Collective License,
    80
VPNs. *See* Virtual private
    networks

Wang Jie, 2
WCT. *See* WIPO Copyright
    Treaty
Weihenstephan, 8
Welles, Terri, 88, 171–173
Windows operating system,
    54–55
Winslow, Samuel, 173–174
WIPO. *See* World Intellectual
    Property Organization
WIPO Copyright and
    Performances and
    Phonograms Treaties
    Implementation Act, 7
WIPO Copyright Treaty, 111
WIPO Performance and
    Phonograms Treaty,
    111–112
World Intellectual Property

Organization, 6, 7, 66,
    100–101, 123, 253
treaties administered,
    101–103
voting structure, 103
website as best first stop
    for research, 225
*See also* TRIPs; *entries
    beginning with* WIPO
World Trade Organization, 6,
    100–101, 254
and patents, 118–119
and trade secrets, 122–123
trademark enforcement,
    115–116
World Wide Web
browsers, 105–106
development of, 105–106
distinguished from
    Internet, 104
*See also* Internet
WPPT. *See* WIPO
    Performance and
    Phonograms Treaty
WTO. *See* World Trade
    Organization

Yi Gyu-bo, 2

# About the Author

**Aaron Schwabach** is a professor of law at Thomas Jefferson School of Law in San Diego, California, where he teaches computer and Internet law. He is the author of ABC-CLIO's *Internet and the Law: Technology, Society, and Compromises.*

5/07

ML